The Renaissance Wind Band and Wind Ensemble

Books by David Whitwell

Philosophic Foundations of Education
Foundations of Music Education
Music Education of the Future
The Sousa Oral History Project
The Art of Musical Conducting
The Longy Club: 1900–1917
A Concise History of the Wind Band

The History and Literature of the Wind Band and Wind Ensemble Series

Volume 1 The Wind Band and Wind Ensemble Before 1500
Volume 2 The Renaissance Wind Band and Wind Ensemble
Volume 3 The Baroque Wind Band and Wind Ensemble
Volume 4 The Classic Period Wind Band and Wind Ensemble
Volume 5 The Nineteenth-Century Wind Band and Wind Ensemble
Volume 6 A Catalog of Multi-Part Repertoire for Wind Instruments or for Undesignated Instrumentation before 1600
Volume 7 Baroque Wind Band and Wind Ensemble Repertoire
Volume 8 Classic Period Wind Band and Wind Ensemble Repertoire
Volume 9 Nineteenth-Century Wind Band and Wind Ensemble Repertoire
Volume 10 A Supplementary Catalog of Wind Band and Wind Ensemble Repertoire
Volume 11 A Catalog of Wind Repertoire before the Twentieth Century for One to Five Players
Volume 12 A Second Supplementary Catalog of Early Wind Band and Wind Ensemble Repertoire
Volume 13 Name Index, Volumes 1–12, The History and Literature of the Wind Band and Wind Ensemble

www.whitwellbooks.com

David Whitwell

The Renaissance Wind Band and Wind Ensemble

THE HISTORY AND LITERATURE OF THE WIND BAND AND WIND ENSEMBLE, VOLUME 2

EDITED BY CRAIG DABELSTEIN

WHITWELL BOOKS • AUSTIN, TEXAS, USA

The Renaissance Wind Band and Wind Ensemble
Second Edition
Dr. David Whitwell
Edited by Craig Dabelstein
www.whitwellbooks.com

Whitwell Publishing
815-A Brazos Street #491
Austin, TX 78701

Copyright © David Whitwell 2011
All rights reserved

All images used in this book are in the public domain except where otherwise noted.

Composed in Bembo Book
Published in the United States of America

The Renaissance Wind Band and Wind Ensemble (paperback) isbn 978-1-936512-19-5

Foreword

This volume is the second of several which together attempt a general History and Literature of the Wind Band and Wind Ensemble. At the time these volumes were first written there was no comprehensive history of the wind band. In addition these volumes together provide library identification and shelf-marks for more than 30,000 wind band manuscripts and early prints before 1900 found in more than 450 libraries. Over several decades it was my practice when conducting in Europe to add some weeks to my trip to visit libraries and examine early works for wind band and many of these scores I worked into the repertoire of my own concerts.

Whereas general music history begins the Renaissance with the fourteenth century, because of developments in Church music, in terms of musical style for wind bands it is the beginning of the sixteenth century when things really change. This was due to rather sudden advances in the art of the crafts of the wood workers and the metal workers which resulted in an almost complete change in the construction of wind instruments themselves during the sixteenth century. In particular, these changes made possible the first true bass wind instruments which, together with the consort principle, led to much more mature and satisfying music. For these reasons, in terms of the history of wind bands it is only the sixteenth century which is truly the Renaissance.

In the first volume one finds the civic and court wind bands developing gradually to become real established wind bands by the fifteenth century. In this volume one finds larger and more artistic wind bands with important bodies of music literature which still exist. In general the civic wind bands reach their climax in the fifteenth century, with the exception of the German-speaking lands where the tradition finds it climax in the seventeenth century.

Wind bands finally began to be accepted in the church during the fifteenth century and in the sixteenth century they seem indispensable and civic wind bands of the Renaissance often had in their contracts the requirement to rehearse with the choir during the week and perform with them on Sundays. The field of musicology has never quite accepted the fact that the great choral music by Josquin and Palestrina should have wind instruments added, not to mention improvisation in the service, but the extant church records are very clear. Fortunately, today there are more and more recordings with winds added to the sacred masterpieces and this allows the modern student to hear this music more like its original performance practice.

Very few court or church records refer to string instruments before 1550, the final decades of the span of years usually called the Renaissance. Therefore, one is on fairly safe ground in saying that in the Renaissance the professional instrumentalist was a wind player.

The real purpose in writing these volumes has been an attempt to demonstrate to band directors everywhere that they represent a medium that has performed at the highest levels of society over a very great span of time and that while all musicians take their turn at functional music wind bands also performed music to be listened to. It is a very great mistake for any band director to assume that his role is limited to only entertaining the public.

David Whitwell
Austin, Texas

Contents

COURT WIND BANDS ... 1

   1 *Court Wind Bands in England ... 15*
        Wind Music in the Elizabethan Theater
        The Music of Holborne

   2 *Court Wind Bands in France ... 61*
        The Published 'Danceries'

   3 *Court Wind Bands in Spain ... 87*

   4 *Court Wind Bands in the German-Speaking Countries ... 97*

   5 *Court Wind Bands in Italy ... 117*

CIVIC WIND BANDS ... 141

   6 *Civic Wind Bands in England ... 147*

   7 *Civic Wind Bands in the Low Countries ... 165*
        Notes on the Repertoire

   8 *Civic Wind Bands in France ... 179*

   9 *Civic Wind Bands in the German-Speaking Countries ... 185*

  10 *Civic Wind Bands in Italy ... 197*

CHURCH WIND BANDS ... 203

  11 *Church Wind Bands in the Low Countries ... 213*

  12 *Church Wind Bands in France ... 217*

  13 *Church Wind Bands in Spain ... 221*

  14 *Church Wind Bands in England ... 225*

  15 *Church Wind Bands in the German-Speaking Countries ... 229*

  16 *Church Wind Bands in Italy ... 241*
        Instrumental Forms in the Italian Church Service
        The Wind Ensemble Music of Giovanni Gabrieli

NOTES ON PERFORMANCE PRACTICE ... 249

NOTES ON THE INSTRUMENTS ... 257

BIBLIOGRAPHY ... 267

INDEX ... 281

ABOUT THE AUTHOR ... 287

Acknowledgments

This new edition would not have been possible without the encouragement and help of Craig Dabelstein of Brisbane, Australia. His experience as a musician and educator himself has contributed greatly to his expertise as editor of this volume.

                    David Whitwell
                    Austin, 2011

PART I
Court Wind Bands

Court Wind Bands

DURING BOTH THE END OF THE MEDIEVAL and the Renaissance Periods,[1] the best wind bands and wind players were associated with the courts of the aristocracy. It is with these bands that one first sees the extraordinary new concept which distinguishes the Renaissance band from the Medieval one: the consort, a prevailing practice during the first half of the sixteenth century which replaced the older 'loud–soft' principle of the Middle Ages. Perhaps originating in an attempt to approximate the consistent tonal color of the polyphonic vocal repertoire, which the wind band was beginning to transcribe for its own use, the development of whole families of from four to eight different sizes of the same instrument made possible a homogenous, matched ensemble sound. Further, the development of these families of instruments resulted in the natural introduction of lower pitched members, giving a darker ensemble sound as compared to the more shrill, heterogeneous medieval sound; it was as if ensemble music added a lower octave after 1500.

The development of the consort principle also solved the most significant aesthetic problem in the medieval wind band, ensemble intonation. By making a complete consort, an instrument maker could guarantee that at least that ensemble could play in tune.[2]

Variety in instrumental color, during performance, was achieved by the alternation of consorts, a practice which accounts for the extremely large collections of instruments owned by many nobles. A typical example of this practice can be seen in the following description by Sir Philip Sidney.

> The musick was of Cornets, whereof one answering the other, with a sweete emulation, striving for the glorie of musicke, and striking upon the smooth face of the quiet Lake, and then delivered up to the castell walls … And when a while that instrument had made a brave proclamation to all unpossessed minds of attention, an excellent consort streight followed of five violles, and as manie voyces.[3]

[1] For the purpose of writing on the history of wind music, I consider the 'Renaissance' as being only the sixteenth century. This is based, of course, on the clear changes in both the music and the instruments which occur at approximately the beginning of that century.

[2] Several European museums contain examples of complete consorts of wind instruments together with their original (single) case. Such an example can be seen in the Brussels Conservatory of Music. Numerous works of art produced during the sixteenth century also picture various consorts of wind instruments, as for example the intarsia (wood inlay), ca. 1510, by Fra Giovanni da Verona, now in the Vatican, which shows five crumhorns in careful detail.

[3] Quoted in Brian Jeffery, 'Antony Holborne,' *Musica Disciplina* 22 (1968): 147–148. A similar example is quoted by Wolfgang Suppan, *Lexikon des Blasmusikwesens* (Freiburg: Schulz, 1973), 28, relative to the letter of a trombonist, ca. 1500, which mentions a performance by consorts of four trombones and two cornets; four trombones and four shawms; eight flutes; and five trombones.

So enthusiastically was this new consort principle adopted by nobles everywhere for their musical establishments, that one Englishman goes so far as to suggest that the best equipped household will even have the dogs in its kennel organized in a consort!

> If you would have your kennels for sweetness of cry then you must compound it of some large dogs that have deep, solemn mouths … which must as it were bear the bass in consort, then a double number of roaring and loud-ringing mouths which must bear the counter tenor, then some hollow, plain, sweet mouths which must bear the mean or middle part and so with these three parts of music you shall make your cry perfect.[4]

[4] Quoted in Elizabeth Burton, *The Pageant of Elizabethan England* (New York: Scribner, 1959), 190.

Certainly this is not to be taken seriously, but can one be sure? Shakespeare, in *A Midsummer Night's Dream*, gave a similar description. 'My hounds,' says Theseus, 'are,'

> Slow in pursuit, but matched in mouth like bells,
> Each under each. A cry more tuneable
> Was never holla'd to nor cheer'd with horn.[5]

[5] William Shakespeare, *A Midsummer Night's Dream*, act 4, scene 1, lines 122–124.

After the middle of the sixteenth century, the aristocratic preference slowly began to move toward the mixed ensemble of strings and winds, the so-called, 'broken consort.' Considering the fact that the wind band had been dominant for more than a century in aristrocratic circles, perhaps part of the explanation for the move to adopt strings into their 'consorts' can be found simply in the need for the noble to distinguish himself from the mere citizen. Thus with the development of very successful civic wind bands during the fifteenth and early sixteenth centuries, affording the middle-classes the opportunity to imitate the entertainments of the aristocracy, the aristocracy moved on to something else—as they would have placed little value on anything available to everyone.[6] Nothing illustrates this possibility better than the history of the basse-dance. First danced only at court, during the sixteenth century the bourgeoisie began to dance the basse-dance, and publications appeared in large numbers to serve this new demand, and soon it was no longer danced at court. It was the wind band which helped make the basse-dance popular and the wind band which was a victim of its own success.

[6] It is only late in the sixteenth century that one begins to read of this aristocratic snobbery. Galilei (the father), partly reflecting his own partiality for the lute, wrote that cornetts and trombones 'are never heard in the private chambers of judicious gentlemen, Signori, and Princes.' (Marcello Castellani, 'A 1593 Veronese Inventory,' *The Galpin Society Journal* 26 (May 1, 1973): 18). Another writer, on the subject of the education of a Lady, writes he would have her 'sing softly and sweetly; in dancing, he would not have his Lady move too energetically; nor would he have her play drums, fifes, trumpets, or other like instruments.' (Charles L. Mee, *Daily Life in Renaissance Italy* (New York: American Heritage Pub. Co., 1975), 65).

The chief factor which caused the breakdown of the consort principle itself was certain weaknesses in some consorts, which therefore invited substitutions. An ideal example can be seen in the trombone consort, which lacked a good upper voice, and in the cornett consort, which lacked a good bass. They combined to make the most popular ensemble of the sixteenth century.

> After midcentury, … musicians often added to an otherwise pure consort one or two instruments from another family. Thus a single trombone could play the bass line beneath a crumhorn or a flute consort. And various instruments, dolzaine, crumhorns, or even flutes or recorders, filled in the inner parts in a trombone-cornett band. By 1589 a great amount of borrowing back and forth was tolerated. By then the consort principle was often diluted to mean no more than that one choir consisted of wind instruments, another of bowed strings, and so on.[7]

[7] Howard M. Brown, *Sixteenth-Century Instrumentation: The Music for the Florentine Intermedii* (Dallas: American Institute of Musicology, 1973), 79.

All this is not to suggest, by any means, that consorts of wind instruments did not continue to exist throughout the sixteenth century, as numerous examples below will demonstrate. Indeed, even as late as 1619, Praetorius gives a detailed list of wind 'complete' consorts.

> 8 cross flute players, 2 on discant, 4 on alto or tenor, and 2 on bass,
>
> 6 bassanelli players, 2 on discant, 3 on alto or tenor, and 1 on bass,
>
> 8 trombone players, 1 on alto, 4 on 'ordinary' trombone, 2 on quart trombone, and 1 on octave trombone,
>
> 7 rackett players, 2 on discant, 3 on alto or tenor, 1 on bass, and 1 on large bass,
>
> 8 bassoon players, 1 on discant, 2 on fagotto piccolo, 3 on chorist bassoon, 1 on quart double bassoon in F, and 1 on quint double bassoon in F,
>
> 9 crumhorn players, 1 on small discant, 2 on discant, 3 on alto or tenor, 2 on bass, and 1 on large bass,
>
> 6 cornamuse players, 1 on discant, 1 on alto, 1 on alto or tenor, 2 on tenor, and 1 on bass,
>
> 13 bombard or shawm players, 1 on the very small shawm, 2 on shawm, 3 on small alto pommer, 2 on large alto pommer, 2 on basset or tenor pommer, 2 on bass pommer, and 1 on avery large bass pommer,
>
> 21 recorder players, 2 on the very small 'exilent,' 2 on discant, a fourth lower, 2 on discant, a fifth lower, 4 on alto flute, 4 on tenor flute, 4 on basset flute, 2 on bass flute and 1 on a large bass flute.[8]

[8] Michael Praetorius, *The Syntagma Musicum*, trans. Harold Blumenfeld (New York: Da Capo Press, 1980), vol. 2, 13.

The full superiority of the string medium does not come until late in the Baroque Period when, on one hand, the winds are needed in the military, and, on the other hand, the arrival of the period of the great string instrument makers occurs. But this is another story, for another volume. During the sixteenth century, the strings had not yet eclipsed the winds and no where is this more clear than in the music of the court.

The dance music of the sixteenth century court was most often played by the wind band, whether the dance was the older basse-dance or one of the forms which followed it. Because members of the string families became more visible during the final third of the century, some earlier writers have left the implication that throughout the sixteenth century a string consort performed the multi-part dance music. Such an implication can not be proven and most writers today acknowledge the role of the wind band in the court dance. Grove, for example, points out,

> Most princes also employed one or more bands of instrumentalists—principally cornettists, trombonists, shawm players and the like—who played for dancing and outdoor entertainments …
>
> …
>
> Doubtless the wind bands of princes played regularly for dancing.[9]

For the first half of the sixteenth century the wind band was by far the preferred medium for the court dance.[10] This is very significant in terms of the dance collections which appeared in manuscript and in print during this period. It is now clear they must be considered as part of the basic extant repertoire of the early wind band.

Of course, isolated occasions may be found when almost any grouping of instruments appeared for dance music. For example, Henry VIII of England and the Duke of Buckingham once danced to an heterogenous ensemble of shawm, rebec, small pipe, and lute, which must have sounded more medieval than renaissance in character.[11] Almost every noble had personal trumpets for ceremonial use and sometimes, as for example the especially festive occasion of a royal wedding, one reads of a dance performed by a trumpet ensemble. For the 1500 marriage of Duke Johann von Sachsen and Sofie von Mecklenburg in Torgau, for example, the princely pair danced and,

[9] Grove, 14:378. All references to Grove refer to George Grove, *The New Grove Dictionary of Music and Musicians*, ed. Stanley Sadie, (London: Macmillan, 1980).

[10] A painting, formerly in the Kupferstichkabinett, Berlin, and lost during the last war, pictured an 'Augsburger Basse danse,' in 1552. One sees here an ensemble of alto and tenor shawm, trombone, cornett, bagpipes, and percussion playing, in addition to a lute player who is *not* playing. Behind them is a banner which contains a typical basse-dance tenor. Perhaps the most famous icon of a sixteenth-century dance wind ensemble is Heinrich Aldegraever's *Three Crumhorn Players*, of 1551 (see picture on opposite page).

[11] John Stevens, *Music & Poetry in the Early Tudor Court* (London: Methuen, 1961), 245. A tapestry from northern France of this period called, 'The Savage's Ball,' pictures two shawms, a trumpet, and two strange natural horns playing (Church of Notre-Dame, Nantilly).

Three Crumhorn Players, by Heinrich Aldegraever, 1551

With great joy the participating guests noticeably listened when the trumpets, in an old custom and tradition, blew the Passamezzo and Saltarella.[12]

Even by the late sixteenth century, there is evidence that many people still associated the wind sound, and not the string sound, with this facet of court life.

Lightly rise and lightly fall, in the motion of your feete;
Move not till our noats doe call you, musicke makes the action sweet.
Musicke breathinge blowes the fyer, which Cupid feeds with fuell …
…

[12] Quoted in Wilhelm Ehmann, *Tibilustrium* (Kassel: Barenreiter-Verlag, 1950), 12.

mit grosser frolockunge der zusehenden ond zuhorenden der vorstendigen personen wan die tromther vbir lang herkommende gewonheit ond alten gebrauch mit Concordanzien gesetzte tentze, passund sprungmasse (Passamezzo und Saltarella) geblasen haben.

One of a series of engravings done by Heinrich Aldegraever, in 1538, pictures two slide-trumpets and a sackbut playing for a dance (see picture p. 8).

8 The Renaissance Wind Band and Wind Ensemble

An engraving by Heinrich Aldegraever, 1538, showing two slide-trumpets and a sackbut playing for a dance

Musicke is the soule of measure, speeding both in equall grace;
Twines ar they begot of pleasure, when she wishly numbered space.
Nothinge is more olde or newer than number all advancinge,
And noe number can be truer, than musick-wynd with dancinge.[13]

[13] John Nichols, ed., *The Progresses and Public Processions of Queen Elizabeth* (London, 1788), vol. 3.

Nothing, he says, could be more natural than wind music and dancing.

Some writers have perhaps been confused, regarding the frequency of the use of the wind band during the sixteenth century, by a failure to understand that from approximately 1400 to 1550, and even beyond, the term, 'minstrel,' usually meant a wind player. Thus the 'minstrels' who performed during the funeral of Henry VII, of England, are the same persons recorded under 'still shalmes' for the coronation of Henry VIII. One early English scribe makes this association of terms very clear.

> For the most parte all maner mynstrelsy
> By wynde they delyver thyr sound chefly.[14]

[14] Quoted in Stevens, *Music & Poetry*, 302.

This preference for the wind ensemble should be no surprise if one remembers that the renaissance musician tended to measure every instrument against 'God's instrument,' the voice.

> ... a consequence of the aesthetic ideal of the Italian Renaissance, which attributed the role of voice-imitation to instruments. This ideal was so well-rooted that, as Pietro Ponzio informs us, even the instrumentalists were called *cantori*. It is not to be denied that Renaissance wind instruments, not so much for their tone color as the way in which the performer breathed and produced the sound, could imitate the human voice better than could string instruments.[15]

[15] Marcello Castellani, 'A 1593 Veronese Inventory,' 18. Nothing is more foreign to the twentieth-century wind ensemble, which is treated almost always as a homophonic-percussive medium!

It was this function of dance performance which gave the wind band its first genuine repertoire, as opposed to the instrumental transcriptions of vocal materials. Functional though it was, it *was* original wind music. Wangermée speaks of this same transition.

> In the sixteenth century, along with certain pieces which had always served as dances, other instrumental pieces retained nothing of dance character except the formal schemes and rhythms, neglecting any functional use and becoming truly a kind of pure music. An important body of material grew out of these, including such forms as the *pavane*, which was composed with high art and was full of harmonic experiment.[16]

[16] Robert Wangermée, *Flemish Music and Society in the Fifteenth and Sixteenth Centuries* (New York: Praeger, 1968), 164.

When a wind band performed for a court banquet,[17] another frequent function, it now had these two bodies of music to play, the vocal motets, chansons, etc., and the original multipart dance music. Some scholars today seem to demean these 'banquet concerts,' as being not concerts but only 'background' music. But I believe one must be cautious in applying twentieth-century definitions to these events. I believe that, while some banquet music was no doubt truly 'background' in nature, there must have been moments, between servings, or after the eating, when the musicians were listened to as we

[17] A typical icon is found in Ammerbach's *Orgel order Instrument Tabulatur* (Leipzig, 1571), where one sees the wind band, together with singers and an organist, performing court dinner music.

listen to 'concert' music today. Why else, as the reader will find below, would a wind ensemble in Rome rehearse for eight days in preparation for one of these banquet performances? I rest my case with a description of a banquet performance in 1555 by Pontus de Tyard. True, it describes a lute player, and is no doubt highly exaggerated, but it does, I believe, reveal that music in general *must* have been something to listen to by this date, and not merely background music – whatever the occasion or medium.

> The tables cleared, he took up a lute and, as if merely essaying chords, he began, seated near the foot of the table, to strum a fantasy. He had plucked no more than the first three notes of the tune when all the conversations ceased among the festive throng and all were constrained to look there where he was, as he continued with such enchanting skill that little by little, through the divine art in playing that was his alone, he made the very strings to swoon beneath his fingers and transported all who listened into such gentle melancholy that one present buried his head in his hands, another let his entire body slump into an ungainly posture with members all awry, while another, his mouth sagged open and his eyes more than half shut, seemed, one would judge, as if transfixed upon the strings, and yet another, with chin sunk upon his chest, hiding the most sadly taciturn face ever seen, remained abstracted in all his senses save his hearing, as if his soul had fled from all the seats of sensibility to take refuge in his ears where more easefully it could rejoice in such enchanting symphony.[18]

[18] Description of Francesco da Milano, by Pontus de Tyard, *Solitaire second*, 1555.

In the succeeding pages, the reader will see the sixteenth-century court wind band in a variety of additional appearances, including the *intermedii* of the theatrical plays, the tournament, and a host of ceremonial functions.

During the sixteenth century, military music began to play a more conspicuous role and thus demands our attention. In this volume I treat the subject under 'court wind bands,' rather than as a separate medium, for two reasons. First, during most of the sixteenth century the military consisted of mercenaries, soldiers hired by nobles for particular battles and wars. It is with the arrival of standing armies, which we associate with the Baroque period, that one finds true military bands for the first time. Only a few accounts during the sixteenth century seem to describe a military ensemble beyond the usual flute-types and drums. One eyewitness, describing a sea battle between Spain and Portugal in 1582, reports having heard trumpets, shawms, and drums.[19] Another eyewitness, Johann David Wunderer, of Strasbourg, wrote of Russian troops, in 1589,

> In battles and parades they use many sackbuts, crumhorns, shawms and other wind instruments which are unknown in Germany.[20]

Second, until that basic change in military organization, military music was primarily 'interval' music, signals, etc. It is again with the advent of standing armies, and the rediscovery of the Greek tradition of co-ordinated marching—for which wind instruments were considered indispensable—that a true repertoire of military music begins to appear.

The roots of this fundamental change, which occurred during the seventeenth century, can already be seen during the sixteenth century. Machiavelli, for example, writing before 1520, recommends the reintroduction of the use of music for co-ordinated marching.

> Then the menne ought to march, accordyng to the Ensigne: and the Ensigne to move, accordyng to the Drumme, the whiche Drumme well ordered, commaundeth to the armie, the whiche goyng with paces, that answereth the tyme of thesame, will come to kepe easilie thorders: for whiche cause the antiquitie had Shalmes, Flutes, and soundes perfectly tymed: For as moche as like as he that daunseth, proceadeth with the tyme of the Musick, and goyng with thesame doeth not erre, even so an armie obeiyng, in movyng it self to thesame sounde, doeth not disorder: and therefore, thei varied the sounde, accordyng as thei would varie the mocion, and accordyng as thei would inflame, or quiete, or staie the mindes of men.[21]

As kings and princes moved in the direction of permanent armies, they took increasing interest in all details of military organization. Field communication, for example, which had for centuries depended on wind and percussion 'signals,' now began to take on a somewhat more complicated form. Machiavelli recommended placing the trumpets, who had the greatest carrying power, close by the commander-in-chief to give the primary orders. These orders were then passed on through the troops by drums and flutes, instruments of more local carrying power.

[19] Quoted in Walter Salmen, *Musikleben im 16. Jahrhundert* (Leipzig, 1976), 98.

[20] Quoted in W. Salmen, 'Russchische Musik und Musiker in Deutschland vor 1700,' *Die Musikforschung* 26 (1973), 175.

> In Schlachten und Zugodtnungen gebrauchen sie viel Posaunen, Grumhörner, Schalmeyen und ander geblass, so in Deutschland unbekannd seindt …

[21] Niccolo Machiavelli, *The Art of War*, trans. Peter Whitehorne, ca. 1560 (New York: AMS Press, 1967), 92–93.

> ... nere (near) the generall capitain, I would make the Trompettes to stand, as a sounde not onely apt to inflame the armie, but apte to bee heard in all the whole tumoult more, than any other sounde: all the other soundes, whiche should bee aboute the Conestables, and the heddes of maine battailes I would, that thei should bee smalle Drummes, and Flutes, sounded not as thei sounde theim now, but as thei use to sounde theim a feastes. The capitaine then with the Trompet, should shewe when thei must stande still, and go forward, or tourne backward, when the artillerie must shoote, when the extraordinaire Veliti must move, and with the varietie or distinccion of soche soundes, to shewe unto the armie all those mocions, whiche generally maie bee shewed, the whiche Trompettes, should bee after followed of the Drummes, and in this exercise, bicause it importeth moche, it behoveth moche to exercise the armie. Concernyngs the horsemen, there would be used likewise Trompettes, but of a lesse sounde, and of a divers vocie from those of the Capitaine.[22]

The earliest of European signals which have come down to us seem to be of Italian origin, spread throughout Europe during the late Middle Ages by Italian mercenaries. Many of the names of signals in other languages are corruptions, or similar-sounding replacements, of the Italian originals. The English signal, 'Boot and Saddle,' meaning to put on the saddles, is derived from the Italian, 'Butte Sella.'[23] This very signal is quoted in the earliest example of military signals which is extant in musical notation. These are found in Janequin's extraordinary vocal composition, 'La bataille,' published in Paris in 1528, probably depicting the French victory at Marignano in 1515.[24]

During the course of the sixteenth century, these signals became more detailed, governing more and more of the soldier's daily life. An English publication (*Rules and Ordynaunces for Warre*) of 1544 notes, for example,

> Euery horseman at the fyrst blaste of the trumpette shall sadle or cause to be sadled his horse, at the seconde to brydell, at the thirde to leape on his horse backe, to wait on the kyng, or his lorde or capitayne.

It goes without saying that the effectiveness of these signals depended on their recognition by the regular soldier and, as one can see in an English regulation of 1557,[25] it was part of the job of the musician to teach them.

---

[22] Ibid., 126–127. The reference to how the flute and drum used to play at banquets (feastes) probably should be taken as a reference to the level of co-ordination achieved by the one-man fife and tabor player.

[23] Lilla Fox, *Instruments of Processional Music* (London: Lutterworth, 1967), 65.

[24] A quotation of this passage may be seen in Grove, 12:317.

[25] Quoted in Grove, 6:540.

(The fifers must) teach the companye the soundes of the marche, allarum, approache, assaulte, battaile, retreate, skirmishe, or any other challenge that of necessitie should be knowen.

But these signals were more than a form of communication, they were part of the formal ritual of war itself. Zarlino, in 1558, wrote,

> Such a custom is still observed in our time, so that one of two fighting forces does not assault the enemy unless urged by the sound of the trumpets and tympani, or by some other musical instrument.[26]

[26] Gioseffo Zarlino, *Le institutioni armoniche* (1558), I, ii.

1 Court Wind Bands in England

Henry VIII

Henry VIII (reigning 1509–1547) was born with all of the capacity to become one of the greatest kings in history; if he did not achieve that, he was certainly one of the more influential. An Italian diplomat who knew him described the king at age twenty-five.

> His Majesty is the handsomest potentate I ever set eyes on; above the usual height, with an extremely fine calf to his leg, his complexion very fair and bright, with auburn hair combed straight and short ... He speaks French, English, and Latin, and a little Italian, plays well on the lute and harpsichord, sings from book at sight, draws the bow with greater strength than any man in England, and jousts marvellously.[1]

I might add that he loved the flute, owning no fewer than one hundred and fifty-four of them when he died.

Henry's coronation festivities occurred on 21–24 June 1509, beginning with a great procession into London. The principal streets were richly decorated, in some cases with sheets of gold cloth, and Henry wore a robe of red velvet, covered with jewels. All the nobles and ladies appeared in the procession, displaying such an abundance of gold and silver cloth, gold chains, etc., that one felt the wealth of dress was, 'in more plentie and abundaunce, than hath been seen, or redde of at any tyme before.'[2]

The actual coronation occurred on Sunday, the day following the procession. While details are lacking regarding the music performed during the coronation, extant Lord Chamberlain's records[3] mention three distinct wind ensembles who participated.

The Styll shalmes

John Chambre, marshall	Thomas Spencer
John Furneys	Thomas Grenyng
Thomas Mayow	John Abys
Richard Waren	Thomas Pegion
Bartram Brewer, mynstrell	

---

[1] Letter dated 30 April 1515, by Piero Pasqualigo, Venetian Ambassador, in Sebastian Giustinian, *Four Years at the Court of Henry VIII* (London, 1854), 1:83.

[2] Edward Hall, *Hall's Chronicle* (London, 1809), 508

[3] Quoted in Henry Cart de LaFontaine, *The King's Musick* (London, 1909), 4.

16 The Renaissance Wind Band and Wind Ensemble

Portrait of Henry VIII, by Hans Holbein the Younger (1498–1543), ca. 1536

Sakbudds and shalmes of the Privee Chambre

Johannes	Alexander
William	Edward

The kyng's trompytts

Peter, marshall of the kyng's trumpetts	John Banke
	John Hert
Jakett	Thomas Wrethe
Franke	John Frere
John de Cecill	John Scarlett
Domynk	John Strett
Christopher	Robert Wrethe
John Broun	

Following the coronation was a banquet, which began as 'the trumpettes blew vp.' The first course was led into the room by the Duke of Buckingham and the Lord Steward, riding into the hall on horses richly decorated in cloth of gold. The food was 'sumpteous, with many subtleties, straunge deuises, with seuerall poses, and many deintie dishes.'

The following day featured a tournament. A gallery (faire house) was specially constructed in the form of a castle with towers and embattlements, to seat the royal couple. It was richly laid with tapestries and was entwined by a 'curious Vine, the leaues and grapes thereof, gilded with fine Golde.' Finally at several points around the castle, 'out of the mouthes of certain beastes, or gargels' did runne red, white, and claret wine.' The tournament was based on a theme of Pallas and her relationship to both War and Wisdom and began with a pageant featuring a wagon constructed in the form of a mountain, drawn by a 'lyon made of Glyteryng gold.' Within this mountain, on horse, were the two chief Challengers. The Answerers entered from the opposite side of the field, led by a silver lioness, and within a constructed castle with a pomegranate tree 'soo cunnyngly' created that all thought the fruit was real. After some speech making, the Challengers rode on to the field to the sound of trumpets, the Answerers, 'with Dromes and Fifes a greate nombre.'

The final event of the coronation festivities featured another pageant, the centerpiece of which was a constructed forest of 'curious Trees made by crafte; with Busshes, Fernes, and other thynges in likewise wroughte, goodly to beholde.' Eight knights were introduced by 'a greate nombre of hornes blowen,' by men dressed in the green cloth of foresters. A fallow deer was let loose in this forest, to be killed by dogs and then presented to the queen. The ensuing hand-to-hand combat among the knights got out of control and became so violent that Henry was forced to call out the guard and halt the proceedings, which they accomplished only with 'grete payn.'[4]

Of all the indoor entertainments available to a King of England, Henry seemed, early in his reign, to enjoy most appearing with his nobles in elaborate disguises. On 28 February 1510, he gave a banquet at which the various nobles appeared dressed as foreign ambassadors. A 'drumme and a fife' appeared, but as there was dancing, no doubt there were more instrumentalists.

[4] Descriptions taken from Hall, *Hall's Chronicle*, 507–512, and Robert Fabyan, A.H. Thomas, and I.D. Thornley, *The Great Chronicle of London* (London: G.W. Jones, 1938), 341–342.

A similar dinner, given for ambassadors of the Emperor Maximilian and the King of Spain, held 14 November in the same year, featured Henry disguised, entering after dinner to hold a 'mumming.'[5] Then 'sodenly entred vi mynstrels, rychely appareled, plaiyng on their instrumentes,' followed by richly dressed members of the court who then held a formal dance.

By far the greatest court celebration held during the early years of Henry's reign was occasioned by the birth of his son. The celebrations, held 12 and 13 February 1511, were announced by an allegorical letter of challenge by a 'Queen Noble Renome' of the land, 'Ceure noble.' The first day featured a tournament, again preceded by an elaborate pageant. First, a wheeled float, twenty-six feet long and sixteen feet wide, representing a forest with 'trees and bowes artyfycyall as hawthornes, okes, mapylles, hasylles, byrches, fern broom, fyrs, with bestes and byrds in bosyd of svndry facyvn.' This vehicle was drawn (apparently) by two constructed animals, a golden lion and a silver antelope, both gilded with gold, with mouths connected with hinges, and tails of iron wire. Mounted on the animals were ladies; leading the animals were four 'wildmen.' Foresters 'blew a moot' on their horns and the tournament itself was announced with 'great noyse, as well of Trompettes as of Dromes.'

The following day another tournament was held, one recorded in a manuscript volume of illustrations called the *Great Tournament Roll*, now housed in the College of Arms.[6] In two illustrations entitled, 'Les Trompettes' (Nrs. 3–4), one sees six mounted players of the short folded trumpet, all dressed in yellow and grey with blue purses at their waists. It is quite rare, for this date, to see one of them is a black man, identified in the Treasurer of the Chamber accounts as, 'John Blanke, the black trumpet.' This group of players appears again (in illustrations Nrs. 27–28) under the title, 'Le son des Trompettes. A l'hostel.'[7] In spite of these representations of six trumpeters, an extant document addressed to the 'keper of oure greate warderobe' suggests that in fact fifteen players participated, which would be consistent with the number of players at the coronation less than two years before.[8]

This tournament was preceded by a pageant led by a tower and jailer holding a great key in his hand. This entry was made in silence, 'without dromme or noyse of mynstrelsye.'[9]

[5] A mumming was the appearance of masked persons who invited the guests to games of dice, which the guests always won.

[6] A modern reproduction of these illustrations can be seen in Sydney Anglo, *The Great Tournament Roll of Westminster* (Oxford: Clarendon, 1968).

[7] 'l'hostel' was a frequent cry at the end of a tournament, meaning 'to the hostel,' or back to quarters.

[8] London, British Museum (MSS. Add. 18.826, fol. 16). Henry R. By the king

> We woll and comaunde you to deliuer or doo to be deliuered vnto oure Trompettes for oure vse fiftene Baners with theire Tasselles.

[9] 'Noise' is a synonym (but not a musical criticism!) for a wind band in English literature of this period.

COURT WIND BANDS IN ENGLAND 19

John Blanke, The Black Trumpeter, an extract from the Westminster Tournament Roll, 1511

Extract from an Exchequer roll of 1507 showing payment to John Blanke, the Black trumpeter. E36/214, f. 109 (7 Dec 1507)

When the tower arrived before the queen, the jailer unlocked it and out rode a noble clad in the coarse habit of a recluse or religious person, requesting permission to be in the tournament, etc.

That evening the king gave a banquet for all the foreign ambassadors which featured singing by men of the Chapel Royal and dancing to the music of the minstrels. Henry slipped out unnoticed to prepare for another 'disguising.' 'Within a littell while after his departing, the trompettes at thende of the Hall began to blow.' In came a huge float, including six children singers of the Chapel, six richly clad ladies, the principal Challengers of the day's tournament, and eight minstrels 'wyth strange instrementes.' One can understand this float was 'mervelvs wyghtty to remevf and karry as yt dyd bothe vp and down the hall and tvrnyd rovnd.' In fact, it was so heavy that when under construction at 'bechop of harfordes plas' it fell through the floor! Eventually, there was more dancing to the music of the minstrels and it was said that the minstrels themselves joined in the dancing so 'that it was a pleasure to beholde.'

Additional jousts were held in Greenwich in May 1511, and June 1512, both with the participation of trumpets, in the latter case, 'a great noyse of Trompettes.'

The year 1513 began with a 'disguising' at Greenwich, featuring a 'mountain,' with six ladies contained within, followed by dinner and a dance. The court Revels Accounts list payment for six minstrels, four tabors, and a rebec for the dance.[10]

Much of 1513 the court was occupied with the war with France and accounts of the various battles contain the usual references to trumpets giving a variety of signals.[11] Henry followed along behind the troops, enjoying a variety of entertainments. A contemporary, John Taylor, lists Henry's own performance on the 'fluto de cythara, lira de flauti and corno' as being among these diversions.[12] After the city of Tournai fell to his armies, Henry entered under a canopy of gold and silk, to the sounds of 'drums and minstrelsy.'[13]

On 1 May 1515, Henry arranged for a disguising by way of which he and his company while out for a ride would be surprised by 'Robin Hood' and his men.

[10] Stevens, *Music & Poetry*, 262.

[11] Hall, *Hall's Chronicle*, 543, 551, 554.

[12] Quoted in Anglo, *The Great Tournament Roll of Westminster*, 61.

[13] Hall, *Hall's Chronicle*, 566.

> Then Robyn hood desyred the kynge and quene to come into the grene wood, & to se how the outlawes lyue. The kyng demaunded of ye quene & her ladyes, if they durst aduenture to go into the wood with so many outlawes … the hornes blewe … there was an Arber made of boowes with a hal, and a great chaber and an inner chamber very well made & couered with floures & swete herbes, whiche the kyng muche praysed.[14]

The king and his company were served a breakfast of venison, accompanied by music of organs, flutes, and a lute. One of the guests, a Venetian, describes the return home.

> … proceeding homewards, certain tall paste-board giants being placed on cars, and … (we) were conducted with the greatest order to Greenwich, the musicians singing the whole way, and sounding trumpets and other instruments, so that, by my faith, it was an extrenely fine triumph.[15]

Yet another Venetian described this return trip as riding, 'in great state in pairs, with big drums, and to the sound of trumpets.'[16] Upon the arrival at Greenwich, a joust was held which an eyewitness describes as lasting three hours, 'to the constant sound of the trumpets and drums.'[17]

Beginning with the tournament of 19–20 May 1516, held in honor of Mary, Queen of Scots, one notices a change in the character of these events. The allegorical and quasi-fantastic pageants which preceded earlier tournaments now disappear, although the sumptuous costumes of the king and knights, and their horses, continue even more extravagantly than before. On this day, Henry wore purple apparel, set with leaves of gold fastened to each other with points of damask gold and bordered with letters in gold bullion. The entry was made with 'trompettes, dronslades and other minstrelsey.'[18]

A joust in honor of Flemish ambassadors, held in July 1517, began with the appearance of twenty-four trumpeters in cloth of silver and caps of white velvet.[19] Chieregato, an eyewitness, reports that the harnesses for the horses of those present were made from pure silver and had required all the smiths in London to work on nothing else for four months before.[20] At the end of the day, a banquet was held in honor of the Flemish ambassadors which Chieregato says lasted seven hours.[21]

[14] Ibid., 582.

[15] Letter of Nicolò Sagudino, dated May 3, 1515, quoted in Giustinian, *Four Years at the Court of Henry VIII*, 1:80.

[16] Letter of Piero Pasqualigo, dated April 30, 1515, quoted in Ibid., 1:91.

[17] Ibid., 1:81.

[18] Hall, *Hall's Chronicle*, 584.

[19] Anglo, *The Great Tournament Roll of Westminster*, 64.

[20] Quoted in ibid., 65.

[21] Ibid., 66.

In October 1518, Cardinal Wolsey entertained the French ambassadors, who were present in London to sign the 'Celebration of Universal Peace.' Wolsey maintained his own private minstrels who were players of wind instruments, as one can see in the following description of a mumming offered by the Cardinal following the banquet for the ambassadors.

> And when the banket was done, in came vj mynstrels, richely disguysed, and after them folowed iij gentlemen in wyde and long gounes of Crymosyn sattyn, everyone havyng a cup of golde in their handes, the first cup was ful of Angels and royals, the second had diverse bales of dyce, and the iij had certayn payres of Cardes. These gentlemen offered to playe at monchaunce, and when they had played ye length of the first boorde, then the mynstrels blew up, and then entered into the chambre xij ladyes disguysed ...[22]

[22] Hall, *Hall's Chronicle*, 595.

Another contemporary describes an appearance by the Cardinal's wind band, during a banquet given for the king, and hints rather darkly of possible foul play in the sudden death of one of the shawm players.

> ... there was not only plenty of fine meats, but also much mirth and solace, as well in merry communication as with the noise of my Lord's minstrels, who played there all that night so cunningly, that the King took therein great pleasure; insomuch that he desired my Lord to lend them unto him for the next night, and after supper their banquet finished, the ladies and gentlemen fell to dancing, among whom, one Madame Fontaine, a maid, had the prize. And thus passed they the most part of the night ere they departed. The next day the King took my Lord's minstrels, and rode to a nobleman's house where there was some image to whom he vowed a pilgrimage, to perform his devotions. When he came there, which was in the night, he danced and caused others to do the same, after the sound of my Lord's minstrels, who played there all night, and never rested, so that whether it were with extreme labour of blowing, or with poison (as some judged) because they were commended by the King more than his own, I cannot tell, but the player on the shalme (who was very excellent on that instrument) died within a day or two after.[23]

[23] Stow's *Annals* quoted in Edmondstoune Duncan, *The Story of Minstrelsy* (Detroit: Singing Tree Press, 1968), 139. One of Wolsey's biographers tells a somewhat different version of what must be the same tale. He, Cavendish, says that when Wolsey was visiting the French court in Paris, in 1527, with his wind band in tow, the King of France, Francis I, who was always on the lookout for good wind players, stole one of Wolsey's shawms. The implication here is that Wolsey, in retribution, was somehow responsible for the death by poison of the shawm player. See George Cavendish, *The Life and Death of Cardinal Wolsey*, ed. Richard Sylvester (London: Oxford University Press, 1959), 60, and Joycelyne Gledhill Russell, *The Field of Cloth of Gold* (New York: Barnes & Noble, 1969), 163.

During the previous several years, Henry and his agents had been enlisting foreign musicians for service in his court. The results of one such recruiting effort can be seen in a letter from Chamberlain, Court-Master of the English merchants in Antwerp, to Paget, First Secretary of the court. He reports that with the help of local merchants he has found five musicians, one of whom can make all sorts of instruments. Four of the musicians are young and would like to join the king's service, but own no instruments. The fifth, who owns the instruments, has with some difficulty been persuaded to go with them. If paid wages and expenses in advance they agree to stay in England until the new year. Chamberlain reports there are also some Italians in the town, but they can only play the viols and therefore, 'are no musicians.'[24]

[24] Stevens, *Music & Poetry*, 308.

The foreign names of some of the wind players are immediately recognizable: the trumpeters Domynyk and Andryan, the flutists Guillam Troche and Piero Guye, and the keeper of the instruments, Philip van Wilder. An extremely interesting document exists, addressed to this last man, which suggests that the wind band played in intimate, indoor situations as well as the great ceremonial ones.

> … paied to phillip of the pryvat chambre for ij sagbuttes ij tenor shalmes and two treble shalmesse. 10.10s.[25]

[25] Ibid., 307. Philip van Wilder was a player of the lute and well-known as a composer as well. An Elegy, 'Of the death of Phillips,' was included in Tottel's *Songs and Sonets*, of 1557.

> The stringe is broke, the lute is dispossest;
> The hand is colde, the bodye in the grounde.
> The lowring lute lamenteth now therfore
> Philips her frende that can her touche no more.

In June 1520, there occurred a summit meeting between Henry and Francis of France, arranged by Wolsey, aimed at creating a new era of peace between the two countries. Henry traveled to the site, between Guisnes and Ardres, in France, with more than five thousand men and women, requiring nearly three thousand horses for transportation. A vast tent city was created so rich in appearance that the entire meeting has been known ever since as the 'Field of Cloth of Gold.' There were fountains running with wine, jousts, tournaments, wrestling (Francis risked ruining the mood by throwing Henry to the ground), music, dramatic events, and banquets. It was, said contemporaries, the eighth wonder of the world. There are many references to trumpets, but no doubt there were many other instrumentalists present. At the first meeting of the two kings, the wind bands of both countries were stationed and ready.

> Then vp blewe the Trumpettes, Sgabuttes, Clarions, and all other Minstrelles on bothe sides, and the kynges descended doune towarde the bottome of the valey of Andern, in sight of bothe the nacions and on horsebacke met and embarsed the twoo kyngeseache other.[26]

[26] Hall, *Hall's Chronicle*, 610.

On another day, the English wind band is described as it went to perform before the Queen of France.

> … the Drunslad plaiers and other minstrels arayed in white, yelowe, and russet Damaske, these minstrels blew and played and so passed through the strete of Arde.[27]

[27] Ibid., 615.

Another reference to the actual instrumentation of Henry's wind band is found in accounts of his celebration of a new title, 'Fidei Defensor,' given him by the Pope. This was an honorary title intended to suggest that Henry might be considered as the next Emperor of the Holy Roman Empire, and as it was proclaimed,

> trumpettes blew, the shalmes and saggebuttes plaied in honour of the kynges new style.[28]

[28] Ibid., 629.

On 28 May 1522, the Emperor, Charles v, returned to England for a visit, resulting in some of the most extravagent festivities of Henry's reign. The great processional entry into London first passed by a dragon and two great bulls, 'whiche beastes cast out fyer continually,' as only the first of numerous elaborate pageants. Further in the procession route, the two kings passed a large group of wind instruments.

> From thence they passed to ye conduite in Cornehill where the strete was enclosed from side to side with ii gates to open & shitte, and ouer the gates wer arches with towers embattailed set with vanes and scutchions of the armes of the Emperor & the kyng, and ouer the arches were two towers, the one full of Trompettes and the other full of Shalmes and sagbuttes whiche played continually.[29]

[29] Ibid., 638.

As a result of this visit, Henry joined Charles in a war against France; six years later Henry would join France in a war against Charles. These wars were expensive in money and lives for England and accomplished virtually nothing for the country. For these years the Hall chronicle contains many references to military music, primarily the trumpet. One sees accounts of the trumpet beginning the various battles, announcing truces, sending signals, and serving diplomatic duties ('well sayd the lorde Admyrall, I will send him answere by my trumpet.').[30]

These great court festivals, disguisings and tournaments became more and more rare as the reign progressed, even though Henry continued to maintain a large number of minstrels. The liveries accounts for 1526 included payment to sixteen trumpeters and eighteen minstrels, of whom ten were trombonists.[31] The rest were probably players of rebec and woodwind instruments. A well-known drawing by Holbein of the 'Musicians gallery,' at Whitehall, pictures three players with shawms, one with a straight trumpet, and one with a slide-trumpet, or perhaps a trombone (see image below). According to Dart, no trace of the viole can be found among the royal instrumentalists before 1526.[32]

[30] Ibid., 648.

[31] LaFontaine, *The King's Musick*, 5. Regarding the ten trombones, see Stevens, *Music & Poetry*, 302. The ceiling of the Chapel Royal at Hampton Court was decorated at the time of Henry VIII with carved shawms.

[32] Thurston Dart, 'Origines et Sources de la Musique de Chambre en Angleterre (1550–1530),' ed. Jean Jacquot, *La Musique Instrumentale de la Renaissance* (Paris, 1955), 82ff.

Musicians on a Gallery, Hans Holbein the Younger (1498–1543), ca. 1524

The rapid trading of wives, for which Henry VIII was so notorious, is associated with the second-half of his reign. The first of these new wives, Anne Boleyn, received from Henry an extraordinarily lavish coronation celebration, partly to help achieve her acceptance by the public and partly, perhaps, to help hide the fact that she was six months pregnant.

The celebration began with a great water procession down the Thames to Greenwich to meet and escort the new queen back to London. The first boat in this procession contained guns to salute the queen, but also a 'great Dragon continually mouyng, & castyng wyldfyer' and a group of 'terrible monsters and wylde men castyng fyer, and makyng hideous noyses.' Next came Mayor Stephen Peacock, 'In which barge wer Shalmes, Shagbushes & diuers other instrumentes, whiche continually made goodly armony.' This reference to the music of the shawms and trombones suggests, as do several references below, that they were playing highly organized, multi-part music and not simple fanfares. To the right of the Mayor's boat was the 'Batchelers' barge, filled with 'trumpettes and diuers other melodious instruments.' These were followed by forty-eight additional boats, each representing a private corporation (guild) in London and each with its own 'mynstrelsie.' After the short trip to Greenwich it appears that these wind bands gave a concert of sorts while waiting for the appearance of the queen, for one reads, 'they rowed douneward to Grenewiche toune and there cast anker makyng great melody.'

When the queen appeared, the entire company made the return trip to London, 'their minstrels continually plaiyng.' They took the new queen to the Tower of London, which was to be her residence before the coronation. Before the Tower there was more music ('makyng great melody'), together with trumpets and guns creating an impression for one Spanish diplomat that, 'verily it seemed as if the world was coming to an end.'[33]

The following day marked the official reception of the queen in London, requiring another procession. All houses on the parade route were richly decorated and even the streets were covered with gravel to prevent any royal horses from slipping. Several fountains ran continuously with wine and pageants appeared at principal intersections. No doubt wind bands were prominent, although the eyewitnesses men-

[33] Carolly Erickson, *Bloody Mary* (Garden City, NY: Doubleday, 1978), 98. The other references to this celebration are taken from Hall, *Hall's Chronicle*, 798–805.

tion only 'swete armony both of song and instrument … a riche pageaunt full of melodye and song.' Certainly one reference to an ensemble playing from a tower must have meant trombones:

> (In a nearby tower) was suche several solemne instrumetes, that it semed to be an heauenly noyse, and was muche regarded and praised.[34]

34 Hall, *Hall's Chronicle*, 802.

The following day, 1 June 1533, the coronation itself occurred. As the party left the cathedral, 'the trumpettes played meruailous freshely,' which I take to mean they must have done a great deal of playing earlier during the service. The following banquet consisted of twenty-eight dishes in the first course, twenty-four in the second, and thirty in the third course. One is reminded of the manners of the day when reading,

> On the left side stood the countesse of Worcester all the dyner season, which diuers tymes in the dyner tyme did hold a fyne cloth before the quenes face when she list to spet.

All during the banquet, 'the trumpettes standing in the wyndow at the netherende of the halle played melodiously.'

The later wives and queens in their very rapid succession made pomp of this magnitude inappropriate. Thus, for Anne of Cleves, for example, one sees only the usual aristocratic instruments. First the queens trumpets,

> went forwarde, whyche were twelue in nombre besyde two kettle Drommes on horsebacke, then followed the Kynges Trompettes.[35]

35 Ibid., 835. The king still had other wind players, for only a few months earlier he had rewarded both the 'old and the new sagbutts.' See Stevens, *Music & Poetry*, 301.

The funeral of Henry VIII, in 1547, was conducted with the full ritual of the Catholic Church and the Latin service. An eyewitness remarked that 'the trumpets sounded with great melody and courage, to the comfort of all them that were present.'[36] The official accounts of the ceremony list participation by twenty-nine singers, eight string and forty-two wind and percussion players.[37] I list the latter, for perhaps it represents a clue to the organization of the wind players in Henry's court during the final years of his reign.

36 Quoted in Duncan, *The Story of Minstrelsy*, 157.

37 LaFontaine, *The King's Musick*, 7, 8.

Trumpettors

John Fisher	Robert Richemound
Henry Stephinson	William Frende
Benedict Browne	Edmond Frere
John Tuke	John Warren
Peter Frauncis	Robert Copley
John Pytches	Richard Lane
John Frere	Henry Ryve
Richard Frende	John Hall
Thomas Newman	Stephin Medcalfe
Thomas Browne	John Graundge
Arthur Skarlett	

Mynstrells

Hughe Wodhouse	Robert Strachon
Thomas Mayewe	Hugh Grene
John Webbes	Robert Norman
Thomas Pigen	

Musytyans

Alinso Bassani	Gespero Bassani
Zuani Bassani	Baptista Bassani
Anthony Bassani	

Shackebuttes

Marck Anthonio Petala	Anthony Syma
Nicholas Dandre	Anthony Maria

Fluttes

John Syvernacke	Nicholas Puvall
Guillam Trochies	Pietro Guy
Guillam Puett	

Fyfer

Olyuer Fyfer

Drume player

Allexaunder

Bage piper

Richard Edward[38]

---

[38] The 'Mynstsrells' are perhaps shawm players, as Thomas Pigen appears as a player of this instrument on an earlier list. The 'Musytyans,' I take to be a family of Italian wind players, as the next generation of this family are so identified.

Finally, I have mentioned above the large number of flutes found in the inventory of Henry's musical instruments made upon his death in 1547. This collection also included a large number of keyboard instruments, fifty strings, and nearly two hundred and fifty wind instruments. Among the latter were twenty-one horns, twenty-two cornetts, twenty-one crumhorns, seventeen shawms, and eleven bassoon-types. One must assume these instruments were used indoors, as the trumpets, trombones, and percussion instruments so frequently mentioned in chronicles of the state ceremonies are entirely missing in this collection and must have been housed separately.

Edward VI

Edward VI (reigning 1547–1553) became a king at age ten upon the death of his father, Henry VIII. Rather than inheriting the robust health of his father, he was more like his frail mother, Jane Seymour, who died during his birth. Edward himself died before completing his sixteenth year.

One sees the royal trumpets of Henry VIII performing at the christening ceremony for Edward in 1537.

> Item, the sergeaunte of the trumpettes with all the company of that offyce were redy with their trumpettes, and did sownde as by the lorde chamberlan thei were commaundid.[39]

[39] Edward, King of England, *Literary Remains of King Edward the Sixth*, ed. John Nichols (London, 1857), I, cclvii.

The trumpets played as the baptism began and again after the blessing. At the conclusion of the ceremony, all the nobles formed a procession to the state apartments, where the young prince was presented to the king and queen.

> Item, after the Prynce his stile proclaymed by the kynges of armes and herauldes, then they retornyng to the quenes chamber wering on their cotes of armes and the sergeauntes at armes berying their masys and all the torcheis then lyghted, every man kepyng ordre in his place; so procedid forthe to the quenes chambre, the trympyttes blowing all the waye; and, the Prynce commen in the said chamber, then the trumpettes standing in th'other courte within the gate, there blowing, and the mynstrelles playing, which was a melodious thing to heare.[40]

[40] Ibid., I, cclx.

The festivities surrounding the coronation of Edward VI began on 19 February 1548, with a procession through London which lasted most of the day. Streets were again covered with gravel to steady the step, houses were hung with cloth of gold, and fountains in several locations ran with free wine. Near the head of the procession were the royal trumpets, probably on horse, two by two ('Then the Trumpetes, clothed all in redde damaske, ij and ij').[41]

The procession began officially at the conduit in Cornhill where actors upon a platform gave two speeches before the king and minstrels stationed there sang a song.

At the Great Conduit in Cheap, another group of minstrels played and actors representing the knight, "Valentyne," and the 'wylde Urson' gave speeches. Further down this street was one of the fountains of wine, on top of which was a 'crowne imperyall of golde, garnished as it stode with ryche perle and stones.' During the course of the day the public, 'with great diligence feched it away.' Here, too, children representing Grace, Nature, Fortune, and Charite, gave speeches. At a 'certain distance' from this pageant stood another with actors, 'richly apparelled like ladyes,' representing the seven sciences.

[41] Coronation details found in ibid., I, cclxxviii-cccv.

> Grammer
> I, Grammer, with the silver key unlocke the doore to science every way.
>
> Logicke
> And I, Logick, dyrectly discusse all thinges uprightly.
>
> Rhetoricke
> And I, the adorned Rhetorick, to bewtefy speeches is much pollityke.
>
> Arsmetricke
> And I, Arsmetrik, through excercise in numbering maketh men wise.
>
> Geomatrie
> I, Geomatry, ordained for measuring, and as necessary for building.
>
> Musicke
> Yet I, pleasant Musicke, for kynges pastime am most lyke.
>
> Astronamy
> I, prudent Astronamy, describeth of planettes the mystery.

At the Standard in Cheap, there were 'trompettes blowing melodiously' and a planned speech was omitted as the king 'passed by spedely.'

At St. Peter's Church, in Cheap, the Mayor of London and his party stood, together with the London Waits, the official civic wind band. Here an actor was dressed as St. George and although his Latin speech was omitted, a song was sung before the king.

> Sing up heart, sing up heart, sing no more downe,
> but Joy in King Edward that wereth the crowne.

Nearby, at St. Georges' Church, a rope had been laid from the tower of the church to the ground. As the king approached, a 'stranger, being a native of Arragon,' came down the rope on his breast, with arms and legs streched out, as if he had 'been an arrowe out of a bowe.' Reaching the ground, he kissed the king's feet, spoke a few words with him, and then climbed back up the rope, performing tricks as he ascended. For the boy king this was, of course, the highpoint of the day. He forced the procession to halt there for some time to watch and this event would become a feature of several later coronation processions.

Next, at Great Conduit in Fleet Street, two child actors appearing as Trewth and Justice spoke, Trewth giving a plug for the Protestant faith which had been newly adopted by England.

> I, auncyent Trewth, which long time was suppressed
> with hethen rites and destable idolatrye, ...

At Temple Bar, a city gate, were 'viii French trumpetts blowing their trumpettes after the fashion of their countrey.' Before the procession ended at Westminster, the king had also observed minstrels playing at Bridgefoot (London Bridge), St. Margaret's Church, The Falcon, Ludgate, St. Dunstans Church, and at still other locations were 'Singingmen.'

The coronation day itself, 21 February, heard music by thirty-three singers, two 'Vialls,' a harp, and a large number of wind players.

Trumpettors

Benedict Browne	John Tucke
Peter Frauncis	John Pytches
John Fryer	Richard Frende
Thomas Newman	Thomas Browne
Arthur Skarlett	William Frende
Edmond Fryer	John Warren
Robert Copley	Richard Lane
Henry Ryve	John Hall
Stephen Medcalf	John Graunge

Musicians

Lewes	Anthony Symon
John	Albertt
Anthony	Marc Anthony
Gasper	Vyncentt
Baptist	Ambrose
Marc Anthony	George
Nicholas Andrewe	Fraunces
Anthony Mary	

The Flutes

John de Severna eke	Piero Guye
Guillam Troche	Nicholas Pewell
Guillam Deventt	

Bagge piper

Richard Woodwarde

The king's majesty's musicians

Hugh Pollard	Robert May
Edward Lake	Allen Robson
Thomas Lye	Thomas Pagington
Thomas Cursson[42]	

[42] I take the 'Musicians' to be a wind ensemble; Anthony Symon, Nicholas Andrewe, Anthony Mary, and a Marc Antony all appear in other court records as trombonists. See LaFontaine, *The King's Musick*, 5–7. The 'king's majesty's musicians,' are perhaps the king's wind band. Lake was a harpist on another occasion, Cursson a 'fyfer,' Pagington a flutist, and May and Robson, trombonists. It is possible that some of the musicians listed in this pay record performed at the banquet the same day and not in the coronation service in the cathedral.

During the coronation, with its processional music and a Mass, the central moment was the placing of three ceremonial crowns on Edward's head.

> Kynge Edwardes crowne, the other the imperyall crowne of his realme of Englande, the third a very ryche crowne which was pourposely made for his grace. Then they set them one after another upon the Kynges hede, and betwixte the puttyng on of every crowne the trumpetts blewe.

The following banquet lasted four hours, and as usual each course came into the hall with the sound of trumpets.

The fragmentary references to wind music during the brief reign of Edward mention only the ceremonial, functional music, such as that heard in 1551.

> To the sound of trumpets and drums, the French and English nobles embraced one another.[43]

It is known, however, that a broader range of wind players were employed among the household staff of Edward VI. For example, the customary presents to the entire household staff for New Year's Day in 1553 (the final year of Edward's reign), one finds listed,

> Item to the Kinges trompiters
> Item to the Kinges drumslades
> Item to the still mynstrelles (shawms)
> Item to the new sagbuttes
> Item to Lewes de Bassiam, Anthony de Bassiam, Jasper de Bassiam, John de Bassiam, and Baptist de Bassiam, mynstrelles
> Item to Guilliam du Warte, Gulliam de Trosse, and Petie John, mynstrelles[44]

[43] Hester W. Chapman, *The Last Tudor King: A Study of Edward VI, October 12th, 1537–July 6th, 1553* (New York: Macmillan, 1959), 219.

[44] Edward, King of England, *Literary Remains*, I, cccxi–cccxiii.

Mary Tudor

During the last years of the reign of Henry VIII, Roger Ascham published a book entitled, *Toxophilus, The Schole of Shottinge*. It debates whether, in the university education, shooting the long bow or music is the more worthy. It concludes shooting is the better choice but concedes, 'if you will needs grant scholars pastime and recreation of their minds, let them use (as many of them doth) music, and playing on instruments.' Caution is needed, however, as some kinds of music are bad, 'leading to sinfulness, effeminacy and dulling of wits.' In particular, the minstrelsy of lutes, pipes, harps and those others requiring 'such nice, fine, minikin fingering ... is far more fit for the womanishness of it to dwell in the court among ladies, than for any great thing of it.'[45]

The author was the Latin secretary to Mary and reflects the opinion that for a cloistered, single lady, with no expectation of holding an important place in society, music was an expected and accepted means of whiling away the days.

[45] Quoted in Walter L. Woodfill, *Musicians in English Society from Elizabeth to Charles I*, (Princeton: Princeton University Press, 1953), 213.

Already at age six, in the early 1520s, the princess had a personal staff of nearly thirty, some of whom were minstrels.[46] In 1537 her Privy Purse Accounts disclose that she was given a concert by the sackbuts at 'Mr. Page's.'[47] These same accounts give her New Year's gifts for 1543, which include payments to,

The new Sagbutts
The Dromslades
The Welsh mynstrels
The Flutes, Yevane and his fellowe
The Recorders[48]

After the brief, abortive attempt to make Jane Gray queen, Mary returned to London in 1553 to assume her reign (1553–1558). She arrived with seven hundred mounted men, including the royal trumpets, to prepare for the coronation in September.

The coronation celebrations began with Mary's arrival at the Tower of London, where one heard music by shawms and trumpets. The following day it was traditional to create new Knights of the Bath. This ceremony had to be altered somewhat, as part of the ritual called for the new knights to jump naked into a bath with the sovereign and kiss his shoulder! On the morning of 30 September, the great coronation procession began with the royal trumpeters leading the way. The procession featured a large number of foreign diplomats and merchants, all richly dressed. Two foreign pageants were especially popular with the public, one a great triumphal arch with four great giants and a fountain of wine, created by the Genoese merchants. The Florentine pageant featured a mechanical angel, dressed in green and carrying a trumpet. When the angel put his trumpet to his mouth, a trumpeter hiding inside played a fanfare, 'to the marveling of many ignorant persons.' A Dutch acrobat performed on the weathercock on St. Paul's and was every bit as popular as the Aragonese who performed at Edward's coronation procession. During the coronation the trumpets blew a triumphant fanfare as successive crowns were placed on Mary's head.[49]

The arrival of Philip of Spain, in 1554, to marry the Queen of England was also a cause of great celebration as everyone hoped it would result in a male heir. One reads of their days being filled with 'minstrels all playing' and the 'sound of trumpets.'[50] Mary went to considerable lengths to try to entertain

[46] Erickson, *Bloody Mary*, 41.

[47] Woodfill, *Musicians in English Society*, 186.

[48] Gerald Ravenscourt Hayes, *King's Music* (London: Oxford University Press, 1937), 52.

[49] Coronation description taken from Erickson, *Bloody Mary*, 317–322.

[50] H.F.M. Prescott, *Spanish Tudor: The Life of Bloody Mary* (New York: Constable, 1940), 351.

her new husband, with whom she shared no language. Among the many court festivities she organized, one notes especially a Spanish game on horses called 'cane game,' played to the music of 'drums made of Ketylles and trumpets,' and a spectacle in which counterfeit apes sat in rows like minstrels apparently playing bagpipes.[51]

The liveries accounts show regular employment of the following wind players during the brief reign of Mary.

[51] Ibid., 355, and Daniel Henderson, *The Crimson Queen* (New York: Duffield and Green, 1933), 227.

[52] LaFontaine, *The King's Musick*, 9–12.

TROMBONES

Nicholas Andrewe	Anthony Mary
Nicholas Coteman	Edward Davis
John Peacocke	Richard Welshe

FLUTES

John Severnake	Guillam Trochie
Guyllam Dovett	Piro Guye
Thomas Paginton	Alyn Robson

MUSICIANS

Anthony Bassanie	Jaspero Bassanie
John Bassanie	John Baptista Bassanie
Augustino Bassanie	

FIFE

Henry Bell	Thomas Curson

DRUM

Robert Brewer

TRUMPET

Benedict Browne	John Tucke
John Pitches	Peter Frauncis
Thomas Browne	Arthur Skarlett
Henry Reve	John Warren
Stephen Medcalf	Richard Lane
Edward Eliott	John Hall
John Winke	Richard Frende
Thomas West crosse	Robert Turren[52]

In addition, there were eight string players and a harpist. These accounts also contain a number of entries regarding the issue of liveries for small numbers of trumpet players who were to accompany various lords on foreign trips. One example was the issue of white and green cloth 'for cassocks and maryners sloppes' for four of the above trumpeters who were to accompany the Lord High Admiral on a sea voyage.[53]

[53] Ibid., 10.

Elizabeth I

The new queen was a twenty-five year old woman, attractive and well educated. Yet, no one looking at this young woman believed her reign would be long or that she was possibly equipped to deal with the extraordinarily complex problems which faced her on every side. Her reign would last forty-five years, with such success and style that today we know this entire period by her name.

Her education centered in theology and languages, her tutor noting, 'she speaks French and Italian as well as she does English, and has often spoken to me readily and well in Latin, moderately in Greek.' Elizabeth herself took this ability in stride, noting, 'it is no marvel to teach a woman to talk; it is far harder to teach her to hold her tongue.' She was also well educated in music and performed well on the virginal, upon which she played at least a pavan every day, or so she told the Ambassador de Maisse.[54] One eyewitness to her keyboard abilities was the courtier, Sir James Melville, who remembered in his *Memoirs*,

> The same day, after dinner, my Lord Huntsdean drew me up to a quiet gallery that I might hear some music (but he said he durst now avow it), where I might hear the Queen play upon the virginals. After I had hearkened a while, I took by the tapistry that hung before the door of the chamber, and, seeing her back was towards the door, I entered within the Chamber, and stood a pretty space, hearing her play excellently well; but she lift off immediately so soon as she turned her about, and came forward, seeming to strike me with her hand, alledging, she was not used to play before men, but (played only) when she was solitary to shun melancholy.[55]

Elizabeth's Musical Establishment

While one can account for some musicians for many years throughout the reign of Elizabeth, the precise composition of her household music is difficult to establish, as no accounts are truly complete. Judging by extant accounts, one can make some reasonably accurate estimations, however, regarding the instrumentation. Trumpets seem to have been maintained in a fairly stable number, averaging seventeen throughout the

[54] Quoted in George B. Harrison, *The Elizabethan Journals* (New York: Doubleday, 1928–1933), 2:242.

[55] Quoted in John Nichols, ed., *The Progresses and Public Processions of Queen Elizabeth*, vol. 3 [these volumes carry no page numbers].

Elizabeth I, 'The Ditchley Portrait', by Marcus Gheeraerts the Younger, ca. 1592.

reign. Three more large consorts seem stable for long periods: a consort of six trombones, until ca. 1593, when it begins to diminish to three or four; a consort of six flutes until 1562, when it gradually diminishes to two regular players; and a consort of approximately eight strings of the treble type. Small numbers of other instruments appear with some regularity, including two drums and a fife, a bagpipe, and a lute or two. During the early years of her reign, a foreign consort appears, all members of the family Bassani (Bassanie, Bassany, de Basson, etc.). This family of six appears until ca. 1564, and then an entirely new generation seems to appear (ca. 1570) for the duration of her reign. Although the actual primary instrument of the first generation members is not known, it was probably a wind instrument, for the second generation were almost always identified as wind players and were, in any case, always listed separately from the string players.

Perhaps the greatest mystery is the apparent absence of the shawm. The Lord Chamberlain records give no less than eleven shawm players participating in the coronation of Henry VIII (1509) and an ensemble of six 'Hoboies and Sagbuttes' for the funeral of Elizabeth (1603) and nothing in between! Perhaps they were paid under a different, now lost, account, or perhaps once again the early scribes failed to accurately distinguish the flute from the shawm. The cornett also fails to appear in the court records, aside from the Chapel, yet Henry VIII owned a large collection at the time of his death.

It seems reasonable to conclude a much wider choice of instruments was available to Elizabeth's musicians than these records indicate. This seems to be reflected in the literature of the period, as for example in Drayton's *Polyolbion*, which describes a musical contest.

> So were there some again, in this their learned strife,
> Loud Instruments that loved, the cornet and the fife,
> The Hoboy, sagbut deep, recorder and the flute:
> Even from the shrillest shawm unto the cornamute.
> Some blow the bagpipe up, that plays the country round,
> The Taber and the Pipe ... sound.[56]

[56] Michael Drayton (1563–1631), quoted in Christopher Welch, 'Literature Relating to the Recorder,' *Proceedings of the Musical Association* 24 (January 1, 1897): 151.

One fact regarding Elizabeth's household musicians seems clear: many were foreign, indeed Woodfill calculates from half to two-thirds.[57] One reason which may have contributed to a shortage of English musicians was a sudden, if temporary, decline in teaching of music in general, related to the closing of monasteries by Henry VIII. Nichols, writing in 1788, makes this interesting observation.

[57] Woodfill, *Musicians in English Society*, 195.

> This Matthew Gwin was a Fellow of St. John's College, studied physic, poetry, chemistry, etc., and made a great figure in almost every part of learning. He was chosen Music Professor of this (Oxford) University in 1582, though he understood not a tittle either of the theory or practice of that science ... The greatest wound, which music ever received in England, was from the suppression of monasteries; after which the Puritans often made it their business to run it down as a relique of popery. For both these reasons, very few Englishmen regarded it in Queen Elizabeth's time. Her own band of musicians were many of them foreigners (Venecians).[58]

[58] Quoted in Nichols, *The Progresses and Public Processions of Queen Elizabeth*, vol. 2.

Wind Music at the Coronation of Elizabeth

Most coronations are festive and Elizabeth's was particularly joyous, as her reign followed that of the rather unpopular 'Bloody Mary.' The observations of an eyewitness to the procession through London, two days before the coronation, communicate a sense of relief which seems to have been widely shared.

> Entrying the Citie (Elizabeth) was of the People received marveylous entirely as appeared by thassemblie, prayers, wishes, welcomings, cryes, tender woordes, and all other signs ... And on thother syde, her grace, by holding up her handes, and merrie countenance to such as stode farre off, and most tender and gentle language to those that stood nigh to her grace, did declare herselfe no lesse thankfullye to receive her peoples good wyll, than they lovingly offred it unto her ... so that on eyther syde there was nothing but gladness, nothing but prayer, nothing but comfort.[59]

[59] Quoted in Alan Ross Warwick, *A Noise of Music* (London: Queen Anne Press, 1968), 18. The eyewitness is not identified, but the tone of the remarks is consistent with other sources.

The official procession began at 2:00 p.m., 13 January 1558, and as usual included a number of official pageants. The first, near Fenchurch, centered on a child actor, who welcomed the queen in English and Latin. Next, at the upper end of Gracechurch Street, was an elaborate pageant with multiple stages where she heard the first wind bands of the day, 'The two sides of the (pageant) were filled with loude noyses of musicke.'[60] This pageant was a kind of personification of Elizabeth's family tree, with actors representing Henry VII, Henry VIII, etc., all connected with branches.

Continuing toward Cornhill, 'as her Grace passed by the conduit, which was curiously trimmed ... with riche banners adourned, and a noyse of loude instrumentes upon the top thereof.' Nearby, the queen arrived at one of several allegorical pageants; here were Pure Religion treading on Superstition, Love of Subjects treading on Rebellion and 'Insolencie,' etc. Another child spoke and two more wind bands played.

> The two sydes over the two side portes had in them placed a noyse of instrumentes, whych immediatlye after the chyldes speache gave an heavenly melodie.

At the Standard in Cheap 'was placed a noyse of trumpettes, with banners and other furniture.' Here also, in front of St. Peters' Church, was a performance by the civic wait band of London, a 'pleasant noyse.'

Several more allegorical pageants were seen and finally the procession ended at Ludgate, 'where she was received with a noyse of instruments.'

The coronation ceremony itself included the participation of all the court musicians, led by the eighteen trumpeters, 'blowinge at every proclamacon.'

Wind Music at Court

The large number of wind instrument players who were part of the regular household staff of Elizabeth suggests they were a constant part of daily court life. Certainly they must have been part of the ceremonial color when the queen traveled within the city of London as well. One reads, for example, of the queen 'crossing over to London side, with drums beating and trumpets sounding, and so to White-hall again' on 11 June 1558.[61]

[60] Coronation quotations taken from Nichols, *The Progresses and Public Processions of Queen Elizabeth*, vol. 1.

[61] Nichols, *The Progresses and Public Processions of Queen Elizabeth*, vol. 1.

No doubt dinner music was a regular duty for the musicians, but it would be a mistake to conclude that this role was always merely functional. One account clearly cites an occasion when the wind band came in after everyone had finished eating to play a concert, or at least music to be listened to. A guest, Thomas Platter, describes first the entry of forty members of the queen's guard, 'they are all very tall, fine young men, and similarly attired, so that I never in my life saw their like.' Each was carrying into the hall one of the main courses, 'and I observed amongst them some very large joints of beef, and all kinds of game, pastries and tarts.' The queen was served in an adjoining room for, except in the case of particularly distinguished guests, 'she ate of what she fancied, privily however, for she very seldom partakes before strangers.' After the third course had been served and taken away, 'the Queen's musicians appeared in the Presence Chamber with their trumpets and shawms, and after they had performed their music, everyone withdrew, bowing themselves out just as they had come in, and the tables were carried away again.'[62]

For state occasions, such as banquets for visiting foreign ambassadors, the emphasis was on the ceremonial royal trumpets. A German guest in 1584 wrote,

> Now eight trumpeters clad in red gave the signal for dinner, and did it very well. Afterwards two drummers and a piper made music according to the English fashion, and we betook ourselves to our lodgings.[63]

A similar account, from another German guest in 1598, speaks of even more trumpets.

> During the time that this guard, which consists of the tallest and stoutest men that can be found in all England, 100 in number, being carefully selected for this service, were bringing dinner, twelve trumpets and two kettle-drums made the hall ring for half-an-hour together.[64]

This particular visitor was most likely astonished by this much 'noise' in the dining hall, for he writes later, rather sarcastically, of the English in general:

[62] Ian Dunlop, *Palaces and Progresses of Elizabeth I* (London: Cape, 1962), 109. Note the rare proof of the existence of shawms.

[63] Lupold von Wedel, 'Journey Through England,' in *Elizabethan People* (London, 1972), 16.

[64] Paul Hentzner, 'Travels in England,' in *England as Seen by Foreigners in the Days of Elizabeth and James the First*, ed. William Brenchley Rye (London, 1865), 106. Kastner, in *Manuel général de musique militaire* (Paris, 1848), 99, attributes a similar quotation to 'Huexner,' but mentions twelve trumpets, two timpani, fifes, cornetts, and tambours, again 'the whole ensemble filled the hall for an half-hour.'

(They are) vastly fond of great noises that fill the ear, such as the firing of cannon, drums, and the ringing of bells, so that in London it is common for a number of them that have got a glass in their heads (qui se inebriaverint) to go up into some belfry, and ring the bells for hours together, for the sake of exercise.[65]

Outdoor entertainments at court, which ranged from picnics to jousts and tournaments, almost certainly demanded wind music.[66] A joust in 1581 at Hampton Court featured, among other pageants, six eagles concealing musicians,[67] and another, in 1584, was described by an eyewitness.

> About twelve o'clock the queen with her ladies placed themselves at the windows in a long room of Whitehall palace, near Westminster, opposite the barrier where the tournament was to be held … During the whole time of the tournament all who wished to fight entered the lists by pairs, the trumpets being blown at the time and other musical instruments … Some of the servants were disguised like savages, or like Irishmen, with the hair hanging down to the girdly like women, others had horse manes on their heads, some came driving in a carriage, the horses being equipped like elephants, … others appeared to move by themselves.[68]

The mask now begins to be a favorite court entertainment and in this early period accounts frequently mention trumpets, fifes and drums.[69] Elizabeth, even to a mature age, loved to dance and we may be sure her household musicians were frequently serving in this capacity. A letter from the Earl of Worcester to the Earl of Shrewsbury comments on the fashion.

> Wee are frolyke heare in Cowrt; mutche dauncing in the privi chamber of contrey dawnces before the Q.M. whoe is exceedingly pleased therwith: Irish tunes are at this tyme most pleasing.[70]

The large number of ceremonial trumpets maintained by Elizabeth were always present at political events, such as Elizabeth's processions to parliament, the proclaiming of peace treaties, and the welcoming of foreign ambassadors. An eyewitness to a dinner honouring the Danish Ambassador's visit to the court in Greenwich in 1586, found,

[65] Hentzner, 'Travels in England,' III.

[66] An icon of Queen Elizabeth at a picnic in 1575, accompanied by hunting horns, can be seen in Turberville, *Booke of Hunting*. (see picture p. 43)

[67] E.K. Chambers, *The Elizabethan Stage* (Oxford: Clarendon, 1923), 1:144.

[68] Ibid., 1:143.

[69] Ibid., 157, 159, 169. Grove (12:53) defines the mask as,

> clearly indigenous in northern Europe but influenced by Italian custom, had as its centrepiece a dance of courtly persons with music played by professionals on loud (haut) instruments.

[70] Letter of September 19, 1602, quoted in Nichols, *The Progresses and Public Processions of Queen Elizabeth*, vol. 3. I have quoted a 1594 English poem above, in the introduction to this section, which suggests that even by this late date the wind band was still the favored court dance ensemble, contrary to many present-day writers who suggest that the string ensemble had taken over this duty.

COURT WIND BANDS IN ENGLAND 43

Turberville's *Booke of Hunting* showing Queen Elizabeth at a picnic in 1575, accompanied by two men, upper right, carrying hunting horns.

> the trumpets sounding, and the drums plaieng thereunto; a marvellous delightsome thing to heare, and a passing gallant sight to behold.[71]

[71] Nichols, *The Progresses and Public Processions of Queen Elizabeth*, vol. 2.

In the accounts of the welcome given Albertus Alasco, Palatine of Siradia (Poland) in Oxford, in 1583, one reads of a rather long wind ensemble concert with repertoire clearly of a non-fanfare nature.

> On the East-gate, wherat he entered, stood a consort of musicians, who, over a long space, made verie sweet harmonie, which could not but moove and delight.[72]

[72] Ibid.

A separate eyewitness confirms that this consort was a wind ensemble,

> which being done, a consort of musicians, that stood over the East-gate, played on their wind-music.[73]

[73] Ibid., vol. 3.

The most elaborate of these political receptions was the welcome given the French Ambassador in April 1581. A temporary building was erected for the banquets, made of canvas and wood, it was three hundred and thirty-two feet long with two hundred and ninety-two windows.[74] Four of the leading nobles of Elizabeth's court were the principal challengers for a tournament, under the name of the 'Four Children of Desire.' For the first pageant on the tournament field, they entered with their personal aids and trumpets and before them was a 'fortress' rolling on wheels, with 'divers kinds of most excellent music' hidden inside. When it stopped, a boy sang, accompanied by cornetts, presumably the hidden musicians.

[74] George Walter Thornbury, *Shakspere's England: Sketches of Our Social History in the Reign of Elizabeth* (London, 1856), 2:372ff.

> Yeeld, yeeld, O yeeld, you that this fort doo hold.
> Which seated is in spotlesse honors feeld.[75]

[75] Nichols, *The Progresses and Public Processions of Queen Elizabeth*, vol. 2.

Then two imitation cannons shot perfumed powder and water, the sound of the cannons being supplied by 'excellent melodie.' Scaling ladders were applied to the walls of the fortress and 'missiles' of flowers and love letters were thrown inside. On another day, the Four Children of Desire appeared again with a 'curiously decked' chariot.

> In the bulke (middle) of the charriot was conveied roome for a full consort of musike, who plaied still verie dolefull musike as the charriot mooved.

'Dolefull,' I suspect, meant trombones.

The armies of Elizabeth also included trumpets, especially when the leaders included one of the great lords. The Earl of Leicester, Governor General of her majesty's forces in the low countries, would appear with almost regal splendor. One sees him celebrating the Feast of St. George there, in 1586, preceded by 'the trumpeters, appareled in scarlet, layd with silver lacae, sounding their trumpets most royally, their banner roles being displayed.'[76] Trumpets were also numerous for Elizabeth's procession to St. Paul's Cathedral in 1588 to celebrate her navy's defeat of the Spanish armada.[77] She was met at Temple Bar by the Lord Mayor and his company, with the London Wait Band playing from the top of the Bar.[78]

For the regular foot company, however, it was the fife and drum which supplied the music. They too appeared when troops were part of great state ceremonies, such as the funeral of Sir Philip Sidney in 1586. On this occasion, three fifes and six drums, covered with black cloth, played, 'very softely.'[79]

While these instruments may be thought of as being rather humble musically, the players were never-the-less selected with some care, As one can see in the sixteenth century ordinance by the Englishman, Ralph Smith.

> (The fife and drumers are to be) of able personage to use their instruments and office, of sundrie languages; for oftentimes they bee sente to parley with their enemies ... which of necessitie requireth language.[80]

This special status is confirmed in another Elizabethan military treatise.

> The best Inne or lodging is to be prowided for the Captain, and the seconde is likewise to be given to the Aunciect bearer (Ensign), and the Sergeant of the bande (company), next unto them must be lodged the Drummeplaiers and Fluite.[81]

[76] Ibid.

[77] London, British Museum (Harleian MSS. 894, fol. 3.b.).

[78] Warwick, *A Noise of Music*, 18.

[79] Account by John Thorpe, Esq., quoted in Nichols, *The Progresses and Public Processions of Queen Elizabeth*, vol. 2.

[80] Grose, *Military Antiquities: Respecting a History of the English Army from the Conquest to the Present Time* (London, 1801), 1:264.

[81] Luis Gutierrez de la Vega, *De re militari* (London, 1582), 3.

This pair was the basic military music in Western Europe before the Baroque period, when one begins to see true military bands.[82]

[82] The following interesting discussion of these sixteenth-century military musical instruments is found in Thoinot Arbeau, *Orchésographie* (Lengres, 1588, modern edition, New York, 1948), 39.

CAPRIOL. But why is the drummer accompanied by one or two fifers?

ARBEAU. What we call the fife is a little transverse flute with six holes, used by the Germans and Swiss, and, as the bore is very narrow, only the thickness of a pistol bullet, it has a shrill note. In place of a fife some use a flageolet called an *arigot*, which has a greater or lesser number of holes according to its size. The best ones have four holes in front and two behind and their sound is piercing; one might call them little *tibiae* as they were originally made from the shin bone and legs of the crane. The players of the said drum and fife are known by the name of their instrument, and we say of two soldiers that one is the drummer and the other the fifer of some captain.

CAPRIOL. Is there a particular way in which to play the fife or *arigot*?

ARBEAU. Those who play them improvise to please themselves and it suffices for them to keep time with the sound of the drum. However, we are told that the Phrygian mode, which musicians call the third mode, incites naturally to anger and that the Lydians used it when going to war. History records that when Timothy played in it upon his *tibia*, Alexander the Great instantly arose like a madman raging for combat. Bacchus, the great leader called Dionysus, taught his soldiers, surrounded as they were by women camp followers, dancing and military marches to the sound of the drum and the Phrygian *tibia*. It was by this means that he subjugated the Indians who advanced in a disorderly mob, screaming and yelling, and consequently were thrown into confusion and easily scattered and vanquished.

Elizabeth's Progresses

Elizabeth, soon after her coronation, began a series of summer travels throughout her realm. Her desire to make these 'progresses' was in part to be seen by her subjects, in part to keep an eye on her powerful vassal lords, and, no doubt, in part to escape the discomfort of London in the Summer. Large numbers of her court, not to mention her personal belongings and furniture, accompanied her and so great was the subsequent cost to the lords and cities that had to entertain her, many prayed she would not pass their way.

The first two of these progresses occurred in 1559, to locations not too distant. On 23 April, Elizabeth went by boat up the Thames to Baynard's Castle, where the Earl of Pembroke resided. Hundreds of boats accompanied her and 'thousands of people thronging at the water side, to look upon her Majesty; rejoicing to see her, and partaking of the musick and sights on the Thames: for the trumpets blew, drums beat, flutes played.'[83] In August of the same year, Elizabeth visited one of her own palaces, the Nonsuch, where the Earl of Arundel was

[83] Nichols, *The Progresses and Public Processions of Queen Elizabeth*, vol. 1.

living. 'There the Queen had great entertainment ... together with a mask; and the warlike sounds of drums and flutes, and all kinds of musick, till midnight.' On the following day, 'a costly banquet, accompanied with drums and flutes; the dishes were extraordinary rich gilt. This entertainment lasted till three in the morning.'[84]

In 1566 the queen visited Oxford, a visit for which at least two eyewitness accounts survive. Both accounts mention a service in the church during which the choir sang a 'Te deum' accompanied by cornetts.[85]

In 1575 Queen Elizabeth took the first of two of these trips for which there is extensive documentation of participating wind bands,[86] the first being a visit to Kenilworth Castle which was inhabited by the Earl of Leicester. The first encounter with wind music occurred in a large tournament field, a tilt yard, which lay between two castle gates, the Gallery Tower and Mortimer's Tower, all laying outside the castle proper. At this, the queen's first entry onto castle property, she was welcomed by a person described as a 'gigantic porter.' Behind him, on the first of the gates leading to the castle, stood six giant statues ('made up') of trumpet players, each playing a huge instrument. Their music was actually played by six live trumpeters hidden behind the statues, but one of the eyewitnesses, Robert Laneham, may have been fooled by all of this, for his account reads like a description of real players.

> (The porter) cauzed his Trumpetoourz that stood upon the wall of the gate thear, too soound up a tune of welcum: which, besyde the nobl noyz, was so mooch the more pleazaunt too behold, becauz theez Trumpetoourz, beeing sixe in number, wear every one an eight foot hye, in due proportion of parson besyde, all in long garments of sylk suitabl, eache with hiz sylvery Trumpet of a five foot long, foormed taper wyse, and straight from the uppor part untoo the neather eend: whear the diameter was a 16 ynchez over, and yet so tempered by art, that being very eazy too the blast, they cast foorth no greater noyz nor a more unpleazaunt soound for time and tune, than any oother common Trumpet, bee it never so artificially (skillfully) foormed. Theese armonious blasterz, from the foreside upon the wallz, untoo the inner; had this muzik maintained from them very delectable, while her Highness all along this Tylt-yard rode.

[84] Ibid.

[85] Ibid., III, and a manuscript (London, British Museum, Harl. MS 7033. f. 139) by Richard Stephens written in 1566.

[86] Descriptions, unless otherwise noted, are taken from the account by Robert Laneham, a Gentleman Usher in the queen's court and 'The Princely Pleasures at Kenelworth Castle,' by George Gascoigne (1575), both quoted in Nichols, *The Progresses and Public Processions of Queen Elizabeth*, vol. 1.

Also within this tournament field a lake had been constructed for a pageant based on the 'Lady of the Lake.' Here a 'floating island' drifted toward the shore upon which the queen waited. The island, blazing with torches, supported two nymphs who addressed the queen in poetry regarding the history of the castle and its owners. This ended with a performnce by a large wind band.

> This Pageaunt was cloz'd up with a delectable harmony of Hautboiz, Shalmz, Cornets, and such oother looud muzik, that held on while her Majestie pleazauntly so passed from thence toward the Castl gate.

Now the queen passed over a bridge into the castle itself and along the sides of this bridge were seven pair of posts, supporting gifta of the Gods to the queen. On the first posts were 'too cumly square wyre cagez' containing birds, a gift of Sylvanus, God of Foul. On the second posts were great silver bowls of fruit, from the Goddess Pomona, followed by bowls of grain, a gift of Ceres. The fourth, fifth, and sixth posts supported grapes and wine, fish, and arms, gifts from Bacchus, Neptune, and Mars. On the final pair of posts,

> wear (were) thear pight (placed) too saer Bay braunchez of a four foot hy, adourned on all sides with lutes, viollz, shallmz, cornets, flutes, recorders, and harpes, az prezents of Phoebus, God of Musik for rejoycing the mind, and of phizik for health to the body.

Once across the bridge and inside the gate, the queen alighted from her horse to the music of 'drummes, fifes and trumpets,' and paused for a performance by a consort of flutes.

> (There) waz her Highnes received with a fresh delicate armony of Flutz.

On the second day, a Sunday, the queen and her party attended the parish church and then spent, 'the afternoon in excelent muzik of sundry swet instruments, and in dauncing of Lordes and Ladiez,' and the evening watching fireworks. Monday was too hot for outdoor activities until the late afternoon, when the queen went hunting. The evening entertainment featured a 'wild man,' called 'Hombre Salvagio,' accompanied by fauns and nymphs.

On Tuesday there was more dancing and music, in particular a concert performed by musicians in a boat while the queen listened from a bridge over the newly constructed lake.

> ... whear it pleased her to stand, while upon the pool oout of a barge fine appoynted for the purpoze, too heer sundry kinds of very delectabl muzik.

The most extraordinary pageant occurred on Monday of the second week.[87] The queen, returning from a hunt, encountered on the lake a mechanical mermaid, eighteen feet long, swimming along with Triton and his trumpet (Neptune's Blaster) on its back. Following this came a mechanical dolphin, large enough to contain a complete consort hidden in its belly. Sitting on top of this twenty-four foot long dolphin was a god, Arion by most accounts, but Protheus according to Gascoigne. Unfortunately the eyewitnesses do not name the instruments heard inside the dolphin, no doubt as they were unseen and the tones perhaps altered by the unusual acoustics. Gascoigne refers to it only as a 'consort of musicke.' Laneham refers to the ensemble with the key word, 'Noise,' which is so often associated with the wind bands during this period in England. One would assume it was an ensemble of wind instruments due to the volume of tone which would be needed to be heard outdoors and from the enclosed belly of the dolphin. Perhaps further confirmation is found in another first-hand account,[88] which mentions that when the god began to sing he found his voice very 'horse and unpleasant, yet he could order (blend) his voice to an instrument exceedingly well.' This I take to mean that such a voice would blend more with winds than strings.

The text of this song, sung to the accompaniment of the mystery ensemble, is extant.

[87] July 18, 1575.

[88] London, British Museum, 'Merry Passages and Jests' (MSS. Harl. 6395).

> O Noble Queene, give eare to this my floating Muse;
> And let the right of readie will my little skill excuse.
> For heardmen of the seas sing not the sweetest notes;
> The winds and waves do roare and erie, where Phoebus seldome floates;
> Yet, since I doe my best, in thankfull wise to sing;
> Vouchsafe (good Queene) that calm consent, these words to you
>   may bring.
> We yeeld you humble thanks, in mightie Neptune's name,
> Both for ourselves, and therewithal for yonder seemely Dame.

A Dame whom none but•you deliver could from thrall:
Ne none but you deliver us from loitring life withall.
She pined long in paine, as overworne with woes;
And we consumde in endless care, to send her from her foes.
Both which you set at large, most like a faithful friend;
Your noble name be praisde therefore, and so my song I ende.

While one will perhaps never know if the ensemble in the dolphin was indeed a wind ensemble, one can be certain it was a fine performance. Laneham, who listened in awe, was very moved by this concert.

(The God) beegan a delectabl ditty of a Song well apted to a melodious noiz; compounded of six severall instruments, al coovert, casting sound from the Dolphin's belly within; Arion, the seaventh, sitting thus singing without. Noow , Syr, the ditty in mitter so aptly endighted to the manner, and after by voys so deliciously delivered; the Song by a skilful artist into hiz parts so sweetlie sorted; each part in hiz instrument so clean and sharpely toouched; every instrument agayn in hiz kind so excellently tunabl; and this in the eeving of the day, resoounding from the calm waters, whear prezens of her Majesty, and longing to listen, had utterly damped all noyz and dyn; the hole amony conveyd in tyme, tune, and temper thus incomparably melodious; with what pleazure ... with what sharpnes of conceyt, with what lyvely delighte, this az ye may; for, so God judge me, by all the wit and cunning I have, I cannot express, I promis yoo ... A, muzik iz a nobl art!

Another well documented trip by Elizabeth was her visit to Norwich in 1578.[89] The queen's first view of Norwich would have been the city gate, richly decorated with the red roses of the House of York and the white roses of the House of Lancaster. By this gate, 'the waites of the citie were placed with loude musicke, who cheerefully and melodiously welcomed hyr Majestie into the citie.' Part of the welcome by this civic wind band was a choral composition, perfomed by 'the Waytes and the best Voyces in the Citie.'

[89] My discussion is based on two eyewitness accounts, one by 'Ber. Gar,' an anonymous paper published in 1578, and an account published in 1578 by Thomas Churchyarde. Both are quoted in Nichols, *The Progresses and Public Processions of Queen Elizabeth*, vol. 2.

The dew of heaven drops this day
On dry and barren ground,
Wherefore at fruitful hearts I sing
Of drum and trumpet sound.
Yield that is due, show what is meet,
To make our joy the more,
In our good hope and her good praise,
We never saw before.

Full many a winter have we seen
And many storms withall
Since here we saw a King or Queen
In pomp and princely pall.
Wherefore make feast and bow quite still
And now to triumph fall
With duty let us show good will.
To glad both great and small.
The dew of heaven ...

The queen entered the city and on the way to her lodging she passed a stage constructed in a church yard, 'over against Maister Peckes dore.' Here a child actor, richly dressed, waited to address the queen, after a performance by another wind band.

> ... which boy was not seene till the Queene had a good season marked the musicke, whiche was marvellous sweete and good, albeit the rudenesse of some ringer of belles did somewhat hinder the noyse and harmonie: and as soone as the musike ended, the boy stepped forth.

This must have been a fine performance for, as the eyewitness notes, the queen listened for some time (a good season). After the boy's address, the band resumed and the queen continued to remain and enjoy this concert.

> Then the noyse of musicke beganne agayne; to heare the which, the Queene stayed a good while.

The official procession through the city featured many pageants for the queen's entertainment, some demonstrated the skills of local crafts and guilds and some were composed of the usual allegorical figures. One in particular attracts our attention for it demonstrates the wind players' ability to perform on a variety of instruments, not to mention singing. The pageant consisted of three constructed gates and over each gate a chamber, 'replenished with musicke.' Here also was a stage supporting five actors dressed as famous women (Esther, Elizabeth, etc.). The musicians performed as a wind band as the queen approached.

> At the first sight of the Prince,[90] and till hir Majesties comming to the pageant, the musitians, whiche were close in the chambers of the saide pageant, used their loude musicke, and then ceassed.

[90] Chauvinistically, Elizabeth was often referred to as a 'Prince.'

The 'women' actors gave their addresses and then the queen moved through the gate while the, 'musitions within the gate, upon their softe instruments, used broken musick, and one of them did sing this dittie:'

> From slumber softe I fell asleepe,
> From sleepe to dreame, from dreame to depe delight,
> Eche jem the Gods had given the world to keepe
> In princely wise came present to my sight:
> Such solace then did sincke into my minde,
> As mortall man on molde could never finde.

Later days saw plays with incidental music (musicke in the meane tyme), dinners, and masks. In one of the latter, six musicians are described, 'all in long vestures of white scarcenet gyred aboute them, and garlnds on their heads playing very cunningly.'

Another extraordinary pageant consisted of a great hole dug in the ground and then covered by canvas. The canvas, apparently painted to look like a cave, could be drawn back by a rope. Buried in this 'cave' was an ensemble of musicians and twelve nymphs.

> And in the same cave was a noble noyse of musicke of al kind of instruments, severally to be sounded and played upon; and at one time they shoulde be sounded all togither, that mighte serve for a consorte of broken musicke ..., which wure had bin a noble hearing; and the more melodious for the varietie thereof, and by cause it should come secretely and strangely out of the earth. And when the musicke was done, then shoulde all the twelve Nymphes have issued togither, and daunced a daunce with timbrels that were trimmed with belles, and other jangling things; which timbrels were as brode as a seeve, having bottoms of fine parchment; and being sounded, made such a confused noyse and pastime, that it was to be wondered at; besides, the strangenesse of the timbrels (yet knowen to oure fore-fathers) was a matter of admiration to such as were ignorante of that new-founde toy, gathered and borrowed from our elders.[91]

In 1591, Queen Elizabeth made a trip to the Cowdray in Sussex where, as so often, she was greeted by a wind band,

> The Queene ... came with a great traine ... on Saterdaie, being the 15 daie of August, about eight of the clocke at night. Where upon sight of her Majestie, loud musicke sounded, which at her enteraunce on the bridge suddenly ceased.[92]

[91] Elizabeth Burton, *The Pageant of Elizabethan England* (New York: Scribner, 1959), 198, gives an undocumented additional note:
   Unhappily, a terrible great cloud-burst rather spoiled the intended effect and half-drowned the subterranean musicians.

[92] Descriptions of the Cowdray visit taken fron an account published by Thomas Scarlet (London, 1591), quoted in Nichols, *The Progresses and Public Processions of Queen Elizabeth*, vol. 2.

A porter, standing between two wooden statues dressed in armour, began his greetings by saying, 'The walles of Thebes were raised by musicke: by musick these are kept from falling ...'

Breakfast the following morning, we are told, consisted of three oxen and one hundred and forty geese. Her days were spent mostly with hunting and riding; on one occasion our observer mentioned, 'the winding of a cornette.'

In this year the queen also visited the Earl of Hertford, in Elvetham. He had prepared for her arrival an especially constructed lake in the shape of a half-moon. There were unique islands, one in the shape of a snail and another in the shape of a boat, with three trees as masts. Six 'tritons' were swimming in the lake with their trumpets (shells?). Interspersed with speeches were performances by three 'virgins, with their cornetts, who played Scottish gigs, made three parts in one.'[93] These young ladies may have also been the musicians heard on the fourth day of the visit.

> On Thursday morning, her Majestie was no sooner readie, and at her gallerie window looking into the garden, but there began three cornets to play certaine fantasike dances.

As she departed, a consort of musicians hidden in a bower accompanied two singers in a final 'dittie,'

> O come againe, worlds starbright eye,
> Whose presence doth adorne the skie.
> O come againe, sweet beauties sunne:
> When thou art gone, our joyes are done.

Queen Elizabeth made her final progresses in 1592. During a stop in Bissam, she heard cornetts sounding from the woods and then a speech by Pan, who, with two virgins, was keeping his sheep on a hill. In his speech he stressed the fact that he was a flute player and not a (mere) lute player.

> Prety soules and bodies too, faire Shephardisse, or sweet Mistresse, you know my sutie, Love: my vertue, Musicke; my power, a Godhead. I cannot tickle the sheepes gutts of a lute, *bydd, bydd, bydd,* like the calling of Chickins; but for a Pipe that squeeketh like a Pigg, I am he.[94]

[93] Descriptions of the Elvetham visit taken from an account printed by John Wolfe (London, 1591), quoted in Nichols, ibid.

[94] From an account printed by Joseph Barnes (Oxford, 1592), quoted in Nichols, *The Progresses and Public Processions of Queen Elizabeth*, vol. 2.

According to Nichols, there was also music to accompany Elizabeth on her final 'progress.'

> In the hour of her departure, she ordered her musicians into her chamber; and died (while) hearing them.[95]

[95] Hawkins (IV, 201), quoted in Nichols, *The Progresses and Public Processions of Queen Elizabeth*, vol. 3.

Wind Music in the Elizabethan Theater

The extant documentation of the wind music in her own residences is all too often given by Elizabeth's accountants only in the form of pay notices. Rarely does one find information regarding the details of the actual role of the various wind consorts in her employ. Fortunately, we have one further source from which we can add to our knowledge of their performances, the great body of literature for the Elizabethan stage. The plays of this period are full of references to wind instruments and I believe their use in the plays may be a reliable reflection of their actual use in court life. One of the important 'new' concepts of writing for the stage at this time was the desire to make the characters and situations more life-like. This, and the consistency from author to author in treating musical subjects, and the fact that the playwright could only strengthen his dramatic logic by using music in situations familiar to the audience, suggest this. Reese also argues for acceptance of these dramatic idioms as documents of court usage.

> Certain dramatic situations had corresponding musical formulas. And it is quite evident that these were taken from contemporary real-life practices in Elizabethan England.[96]

[96] Gustave Reese, *Music in the Renaissance* (New York: Norton, 1959), 879.

Perhaps the most conspicuous example of the close relationship between the appearance of music in the dramatic literature and in actual court usage is found in the treatment of the trumpet. The trumpet, while the most frequently mentioned of all instruments, is never included when 'music' is called for, nor is it found accompanying references to the military (this being the fife, drum, and bagpipe).[97] Rather, the trumpet is reserved exclusively for associations with royalty, most fre-

[97] John Manifold, 'Theatre Music in the Sixteenth and Seventeenth Centuries,' *Music & Letters* 29, no. 4 (1948): 370. Of the many publications dealing with music and theater of this period, this one contains the most detailed discussion of the use of wind music.

quently to announce the arrival of some great person. If he were a king, timpani as well are usually present, as in *Hamlet* (act 1, scene 4, line 8).

>(A flourish of trumpets, and two guns go off)
>HAMLET. The king doth wake tonight and takes his rouse,
>   Keeps wassail, and the swagg'ring upspring reels,
>   And as he drains his draughts of Rhenish down,
>   The kettledrum and trumpet thus bray out
>   The triumph of his pledge.

'Flourishes' and 'alarums' are met with great frequency in Elizabethan plays, including more than seventy occurrences in Shakespeare alone, although it is not understood today precisely what kind of musical fragments they were. Two specific kinds of flourishes seem to have been the 'tucket' and 'sennet,' no doubt deriving from the Italian, 'toccare,' and 'sonare.' The sennet, whatever it was, seems to have been the longest of the flourishes. Additional clues to kinds of music played by trumpets are found in such stage directions as, 'The trumpets sound a dead march,' found at the end of Kyd's *Spanish Tragedy*.

When the dramatic action dwelt with those moments of aristocratic life in which the trumpets played an inseparable part, the playwright builds the sounding of the instrument into the very heart of the dialog. Thus, in Shakespeare's *Tragedy of King Richard II* (1.3) a scene dealing with a trial by combat would seem incomplete to the sixteenth-century audience, if trumpets were not present.

>(*Flourish, Enter King ... Then Mowbray in armour, and Herald*)
>   ...
>   (*Tucket. Enter Hereford and Herald*)
>1ST HERALD. Harry of Hereford, Lancaster, and Derby
>   Stands here ...
>2ND HERALD. Here standeth Thomas Mowbray, Duke of Norfolk,
>   ...
>   Attending but the signal to begin.
>MARSHAL. Sound trumpets, and set forward combatants.
>   (*A charge sounded*)
>   Stay, the king hath thrown his warder down.
>RICHARD. Let them lay by their helmets and their spears
>   ...
>   Withdraw with us, and let the trumpets sound

> While we return these dukes what we decree.
> (*A long flourish*)
> …
> And for our eyes to hate the dire aspect
> Of civil wounds ploughed up with neighbours' swords;
> …
> Which, so roused up with boist'rous untuned drums,
> With harsh-resounding trumpets' dreadful bray.
> …
> Cousin, farewell; and uncle, bid him so.
> Six years we banish him and he shall go.
> (*Exit. Flourish*)

A similar duel is found in Shakespeare's *Troilus and Cressida*, (act 4, scene 6).

> AJAX. Thou, trumpet, there's my purse.
>   Now crack thy lungs, and split thy brazen pipe;
>   …
>   Come, stretch thy chest, and let they eyes spout blood;
>   Thou blow'st for Hector.
>   (*Trumpet sounds*)
> ULYSSES. No trumpet answers.
> ACHILLES. 'Tis but early days.
>   (*Trumpet within*)
> ALL. The Trojan's trumpet …
>   (*Alarum*)
> AGAMEMNON. They are in action …
>   (*Trumpets cease*)

In summary, one could say the role of the trumpet was one of providing information about the presence or activity of the highest levels of nobility.

Lesser nobility and minor dignitaries are sometimes introduced by cornetts, as if the instrument itself were considered, in Elizabethan England, a 'lesser trumpet.' In the plays of Marston, for example, one finds, 'The Duke is is entering … So, cornetts, cornetts!,' or 'The cornetts sound a synnet and the Duke goes out in state.'

On occasion, when a very long 'florish,' such as an extended processional march, is needed, one finds the cornett substituting for the trumpet. Since it is widely believed that the royal trumpeters played a memorized repertoire of rather short signals at this time, it may be that they could not read the music necessary for such dramatic moments.

Cornetts are also found in the plays, on occasion, when dancing is required. Manifold believes a final, if rare, use of the cornett is in association with the noun, 'cuckold.'

The horn is associated exclusively with references to, or scenes involving, the hunt; chronologically, it is too early to be part of 'music.' When a more rustic citizen is encountered on the hunt he is likely to be carrying the original cow-horn (and pre-cornett), the 'sow-gelder.' One play, *The Return from Parnassus*, gives a first-hand description of the use of the horn.

> When the fox is earthed you must blow one long, two short; the second wind, one long two short. Now in blowing every long containeth seven quavers, one short containeth three quavers ... (When you return home) you must sound the relief three times ... Your relief is your sweetest note ... You must sound one long and six short; the second wind, two short and one long; the third, one long and two short.[98]

[98] Quoted in H. Macaulay Fitzgibbon, 'Instruments and Their Music in the Elizabethan Drama,' in *The Musical Quarterly* 17, no. 3 (1931): 326–327.

The shawm (Hautboy) ensemble, conforming to its known role in the palace, is almost always found indoors in an atmosphere of hospitality or entertainment, often a banquet. Thus in the stage directions for the beginning of act 1, scene 7, of *Macbeth*, the shawms appear with the food.

> A lobby in Macbeth's castle. Hauboys and torches. Enter a Sewer, and divers Servants with dishes and service.

The various members of the flute family also appear in the Elizabethan plays as they did in real life. The fife is used in military associations and the pipe and tabor for the dance (as in *The Tempest*, act 3, scene 2). The recorder ensemble is almost always found in church scenes, especially if there is an association with mourning.

Before leaving the subject of the Elizabethan stage, a few comments on the organization of this music should be made. The plays seem to have begun with three blasts, or perhaps short fanfares, on the trumpet. It was this tradition which resulted in the magnificent piece for brass ensemble in *Orfeo*, which Monteverdi specifies is to be played three times. In the summer, when there was enough light, the musicians apparently provided music after the conclusion of the play.

These musicians were usually not situated on the playing surface of the stage, but in a separate 'music-room,' found behind, below, or above the stage. In Rowley's *Thracian Wonder* (ca. 1600), a stage direction carries the suggestion that a curtain may have separated the musicians from the audience.

> Pythia speaks in the Musick-room behind the Curtains ... Pythia above, behind the Curtains.[99]

[99] Quoted in Phyllis Hartnoll, ed., *Shakespeare in Music* (London: Macmillan, 1964), 27.

But who were these musicians? In the case of the simple trumpet fanfares, it is possible to believe the actors themselves might have acquired the ability to perform (which might also account for several uncomplimentary references to the instrument's tone). But in the case of the more complicated shawm, cornett, or recorder, authentic musicians must have been engaged. As it turns out, there is abundant evidence to establish that, in most cases, these musicians were the wind players of the various civic wait bands.[100]

[100] Examples of this evidence are given below under the discussion of English civic wait bands.

I can not leave this discussion of the Elizabethan theater without quoting a description of conductors, found in Gasson's *School of Abuse* (1579). They are represented by,

> costly apparel, to flatter the sight; effeminate gesture, to ravish the sense; and wanton speache, to whet desire to inordinate lust.[101]

[101] W.J. Lawrence, 'Music in the Elizabethan Theatre,' in *The Musical Quarterly* 6, no. 2 (1920): 200.

The Music of Holborne

In 1599, Antony Holborne published in London his *Pavans, Galliards. Almains. and other short Aeirs both grave and light, in five parts, for Viols, Violins, or other Musicall Winde Instruments*. This work is among the earliest volumes of consort music published in England and is the most important source for wind band literature of the Elizabethan era.

The volume consists of sixty-five dances, the first fifty-four of which are alternating pairs of pavanes and galliards, each in the same minor or major mode. A few of the compositions carry titles other than the usual dance names, such as

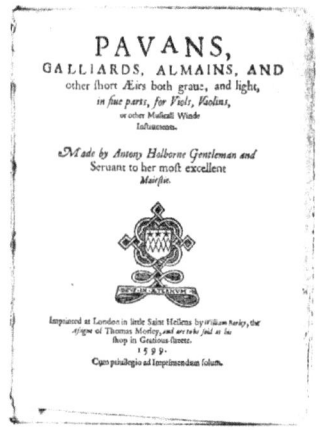

'The New-Yeeres gift,' 'The Widowes myte,' and 'Last will and testament.' It is quite possible that all of the pieces with such titles are in some way related to the Elizabethan theater. Indeed, Jeffery associates two of the tunes, 'As it fell on a holy eve,' and 'Heigh ho holiday,' with specific plays by Spenser.[102]

Both the possible association with the theater and the dance character of the music point in the direction of the wind band rather than the string ensemble.[103] Anthony Baines has suggested that at least six of the compositions were intended for a consort of crumhorns, as they have a compass of only nine notes.

Although the title page of the 1599 edition calls Holborne the 'Genleman and Servant to her most excellent Maiestie,' these works were in all probability composed not for the queen, but rather for the wind band of one of the nobles of the court, Sir Richard Champernowne.[104] The edition is dedicated to Champernowne and correspondence from the composer to Champernowne indicates not only Holborne's past service ('from the experience of many years'), but indicates that at least some of the works date from an earlier period and some from after the employment under him.

> (Holborne has now) bundled up into a catalogue volume, accompanied with a more liberall and enlarged choice than hath at any time as yet come to your refined ears.[105]

On one occasion the queen heard Champernowne's wind band as it played on the Thames River and wanted it for herself. Champernowne, foreseeing the possible permanent loss of his musicians, had to take diplomatic steps to evade the request.[106]

Other than his title from the queen and his implied tenure under Champernowne, little is known of the life of Holborne. He was married in 1584 and between 1584 and 1596 was living in Westminster; he was dead by 1606.

[102] Brian Jeffery, 'Antony Holborne,' *Musica Disciplina* 22 (1968): 141–142. This article also includes extensive sources for all of Holborne's music.

[103] The title, as was often the case, indicated a broad possibility of performance to encourage sales. The phrase, 'or other,' used in the title in reference to the instrumentation, was used in the not uncommon Elizabethan sense of 'or else.' See Andrew Kazdin, in the cover notes for *The Glorious Sound of Brass* (Columbia Records, MS 6941).

[104] Kazdin, cover notes for *The Glorious Sound of Brass*.

[105] Jeffery, 'Antony Holborne,' 134.

[106] Ibid.

2   *Court Wind Bands in France*

Louis XII

THE REIGN OF LOUIS XII (1498–1515) was one of great prosperity for the people of France, due to the unusual character of this king. He abolished the sale of offices, lowered taxes considerably, and spent little on himself, explaining, 'I had rather make courtiers laugh by my stinginess, than make my people weep by my extravagance.'[1]

Louis was a singer and a discerning enough musician to employ the great Josquin. There exists a composition by Josquin with a part labeled, 'vox regis,' consisting of a single pitch repeated throughout.[2] One does not know if this part is a reflection of Louis's good sense of humor, or the quality of his singing! There is also extant a work by Josquin, 'Vive Le Roy,' which was surely part of the repertoire of the king's wind band.

It is perhaps due to this king's acknowledged 'stinginess,' that so few accounts of his musical establishment can be found. His Italian expeditions, otherwise the black-mark of his reign, began a healthy period of influence on the French court by the more artistically advanced peoples of the south.[3] If the extensive organization of wind consorts which are found early in the reign of the following king were begun under Louis XII, it can no longer be documented.

The accounts which survive speak only of the more ceremonial uses of music. An icon depicting his coronation shows only four clarion trumpet players in the balcony, with cheeks puffed out and banners hanging from their instruments.[4] An eyewitness who saw Louis' army music in Rome, in 1508, speaks of 'trumpets, clarions, and big Swiss drums.'[5] An almost identical ensemble marched through the streets of Paris as part of his funeral procession.[6]

[1] Francois Pierre Guillaume Guizot, *The History of France* (London, 1872), 2:627.

[2] Gustave Reese, *Music in the Renaissance* (New York: Norton, 1959), 229.

[3] Bertrand de la Laurencie, 'Les Dubuts de la Musique Chambre en Franch,' quoted in *Revue de Musicologie* (1934), 25.

[4] Paris, Musée de Cluny (Inv.-Nr. 822b).

[5] Jean Auton, *Chroniques de Louis XII* (Paris, 1889), 2:36.

[6] Francis Hackett, *Francis the First* (New York: The Literary Guild), 129.

The Coronation of Louis XII, sixteenth century

Francis I

There is an eyewitness description of Francis by none other than Henry VIII of England, written on the occasion of their famous meeting in 1520, called, 'The Field of Cloth of Gold.' He tells us that Francis was, in that year,

> stately of countenance, mery of chere, roune coloured, great iyes, high nosed, bigge lipped, faire brested and shoulders, small legges, and long fete.[7]

7 Edward Hall, *The Triumphant Reigne of Kyng Henry VIII* (London, 1542), 1:200.

Francis was of good temper and his vivacity and charm helped make him the synthesis of chivalry and the Renaissance.

Portrait of Francis I, by Titian (1490–1576), 1539

History, in treating Francis I, concentrates on his life-long struggle against the forces of the Emperor Charles V. As politics go, it makes a great story: Francis' great victory at Marignano in 1515, a stunning defeat ten years later at Pavia, his imprisonment by Charles V, and his exchange of his two young sons as hostages enabling him to leap on a horse and cry, 'I am a king again!' Bouchet describes the joyous celebration in Paris upon the release of Francis.

> Echoing from all corners was such a grand and marvellous noise of muskets that one could not hear one from the other. There was also the noise of the Swiss tambors which were with the French, ensembles of fifes, trumpets, clarions and other demonstrative and joyous instruments.[8]

But the reign of Francis I (1515–1547) was more than politics, it was the Renaissance in France, produced in part by the musicians and art which he brought back with him from his military travels.[9] A famous description of him finds him in his principal palace gallery, drawing aside a curtain to the sound of trumpets, to give his court their first look at newly acquired paintings by Raphael.[10]

It is under the reign of Francis that the administrative organization and the actual wind bands are formed which remain essentially the same until the revolution at the end of the eighteenth century.[11] The musicians were organized under two administrative sections, the Chambre and the Écurie, and wind bands and ensembles are found under both.

Under the Chambre there was first a category called 'Les officiers domestiques,' which included singers, organists, and lute players. A separate category was called, 'Les cornets,' but seems to have usually been only two players at a time. These players, however, held a place of honor as virtuosi and their pay was the equal of any musicians in the employ of the court. During the sixteenth century, these cornett players appear nearly always to have been from Italy, primarily from Verona.[12]

Another group of players under the Chambre was called, 'Les flutes hautbois et trompettes.' This group, and the following one, were not considered virtuosi (and were thus paid less), but were the humble players of ceremonies.[13] The oboe players

---

[8] Bouchet, *Annales d'Aquitaine*, quoted in Georges Kastner, *Manuel général de musique militaire* (Paris, 1848), 93.

> Redondoit de tous cotes un si grand et merveilleux bruit des arquebusiers qu'on ne se pouvoit ouïr l'un l'autre. Aussi pour le bruit des tabourins suisses qui étoient avec les gens de pied françois, ensemble des fibres, trompettes, clarons, et autres instruments démonstratifs de joie.

[9] He reminds one of his most famous successor, Napoleon, who was also a notorious art thief.

[10] Catherine Hannah Charlotte Jackson, *The Court of France* (Boston: Grolier Society, 1900), 113.

[11] It can not be established exactly when this organization took place, but it is clear that the basic structure was in place by about 1530. An extensive study of this period has been published by Henri Prunières, 'La musique de la Chambre et de L'Écurie sous le Regne de Francois Ier,' in *L'Année Musicale* (1911): 215–250.

[12] The names of these players can be found in several manuscripts in the National Library, Paris, among them: Ms. fr. 21459, fol. 7ff; Ms. fr. 3132, fol. 65v; and Ms. fr. 7856, p. 956. The earliest players of record are Augustin Champaign de Verone and Jehan-Baptiste de Verone, of 1516. Augustin is found at the beginning of the century in Spain. See Michel Brenet, 'Notes sur l'introduction des instruments dans les eglises de France,' in *Riemann-Festscrift* (Leipzig: Max Messes Verlag, 1909).

[13] References to these players can be found in the National Library, Paris, under Ms. fr. 21450, fol. 5, 106, 173v, and 195v; and Ms. fr. 3132, fol. 57.

do not seem to appear on a regular basis among these particular players. It was perhaps these fifes and trumpets who played for the ceremonies of the private family members, such as the reference to these instruments at the baptism of Francis, Duke of Orleans (Francis II) in 1518[14] and the coronation of Queen Claude, when they are described as 'sounding together very melodiously, as a sort of decorous recreation (récréation honnête) according well with Te Deums.'[15]

Early during the reign of Francis, there appeared a separate ensemble called, 'Les fifres et les tabourins,' although such players appear only in the Écurie after ca. 1532. In an early list of these fife players (1516), one can again see the prominance of Italian, German and Swiss names,[16] although two accompanying tabor players have French names.[17]

If the musicians of the Chambre were the virtuosi, the musicians of the Écurie were the more functional providers of music for ceremonies, festivals, tournaments, and the dance. Their life was more difficult; they were paid less and had to be away from home for long periods when the king traveled. In one year alone, they traveled with him to Lyon, Nice, Marseille, Montpellier, Compiègne, and Aigues-Mortes.[18] More remarkable yet is the fact that there is some evidence that they made these trips by foot, slowly accompanying the great pack horses.[19]

It is under the Écurie that one first finds the most important wind band in the early history of France, the ensemble which would become the 'Grands Hautbois' of Louis XIV, during the seventeenth century, and would become the most important model for all court and military bands in the late Baroque. In 1529, in the earliest complete list of these players, one finds eight players of shawm and sackbut under the title, 'Joueurs d'instrumens de haulxbois et sacqueboutes.'

Bartolommeo da Firenze
Pietro Pagano
Christoforo da Piacenza
Masone da Milano
Francesco da Birago
Nicolo da Brescia
Simone (?) da Piacenza
Francesco da Cremona[20]

[14] Dorothy Moulton Piper Mayer, *The Great Regent: Louise of Savoy, 1476-1531* (New York: Funk & Wagnalls, 1966), 112.

[15] *Journal d'un Bourgeois de Paris* (1517), quoted in Jackson, *The Court of France*, 107.

[16] Nicolas Hoster, Melchoir Gorgesallée, Simon Guérin, Thomas de Seler (sometimes, 'de Selles'), and Jehan Waure (called, 'Chichouan' in Ms.fr. 7856, p. 956, Paris, National Library).

[17] Giraut Olivier and Gacien Gerbier.

[18] Prunières, 'La musique de la Chambre et de L'Écurie sous le Regne de Francois Ier,' 236ff.

[19] Paris, National Library, Ms. fr. 3132, fol. 58.

[20] The original Italian form of the names constructed by Prunières, 'La musique de la Chambre et de L'Écurie sous le Regne de Francois Ier,' 241.

As one can see, every player in this wind band was an Italian and it is quite possible that either Louis XII or Francis, on one of his trips to Italy, hired a complete band. A few French names appear during the sixteenth century, but for the most part this ensemble retains its tradition of Italian performers. While extant records do not permit one to know when this band first appeared in the French court, it is first mentioned during the reign of Francis as appearing in his coronation procession. As Francis, dressed in silver, rode throwing handfuls of gold and silver pieces to the crowd, music was provided by the band of shawms and sackbuts, who were uniformly dressed in white, in addition to the royal trumpets.[21]

For the funeral of Francis, in 1547, this band is given as only six players,[22] but it continues as an independent ensemble throughout the century. By 1580, under Henry III, it had arrived at a membership of twelve players, the number we associate with it during the seventeenth century.

Several sources report the appearance of this band at the Conference of Cambrai in 1529. Vander Straeten reports that Francis took with him on this occasion a nine-member band of shawms, sackbuts, and cornetts; a consort of four 'grosses fleutes'; a consort of four viols, and his royal trumpets.[23]

A final ensemble found under the Écurie was the 'Les fifres et les trompettes.' The most complete listing of these players is found relative to the funeral of Francis. There, five players of the fife are given[24] with six royal trumpeters.[25]

The royal trumpets, one may assume, were always on hand to perform a fanfare announcing the appearance of Francis. I have mentioned, above, their appearance in the coronation procession in 1515. In that same year they announced Francis at the wedding of Diane de Poitiers and three years later eight trumpets led him to a banquet.[26] The trumpets appear again for the wedding of the Duc de Clèves with the Princess of Navarre, at Châtellerault in 1541, together with 'flutes, horns, clarions, fifes and tabors.'[27] These royal trumpeters, who finally performed the 'De Profundis' at the funeral of Francis,[28] are themselves immortalized in a relief of 'Ronown' on the Louvre, by Jean Goujon. Ronsard wrote of this work,

> For the King's glory you have carved aloft
> A goddess on the palace of the Louvre,

[21] Mayer, *The Great Regent*, 79. The original text is found in Emile Rhodes, *Les Trompettes du Roi* (Paris: Picard, 1909), 33.

> après étaient les sacqueboutes et hautbois du Roy vêtus de damas blanc, jouant de leurs instruments incessamment. Avec eux, les Trompettes du Roy, vêtus de même, sonnant tout le long des rues.

[22] See Prunières, 'La musique de la Chambre et de L'Écurie sous le Regne de Francois Ier,' 243.

> Nicolas de Lucques (hired in 1533)
> Dominique de Lucques (hired in 1533)
> Nicolas Mutet (hired in 1555)
> Guyon Hue
> Barthelemy Brullet
> Pierre Boullant

[23] Edmond Vander Straeten, *La Musique aux Pays-Bas avant le XIXe Siecle* (1867–1888, reprinted in New York: Dover, 1969), 4:189. Also, Grove, 17:242 ('les ix compaignons Italiens, serviteurs du roi de France, joueurs de hautbois, sacbottes et cornets'). Prunières, 'La musique de la Chambre et de L'Écurie sous le Regne de Francois Ier,' 241, mentions an appearance during a festival given for the Queen Mother, held at this time, and Vander Straeten mentions an additional appearance before Margaret of Austria, the Regent of the Low Countries.

[24] Bertrand Peffier, Pierre Du Val, Leonard de Combe, Nicolas et Gaspard de Chanzemezelles

[25] François Meunier, Dominique de Branque (hired in 1533), Guillaume de Zanzac, François de Rivet, Pierre Chancel (hired in 1537), Gerard de Rivet

[26] See Grace Hart Seely, *Diane the Huntress: The Life and Times of Diane de Poitiers*, (New York: D. APpleton-Century, 1936), 1, and Francis Hackett, *Francis the First*, 200.

> Who through her trumpet of Renown, with cheeks
> Full rounded, blows forever.[29]

I have mentioned above, under the discussion of Henry VIII of England, the historic meeting in 1520 between that king and Francis I. Given the rich musical resources mentioned above, it is no surprise to find the French king with large numbers of his musicians on hand to impress Henry VIII.

We first see them at a banquet, given by Francis in Ardres for Henry VIII, when no fewer than twenty-four trumpets marched in from the kitchen, with various court officials.[30] The chronicles are not very specific regarding the music during this meal, but one account of such music during the final banquet indicates an ensemble of primarily winds.

> During the meal, the royal musicians played in turn; trumpets, cornetts, fifes, sackbutts, trombones, sourdines, a tabor, a viol, and a 'tuifolo.'[31]

When the aristocracy danced there, as nearly everywhere at this date, a wind band provided the music. Thus, when Henry VIII hosted a dance at the village of Guines, where he was residing,

> King Francis led a dance, in the Italian fashion, to the music of his own fifes and sackbutts, the usual accompaniment of dancing in this style.[32]

Based on all similar sources, one must again assume that the 'fifes' mentioned here were actually shawms. However, one mask seems to have included the real fifes.

> The maskers had been escorted to Ardres by … the customary loud instruments, drums and fifes in one account, 'drumslades' only in another, with other minstrels to accompnay the mask and the dancing which followed. Six drummers, clad as lansquenets, and other minstrels in white, yellow and russet damask 'blew and played through Ardres.' The drums and fifes would also announce the entry of the maskers when the mask commenced.[33]

[27] Jehanne D'Orliac, *The Moon Mistress*, trans. F. McCurdie Atkinson (Philadelphia: J.B. Lippincott, 1930), 162.

[28] Seely, *Diane the Huntress*, 139.

[29] Henry Dwight Sedgwick, *The House of Guise* (New York: Bobbs-Merrill, 1938), 90.

[30] Joycelyne Gledhill Russell, *The Field of Cloth of Gold* (New York: Barnes & Noble, 1969), 160.

[31] Russell, ibid., 177. 'Fifes,' in this context, must surely be a mistranslation and must mean shawms.

[32] Ibid., 164.

[33] Ibid., 167.

The royal wind players of Francis also appeared during the church observations which fell during this week. One reads of singers, organists, sackbutts, cornetts, and fifes (shawms?).[34] Another account says the Mass, composed by Perino, was performed on organ, sackbutts, and cornetts.[35]

The interest of Francis in his own wind bands is complimented by his gifts to visiting wind bands. In 1538 alone, he rewarded a visiting band of cornetts, belonging to the Queen of Hungary; an oboe band of the Duke of Mantoue[36]; and no fewer than four wind bands, two of trumpets and two of oboes, of Pope Paul III.[37]

The Published 'Danseries'

Beginning with the *Six Galliardes et six Pavanes*, published by Pierre Attaingnant in Paris in 1530, a series of editions has preserved for us a vast repertoire of what I consider to be authentic wind band literature. The publication of this music during the sixteenth century indicated a wider usage was made of it, which I shall discuss below,[38] but the origin of this music is most likely the wind band of the king. Two of the compilers were members of the king's musical establishment, Claude Gervaise and Jean d'Estrée, the latter an oboist (shawm) in the king's wind band. Heartz adds,

> Enjoying good relations with the main musicians of the Chapel Royal and Sainte-Chapelle, Attaingnant naturally profited from the repertory of these organizations, which furnished his mainstay. In the early years, access to the manuscripts used by the royal musicians was perhaps by way of the mysterious 'P.B.,' … who has been identified with the Pierre Blondeau serving the function of scribe to the Chapel Royal in 1532.[39]

The editions themselves do not specify an instrumentation; why then do I call this wind band literature? I have cited numerous examples of proof in this volume which clearly suggest that before 1550 the dance ensemble was still a wind ensemble, as it was almost exclusively during the fifteenth century. Dr. Caroline Cunningham, a leading scholar in this field, confirms that the early part of the century belongs to the wind sonority.

---

34 Ibid., 172.

35 Ibid., 175.

36 Quoted in Prunières, 'La musique de la Chambre et de L'Écurie sous le Regne de Francois Ier,' 238.

> A Pierre Anthoine et ses compaignons, joueurs de haulxboys du Duc de Mantoue, 45 livres.

37 Discussed below, under Court Wind Bands in Italys.

38 Under Civic Wind Bands in France.

39 Daniel Heartz, *Pierre Attaingnant: Royal Printer of Music* (Berkeley: University of California Press, 1969), 91.

The iconography shows a gradual switchover from pure wind bands, both loud and soft, to various combinations of strings, both viols and violins, amplified as the century goes on by plucked instruments: lute and keyboard.[40]

These observations are precisely confirmed in the most important contemporary treatise on the dance, the *Orchésography* (1588), by Thoinot Arbeau. Speaking of his own period, the latter part of the century, he says,

> CAPRIOL. Must the tabor and flute necessarily be used for pavans and basse dances?
> ARBEAU. Not unless one wishes it. One can play them on violins, spinets, transverse flutes, and flutes with nine holes, hautboys and all sorts of instruments. They can even be sung.[41]

However, when reflecting on an earlier period (he hopes these dances will be 'reinstated'), he describes exactly the kind of wind band I have referred to so often in this volume.

> ARBEAU. On solemn feast days the pavan is employed by kings, princes and great noblemen to display themselves in their fine mantles and ceremonial robes. They are accompanied by queens, princesses and great ladies, the long trains of their dresses loosened and sweeping behind them, sometimes borne by damsels. And it is the said pavans, played by hautboys and sackbuts, that announce the grand ball and are arranged to last until the dancers have circled the hall two or three times …
> CAPRIOL. Pray write down the tunes of a pavan and a basse dance for me.
> ARBEAU. I shall do so willingly, in the hope that such honourable dances are reinstated and replace the lascivious, shameless ones introduced in their stead.[42]

After then giving some of these dance tunes, as he had promised, Arbeau makes a direct reference to the body of published dances discussed below as the very body of literature he had in mind above when he referred to those played by the wind bands of 'hautboys and sackbuts.'

> You will find plenty in the books on dances printed by the recently defunct Attaignant, who lived near the church of St. Cosmo in Paris, and in the books of the late Master Nicolas du Chemin, printer in the said Paris at the sign of the Silver Lion.[43]

---

[40] Letter to the author dated April 20, 1980. Much of this material is based on her excellent study, *Estienne du Tertre, 'Scavant Musicien,' Jean d'Estree, 'Joueur de Hautbois du Roy,' and the Mid-Sixteenth Century Franco-Flemish Chanson and Ensemble Dance* (Unpublished dissertation, Bryn Mawr, 1969).

[41] Thoinot Arbeau, *Orchésography*, trans., Mary Stewart Evans (New York: Kamin Dance Publishers, 1948), 67.

[42] Ibid., 59.

[43] Ibid., 75.

It seems very clear to me, both from this direct association with wind bands by this contemporary authority and the numerous examples of confirming evidence presented in the present volume, that the published 'Danseries' before mid-century must be considered as representative of wind band literature of that period.

The repertoire of these published collections include dances with direct relationships to earlier chansons as well as chansons presented directly for instrumental performance. In other words, the literature here coincides exactly with the known first stages in the development of original wind band literature: first, the direct instrumental performance of multi-part vocal works; next, the re-arranging of vocal materials into new instrumental forms; and finally, the composition of original literature. This French literature of the sixteenth century allows us an extraordinary view of the first two of these steps.

The compositions which are instrumental dances are equally interesting. The music for the basse dance, for example, which we know in the late fifteenth century exists only as single tunes played by the sackbut or slide-trumpet.[44] We know the upper parts were improvised by the shawms, but, with an exception or two, they do not exist in manuscript or in print. Now, in this sixteenth-century French literature one sees the basse dance fully harmonized. The basse dance was, by the time of its appearance in this body of literature, somewhat old-fashioned. One must assume that by 1530 it was no longer danced the same as in the fifteenth century, and perhaps not played with as complex counterpoint. Nevertheless, this is authentic instrumental music, authentic multi-part wind band music in the oldest extant French form.

This series of publications begins in 1530 with the *Six Galliardes et six Pavanes* and the *Neuf basses dances deux branles*. The latter actually contains, in order: nine basse dances (three with following bransles), nineteen pavanes, fifteen gaillardes, and six more pavanes. In these collections the pavanes, gaillardes and branles are rather homorhythmic, while the basse dances and tourdions contain more interesting counterpoint. The basse dances with Italian titles tend to be less interesting.

[44] See Volume 1 in this series.

Next come the chansons which are suggested for flute consorts. They are the twenty-three *Chansons musicales a quatre parties desquelles les plus convenables a la fleuste ...* and the twenty-eight chansons in the *Vingt a sept chansons Musicales a quatre parties desquelles les plus convenables a la fleuste*, both of 1533.[45]

The next volume appears in 1547, a volume of fifty dances, of which at least ten are known to have earlier vocal prototypes. Whereas the earlier publications were in separate part-books, here one has a single volume.[46] It is also the only example which is ordered according to mode. Nearly half of these dances are of the bransle type, reflecting the new popularity of this dance.

During 1549–1550, three separate collections, containing eighty-seven chansons, appear, each volume recommending that they are effective for all musical instruments (*Convenables a tous instrumentz musicaulz*).[47] Why, of all the many separate publications of chanson volumes, did Attaingnant specify these three for instrumental performance? The answer seems to be that these were the ones most frequently performed in this fashion in actual practice, as each volume carefully states (*Pour les meilleures & plus frequentes, es cours des princes*).

The year 1550 also saw the printing of two more instrumental volumes of dances, the *Quart livre de danceries, a quatre parties* (19 August 1550), containing nineteen pavanes and twenty-three gaillardes, and a volume of fifty-three bransle, *Cinquiesme livre de danceries, a quatre parties* (28 August 1550). These volumes introduce us for the first time to Claude Gervaise, who, the title page tells us, has 'seen and corrected' these compositions. Here he may have been only an editor, but in 1555, in *Six-ième livre de Danceries*, he has 'put into music' (*mis en musique*) the dances.

Gervaise has been assumed to have been a viol player, on the basis of a surviving publication for that instrument; but there is nothing to suggest the collections of 1550 are intended for strings. Cunningham believes the increasing 'flourishes, scale passages, turns and ornsmentation' in the 1555 volume possibly indicates Gervaise was beginning to develop idiomatic melodic writing for strings.[48] I see no such suggestion here, indeed the same characteristics can be found in the wind writing of Gabrieli. Quite the contrary, the existence of a hand-written note on the contra tenor part of the only surviving copy of

[45] Another volume (ca. 1535) in two parts recommended for flutes is lost and known only through its mention in Conrad Gesner, *Pandectarum* (Zurich, 1548), fol. 85.

[46] A matter of economy: the publisher cuts down the paper costs by seventy-five per cent and the customer must buy four of each books for performance.

[47] *Second livre contenant xxix chansons* (1549), *Premier livre des chansons esleves* (1550), and *Tiers livre ... xxviii chansons* (1550).

[48] Cunningham, *Estienne du Tertre*, 171.

the *Sixième livre* (*Qui est fait bonne pour les violons*), suggests to me that these were still thought of as wind band works. The author of this manuscript note is clearly going out of his way to suggest an *alternative* instrumentation; if it were common practice no such note would be necessary.

Two final publications appear under the name of the publisher Attaingnant, the *Troisième Livre de Danceries* ('seen by Claude Gervaise') and the *Septième Livre de Danceries* ('set to music by Estienne du Tertre'). Although both are dated 1557, they may well be reprints, as is suggested in the title of the Gervaise work (nouvellement imprime) and in the conservative quality of the du Tertre music.[49]

Another Parisian publisher, Nicolas du Chemin, published in 1559 and 1564 four additonal volumes of instrumental dances which are very important in the history of the wind band. These additional one hundred and ninety-eight dances are the work of Jean d'Estrée, royal oboist to the king and a member of the St. Julien minstrel guild which performed similar music for civic, rather than royal, occasions. The apparent bare harmonic structure of these works suggest that perhaps these are truly intended for dancing, rather than for listening to in concert or 'at the table.' One can not judge them fairly, as no complete copy survives—only the Superius and Bass parts being extant. The only form in which one can study them is in the plagiarized form in which fifty-two of them appear in the 1571 edition by the Flemish publisher, Phalèse.[50]

Perhaps a further insight might be found in the performance activities of d'Estrée himself. Cunningham notes that he was not only,

> a member of the king's *musicque de l'écurie* as 'joueur de hautbois du roi,' but he could further augment his salary as a royal musician by playing in small dance-bands for non-court functions, and by making perhaps even more money in editing and arranging the *Danseries* for Nicolas du Chemin. Sixteenth century Paris was a small place, and the boundaries between the activities of musician, courtier, printer and composer were evidently not as great as we might think.
>
> In any case, d'Estrée appears in one of the above-mentioned contracts as a member, with nine other players, of a group playing for banquets and fetes in Paris between 1552 and 1558. Other members of the group ... were another oboist and friend of Gervaise's, Julien le Maistre, and du Tertre's friend, also a court-musician, Pierre Joly ... d'Estrée

[49] du Tertre apparently replaced Gervaise, who died sometime in 1556–1557.

[50] Cunningham, *Estienne du Tertre*, identifies these fifty-two works.

lived in the Saint Herd district of Paris on the right bank, along with so many other members of the Confrèrie St. Julien. His death-date has been recorded ... as before ... 1577.[51]

It seems probable, therefore, that the music of d'Estrée is not to be thought of as the repertoire of the king's band, but rather a 'special edition' designed for the less gifted players who performed in similar civic wind bands throughout France. This might explain the very simple harmonic and rhythmic settings of the tunes in this collection. Confirmation of this hypothesis may perhaps be seen in the fact that it was in Phalèse's collection that fifty-two of these works reappear in 1571, in a collection intended for the civic wind bands of the low countries.

Leaving aside then the collections of d'Estrée, one still has twelve published collections of instrumental music which must be considered as repertoire appropiate to the royal wind bands under Francis I and Henry II of France.

Henry II

Beginning with Henry II (reigning 1547–1559) there were four kings with relatively brief reigns. Their time was filled with religious and political strife, leaving little time to develop or enjoy their musicial establishments.

The continuing publications after 1547 suggest that Henry maintained the wind band of his father and indeed this is confirmed in a document from 1552 which mentions the shawm and sackbut band.[52] No doubt they were among the 'Noises of loud instruments' at the coronation in Rheims mentioned by an eyewitness.[53]

Henry visited Lyons, in 1548, and one of the *Intermedii* composed to celebrate this visit was, 'Io che del Bronzo fui,' by Piero Manucci, which was sung by four voices and accompanied by three crumhorns and a sackbutt.[54] For part of these celebrations, the River Saône was transformed into a fairyland of ships and sailors, all in the colors of the king. As Henry sailed up river, he saw allegories, Greek temples and centaurs, obelisks, fountains of wine, and foremost, a great artificial forest. From the forest Diana appeared with her nymphs and with an ensemble of trumpets.[55]

[51] Cunningham, *Estienne du Tertre*, 191.

[52] Paris, National Library, Ms. fr. 21451, fol. 53, 54.

[53] Quoted in Seely, *Diane the Huntress*, 140.

[54] Brown, *Sixteenth Century Instrumentation: the Music for the Florentine Intermedii*, 95.

[55] Edith Sichel, *Women and Men of the French Renaissance* (Port Washington, NY: Kennikat Press, 1970), 358.

The royal trumpets form an ironic footnote to Henry's accidental death in a tourney, cutting short his life and reign. The trumpets were, of course, an inseparable part of the tournament, but just before the round during which the king was killed, for once, as if by prescience, no trumpets and drums played.[56]

56 E.R. Chamberlin, *Marguerite of Navarre* (New York: Dial Press, 1974), 3.

Charles IX

Francis II, who ruled only a year, was the husband of the much better known Mary Queen of Scots. With his death, his young brother, Charles IX, became king at age ten, but the power rested in his mother, Catherine de Medici. It was during his reign (1560–1574) that the religious strife reached its climax in the infamous St. Bartholomew's Day Massacre. These religious hangings, burnings, and killings often were elaborately staged 'state' events and, as such, one must assume the 'state' wind bands participated. At Pau, when, for example, the governor hung ten Huguenots without a hearing, we read of 'Drums and fifes playing gay airs during the executions.'[57]

Portrait of Charles IX of France, anonymous, after François Clouet, sixteenth century

The best opportunity to observe the wind players and wind ensembles under Charles IX occurs in the accounts of celebrations held during Charles' great tour of 1564–1566. Following the period of religious wars in France and their conclusion with the Treaty of Amboise (19 March 1563), Charles was declared of age in official ceremonies at Rouen in the fall of 1563. Following this ceremony, the Queen Mother decided to undertake, with the entire court, a great tour of the kingdom. In addition to attempting to reunite discordant factions in the provinces, she hoped to stage a great meeting with Philip II of Spain, not unlike the famous meeting in 1520 between Henry VIII and Francis I. As it turned out, Philip did not attend, but sent his wife, Elizabeth (who was a daughter to Catherine) and his advisor, the Duke of Alba.

57 Paul Van Dyke, *Catherine de Medicis* (New York: Scribner, 1922), 2:14.

The grand tour began with a series of entertainments held in the Fontainebleau area. Of particplar interest to us is a day spent by the king at the palace of the Duc d'Orléans, his brother. The day, 14 February 1564, began at 9:00 a.m. with the king's arrival. Located between two canals, he heard, in addition to the usual poems of celebration, a consort of cornetts.

As the king entered, he heard a concert of very excellent cornett players. And meanwhile from the end of the main canal came three Sirens, who were three young children having excellent voices and looked so natural that they appeared to be nude, their navels lower than their long gilded braids, in silver and azure, decorated like Dolphins, in the way in which Sirens are ordinarily painted, and swam in the middle of the water upright, with admirable guile. As they came in front of the king, the cornets stopped.[58]

Following this, the first poem was recited and then Neptune appeared in a floating chariot, drawn by four marine horses,[59] to the music of another wind ensemble.

(When the poems were finished) they discovered at the head of the other canal, a Neptune, holding a Trident in hand, seated on a chariot pulled by four marine horses, swimming with similar guile to the Sirens, and as they came slowly, they heard a concert of two shawms and a sackbut (deux hault boys, et une saqueboutte). And as it came in front of the king, the concert stopped.[60]

Later that evening a great banquet was given and the first of a variety of ensembles performing was an ensemble of cornetts and a sackbut.

The king was seated at the table, having the direct view of the long table where were seated Princes and Ladies, and as the first service was presented, there began a concert of cornetts and a sackbut.[61]

In some of the smaller of the hundred or so places visited by the royal party the festivities were concentrated around the entry procession. A chronicle which describes such a procession into Troyes, in March 1564, mentions none of the wind instruments used in church or chamber, but rather the lower order of fifes and tambors.

Among them marched a great number of savages, properly contained … The tambors sounded and the savages (were) in good order, some of them mounted on asses, the others on goats, very pleasing to see … Near them was the Colonel of the Swiss with the tambors and fifes, who led the Guard of the King with great order.[62]

[58] *Le recueil des Trimnphes et Magnificences qui ont estez faictes au Logis de Monseigneur le Duc Ddorleans, frere du Roy* … (Troyes, Trumeau), 1. The only extant copy of this print is in the Bibliothèque Méjanes, Aix-en-Provence.

[59] The reader has seen in these pages so many instances of mechanical animals swimming through the water during the sixteenth century. Incredible as it may seem that they were capable of such constructions, I have found only one case in which the contraptions refused to operate. During the reign of Henry III, a celebration given by the Cardinal de Bourbon for the marriage of the Duc de Joyeuse included small boats disguised as sea-horses which contained trumpet, clarion, violin and shawm players. When the grand moment came, the sea-horses refused to leave their mooring; the king waited more than two hours and finally left weary and angry. See Catherine Hannah Charlotte Jackson, *The Last of the Valois* (Paris: Grolier Society), 2:155.

[60] *Le recueil des Triumphes* (Troyes, Trumeau), 2.

[61] Ibid., 5.

[62] 'Ordre du Marcher tenu et observé en l'entrée faicte par le Roy Charles IX en la ville de Troye …', Paris, National Library, Ms. fr. 4318, 23419, and n.a. 7237.

In Bayonne the court stayed for almost two months and participated in many spectacular festivities. They were all the more elaborate owing to the international character of this meeting between the King of France and the Queen of Spain. Catherine de Medici made sure that no expense was spared in impressing the Spanish guests with the wealth and cultural resources of France. This first meeting occurred on the banks of the river which separated the two countries and where, for the occasion, Catherine had had erected a beautiful pavilion in which there was spread 'a very rich luncheon of fine hams and tongues, pastries, all sorts of fruits, salads, sweetmeats, and a great abundance of good wine.'[63]

The Spanish company arrived with three hundred mounted archers, the French began firing repeated salvoes, and the king escorted his sister to a barge in the middle of the river. The couple spent an hour at lunch to the sound of a wind band. One source describes this band as 'tabourins, trompettes, (and) hault-bois sounding noble melody from all around.'[64] Another source describes the ensemble as 'trompettes, doulcines, et clairons' sounding 'around the canopy, echoing on the shore their high and gracious fanfares.'[65]

On the following day, 15 June 1564, Elizabeth made her formal processional entry into Bayonne. Before retiring to her lodging, she attended a Te Deum in the cathedral, performed by the king's sisters and accompanied by 'excellent cornetts.'[66]

The first great entertainment was the 'Tournament of Diverse Nations.' These occasions almost always included trumpets, but the cornetts here are somewhat of a surprise.

> As the Majesty had accorded and bestowed to them, the Gentlemen and Ladies were led to a large place, in the city, in the middle of which was an enclosed area for them: When the two queens arrived, and had climbed the platforms, which were on either side ... (later) entered into the arena six trumpets and six cornetts dressed the same.[67]

The king entered dressed as a Trojan and his brother, the Duc d'Orléans, as an Amazon. As the tournament continued, the court appeared in an extraordinary variety of disguises, at times representatives of civilization—classical and modern,

[63] Van Dyke, *Catherine de Medicis*, 1:318.

[64] Abel Jouan, *Recueil et discours de voyage du Roy Charles IX* (Paris, 1566), 46.

[65] *Ample discours de l'arrivee de la royne catholique soeur du roy a sainct Jehan de Lus: de son entrée à Bayonne ...* (Paris, 1565), 4.

[66] *Recueil des choses notables, qui ont esté faites à Bayonne ...* (Paris, 1566), 8. A copy of this print can be found in Victor E. Graham and W. McAllister Johnson, *The Royal Tour of France by Charles IX and Catherin de' Medici: Festivals and Entries, 1564–6* (Toronto, 1979), 328ff.

[67] Ibid.

pagan and Christian; as exotic or fantastical types, including some dressed as women; as fierce warriors encountering supernatural creatures; and again dressed as women, now Nymphs.

The second major festivity occurred on 21 June 1564, and consisted of an elaborate (indoor) mock attack on a castle, which represented the temporary victory of War over Peace. The king, of course, proved the only knight capable of reaching the castle, thus establishing peace. Upon entering the castle the king found many of his gentlemen and ladies,

> had been taken hostage by a giant: he delivered them from their captivity and they left the castle, to the harmonious sound of fanfares and joyous sounds (allegresses faictes) of trumpets, clarions, and other 'gracious instruments.'[68]

[68] *Ample Discours* (Paris, 1565), 9.

After this 'rescue' things became even more fantastical. Some knights had been turned into rocks and some ladies into orange trees, the result of a spell cast by Merlin. In time all was set straight by the appearance of Amour, seated in a chariot with a lion and a dolphin (representing Amour's power over all life on land or sea).

On 23 June, the court journeyed, in an elaborate boat built like a castle, upriver from Bayonne to an 'enchanted island.' On the way the court encountered many aquatic spectacles, as for example a whale which blocked the river and had to be killed by a group of local whale hunters! Of the greatest interest to us was the encounter of Neptune, richly costumed and riding in a magnificent shell boat drawn by three marine horses. Neptune greeted the company with a poem, which was followed by six 'Tritons' who,

> made a consort of their six cornetts, and they were very pleasant to the ear.[69]

[69] *Recueil des chose notables* (Paris, 1566), 50ff.

This finished, another recitation and another six cornetts. This occurred still again, giving a total of eighteen cornett players, organized into three separate consorts. Several consorts of violins followed as part of this same pageant by Neptune.

On the island itself a dance was given to the music of six 'excellent *cornemuse* players' (here, I believe, bag-pipes). This would not catch our attention except for the fact that soon after there was an appearance of six 'excellent musette' players. I believe this may be an early instance of the use of an instrument which would long be a favorite of the French court. The musette, in the French court during this period, apparently meant at times the performance of only the chanter of the bag-pipe. It was for all effect a small oboe and, I might add, some European oboe players today consider this repertoire as part of the repertoire of the oboe proper. This is all confirmed in the *Mémoires* of an eyewitness, Marguerite de Valois, who describes the festivities on the island in detail. In discussing the various dances, she mentions 'les Poitevines avec la cornemuse' and later the appearance of 'le petit hautbois,' the little oboe.[70]

The final great festivity of the visit to Bayonne was another tournament, this one named in honor of 'Virtue and Love.' The king entered the arena accompanied by nine trumpets, dressed in skirts of damask, speckled with golden nuggets.[71] The Duc d'Orléans was introduced by another nine trumpeters.

Nothing in the remainder of the tour could equal the diverse role of music we have seen in the Bayonne festivities. Usually, one finds only the trumpets and clarions anticipated when the king appears. A chronicle of the subsequent visit to Tours, for example, describes the local trumpets and clarions in a category with noisy pistols and field guns, but carefully describes the trumpets of the king's Swiss guards as 'sounding joyous.'[72]

There is another extensive picture of the wind performance at the time of Charles IX, found in the descriptions of his official entry procession, and that of his Queen, Elizabeth of Austria, into Paris following his coronation. Originally scheduled at the time of his coronation, in 1561, these processions were delayed ten years, due to both political and actual climate.

The king's procession, which began at the Porte Saint-Denis and ended at the Pont Notre Dame, was organized into four divisions: representatives of the Church, the University, civic officials, and the royal representatives. The civic division began with nearly two thousand representatives of trades marching seven abreast. To help them the city had arranged for them to be 'accompanied by fifes and tambors , in good numbers, marching seven by seven, holding their ranks so well that it could not be possible to do it better.'[73]

[70] Quoted in Graham and Johnson, *The Royal Tour of France by Charles IX and Catherin de' Medici*, 44.

[71] *Recueil des choses notables* (Paris, 1566), 33.

[72] Ollivier Tassoreau, *La Description de l'Entée du Treschrestien Roy Charles IX du Nom en sa Ville de Tours* (Tours, 1565), 4ff.

[73] Simon Bouquet, *Bref et sommaire recueil de ce qui a esté faict, et de l'ordre tenüe à la joyeuse et triumphante Entrée de Prince Charles IX de ce nom Roy de France, en sa bonne ville et cité de Paris* ... (Paris, 1572), 40. An extensive list of the names of these players, together with payments, etc., can be found in Paris, National Library, Ms. fr. 11691, pp. 69–70.

The civic portion of the procession continued with various minor civic officials and then three groups of civic militia. The militia were accompanied by mounted trumpeters, some of whom were borrowed from members of the aristocracy.[74] Concluding the civic portion of the procession were one hundred and twenty sons of wealthy middle class merchants, richly mounted on horses, and then more civic militia.

The Paris City Treasurer accounts also mention payment to what must have been the king's wind band, an ensemble we know existed from another source[75] as including a band of fifteen 'sacquebutes, hautbois et cornets,' in addition to twelve trumpets, and ten players of 'phifres, tabourins et cornemuses.'

> To Jehan Gentilz, oboist of the king, more for him than his campanions, the sum of 15 pounds … for playing their oboes (instruments de haultbois) on the king's entrance day at the triumphal arc on the street Saint Denis, near St. Jacques Hospital.[76]

Finally, an epic poem, *La Renommée*, by Charles de Navieres, describes the king's procession at great length. In a poem, of course, one can not know what is fact or fiction, but this account would not be complete without quoting some of his descriptions. One line in particular catches the eye, 'Eight trumpets and eight sounds filled the air.' The poet seems here to want to make the point very clear that the royal trumpets played in eight-parts and not in unison.

> To the King, the motto and the vessel of Paris:
> To the sound of Tambors, and to the sound of
> Fifes resounding, marching in good order,
> This order of soldiers bravely in rank,
> Who, charging forthwith their lances,
> To the bastions of fire, where the thunderous din ceases not
> And the surprised people are quickly amazed
> ......
> Here the eight oboes and cornetts resounded
> And filled the strains, the music furnished
> Was titillating with sweet harmony to all ears.
> Eight trumpets and eight sounds filled the air.[77]

A few days later this great procession was repeated for the official entrance into Paris of the queen. The order of march seems to have been substantially the same with only

74 Ibid., 70ff.
> To Claude de la Vallée, Remon de la Mathe, Michel Noiriet, Pierre Doulcet, Jehan de la Vallée and Francisque de Modene, trumpets of the Duke of Lorraine, and other *seigneurs*, the sum of 48 pounds, 12 solz, for their work, salaries and vacations for playing their trumpets for the entrance of the King in front of the troop of the Sons of Paris, and for overcoat, jumper, cap, plume and scarf.

75 *L'estat de l'Écurie* (1571), quoted in Prunières, 'La musique de la Chambre et de L'Écurie sous le Regne de Francois Ier,' 246–247.

76 Ms. fr. 11691, ibid.

77 Charles de Navières, *La Renommée … sus les receptions à Sedan, Mariage à Mezieres, couronnement à Saindenis, et entrees à Paris du Roy et de la Royne* (Paris, 1571), 4:64ff and 200ff.

minor variations, such as the appearance of nine of the king's trumpets marching before the archers and crossbowmen of the city.[78]

During the fourth, and royal, division of the procession, one sees a contingent of musicians who may well have been members of the king's wind band.

> Afterwards marched the oboes, cornetts, trumpets, and clarions (haulbois, et cornetz à boucquin, et les trompettes et clairons) were there, playing their instruments without cease.[79]

No doubt these same players were those found in the Notre Dame Cathedral where the queen was welcomed following the procession.

> And (she) was led through a gallery expressly made, to the door of the church up to a great stairway, decorated and ornamented very magnificently, by which she climbed to the great room prepared for this effect, whereupon entering she was greeted by a great number of trumpets, clarions and cornets, witness to the incredible joy that everyone felt in her presence.[80]

Finally, there was an interesting entertainment featuring folk music, which was given as part of the festivities in welcome of the visit of Polish ambassadors, on 15 September 1573, which featured musicians from several provinces playing in their various traditions.

> les Bretonnes, (playing) le passepied; les Auvergnates, la bourrée; les Provencales avec leurs cymbales, la farandole; les Poitevines avec leurs cornemuses, le menuet; puis les danses bourguignonnes et champenoises, avec le hautbois et le tambourin.[81]

The audience, we are told, received this with 'profound admiration.'

[78] Ms. fr. 11691, 71, 72.

[79] Bouquet, *Bref et sommaire recueil*, 3:17.

[80] Ibid., 21.

[81] Georges Pillement, *Paris en Fête* (Paris, 1972), 190.

Henry III

The tragic Henry III (reigning 1574–1589), brother to Charles IX, followed and with this king the affairs of both state and family fell to the lowest ebb of the century. A brief description of this king will demonstrate this point.

> The Court of Henry III was a mass of corruption. The King had his pimps and minions, and did not much discriminate between male and female bedfellows, frequently following his orgies of lust with public exhibitions of repentance,[82] when he dressed in sackcloth and scourged himself with whipcord … When some of his male lovers were murdered by the followers of his brother, he gave them state funerals and raised marble monuments over their graves … Rings, bracelets, and earrings adorned his person; his body was anointed with perfumes, his face painted and powdered; and occasionally he dressed as a woman, with a pearl necklace on his open bosom, being waited on by court ladies attired as men.[83]

One must assume it was the dances of this court that Arbeau was thinking of, in the passage quoted above,[84] when he referred to the 'lascivious, shameless ones,' which were currently in vogue at the time of his writing (1588).

Although it was under Henry III that the string instruments began to rise to importance in the French court, we know he maintained the basic wind band of his predecessors. An icon picturing the procession of the Knights of the Holy Ghost, in 1579, shows, in addition to trumpets and drums, a nine-member band called, 'fifes and hautboys,' with several sizes of the shawm instrument (see image page 81).[85] This wind band, under its usual name at this time, 'hautbois, sacquebutes, cornets à bouquin,' consisted of twelve members in 1580, led by Dominique de Lucques and Salomon Darlione.[86]

Arbeau also gives a very interesting description of French military music at this time. He lists an unexpectedly large variety of instruments as being used in the military: four kinds of trumpets, horns, cornetts, shawms, two kinds of fifes, and percussion.[87] No other source speaks of the French as having so apparently large military bands at this time and it is difficult to believe large bands were general. Perhaps he was only commenting on the variety of instruments he had seen, especially in view of the fact, as Kastner points out,[88] the French at this time were using a large number of hired foreign military

[82] I might add that on one of these moments of repentance, in 1583, he, 'troubled in soul by fear of God,' instituted a brotherhood of penitents, made a barefoot pilgrimage from Chartres to Notre Dame de Cléry, and dismissed his musicians! See Jean Mariejol, *A Daughter of the Medicis: The Romantic Story of Margaret of Valois* (New York: Harper & Bros., 1929), 146.

[83] Hesketh Pearson, *Henry of Navarre: The King Who Dared* (New York: Harper & Row), 20.

[84] Page 71.

[85] Paul Lacroix, *Military and Religious Life in the Middle Ages and the Renaissance*, 200.

[86] Paris, National Library, Archives curieuses, 1re série, t. X. p. 427ff.

[87] Arbeau, *Orchésography*, 18ff.

> Les instrumens servans à la marche guerriere sont les buccines et trompettes, litues et clerons, cors et cornets, tibies, fifres, arigots, tambours et autres semblables, mesmement lesdicts tambours.

[88] Kastner, *Manuel general*, 98.

Procession of the Knights of the Holy Ghost from Paul Lacroix's *Military and Religious Life in the Middle Ages and the Renaissance* (D, trumpets; E, drums; F, fifes and hautboys).

troops. Nevertheless, Arbeau's discussion is very interesting in its description of the period when co-ordinated marching was just beginning to come into practice. Here it is still too early to find troops marching to actual band music, but they have begun to march to a beat from the percussion. Once the next step is taken, during the Baroque period, and troops march to actual band music, a whole new era in the wind band will have arrived.

> ARBEAU. The Persian drum (used by some Germans who carry it at the saddle bow) consists of a half sphere of leather closed with strong parchment, about two and a half feet in diameter, and it makes a noise like thunder when the skin is struck with the sticks. The drum used by the French, and familiar enough to everyone, is of hollow wood about two and a half feet deep, closed at each end with parchment skins secured by two bands, about two and a half feet in diameter, and bound with cords to keep them taut. It makes, as you have often heard, a great noise when the skins are beaten with two sticks which the drummer holds in his hands. The appearance is well known by all …

CAPRIOL. (What are) the little straps and buckles at each crossing of the cords on the drum?

ARBEAU. This is to tighten the skins when one wishes to beat the drum … The sound of these various instruments serves as signal and warning to the soldiers, to break camp, to advance, to retreat, and gives them heart, daring and courage, both to attack the enemy and to defend themselves with manful vigour. Now, without them, the men would march in confusion and disorder, which would place them in peril of being overthrown and defeated by the enemy. This is why our Frenchmen are instructed to make the rankers and bondsmen of the squadrons march to certain rhythms.

CAPRIOL. How is that?

ARBEAU. You are a musician and well know that it is to the beats of time. Some are duple others are triple, and either of these in their turn may be slow, moderate, or quick.

CAPRIOL. That is true.

ARBEAU. You will concede that if three men are walking together and each one moves at a different speed they will not be in step, because to be so they must all three march in unison, either quickly, moderately, or slowly.

CAPRIOL. There can be no doubt about it.

ARBEAU. That is why, in military marching, the French make use of the drum to beat the rhythm to which the soldiers must march, especially as the majority of soldiers are no better trained in this than they are in other branches of the military art. Wherefore, I shall not delay in setting down the methods. The drum rhythm contains eight minims, the first five of which are beaten and struck. The first four of these with one stick only and the fifth with both sticks at once. The other three beats are silent.

During the time occupied by the five minims and three rests the soldier takes one pace, that is to say, on the first note he places his left foot on the ground, and during the succeeding three notes raises his right foot so as to bring it down on the fifth note. During the three rests, which are the equivalent of three notes, he raises his left foot to recommence another pace as before. Consequently, if the march continues for two thousand five hundred drum beats, the soldier will have covered one league.

CAPRIOL. Why do you start off with the left foot?

ARBEAU. Because most men are right footed and the left foot is the weaker, so if it should come about that the left foot were to falter for any reason the right foot would immediately be ready to support it.

Henry IV

The last French king of the sixteenth century (reigning 1589–1610) also loved the drama and excitement of war, 'the rolling kettledrums and shrilling fifes.'[89] On one occasion, in 1590, the first detachment of his amy passed near the city of Paris and played the *réveil* early one morning with 'drums, trumpets, clarions, and hautbois.' The city was alarmed.

[89] Desmond Seward, *The First Bourbon: Henri IV, King of France and Navarre* (Boston: Gambit, 1971), 94.

> This caused a terrible panic; the people rose from their beds in great haste, fancying that the Huguenots had taken the city by surprise.[90]

[90] Jackson, *The Last of the Valois*, 2:336.

One first sees this Henry when, as King of Navarre, in 1572, he was married to Marguerite of Valois in Notre Dame Cathedral. Several accounts mention the perfomance of 'trumpets, clarions, and hautboys' before and after this ceremony.[91]

[91] Marcelle Vioux, *Henry of Navarre*, trans., J. Lewis May, New York: Dutton, 1937), 10, 13; and Irene Mahoney, *Royal Cousin: The Life of Henry IV of France* (Garden City, NY: Doubleday, 1970), 39.

Henri IV, King of France, by Frans Pourbus the younger

These 'hautboys' must certainly have been the twelve-member shawm and sackbut band which is known to have existed under Henry III and which appears still by the end of the reign of Henry IV, for the coronation of Louis XIII, in 1610.

Henry was, on this day, dressed in yellow doublet satin and wore a white plumed hat while Marguerite, as she wrote later in her *Mémoires*, 'blazed in diamonds.'[92] It is said that during the vows, after a loud 'yes' by Henry, Marguerite lost her courage and stood in tense silence. Charles IX in a fit of fury struck her a blow with his clenched fist on the back of her neck, which she lowered with a moan. The crowd began to mumur with resentment, so the officiating Cardinal hurriedly pronounced them man and wife!

When Henry, in 1589, found himself king, by law and tradition, he saw it would be quite impossible, as a protestant, to maintain his reign over a nation which was ninety per cent catholic. The only pragmatic solution was to become a catholic, which he did in 1593. He appeared at the church, as a newly 'purified heretic,' dressed entirely in white, but with black cape and hat, and led to the church by his royal trumpets.

When Henry visited Rouen, in October 1596, he entered as part of a great procession, with representatives of several religious orders, judges and civic officials, civic militia, and the local aristocracy. Then came the 'Bachelors and Masters of Art, Doctors of Physic, Civil Law and Divinity, clothed in very fair and reverent garments of damask, satin and black velvet, and for the most part riding upon mules.'[93] Henry followed his guard, with their drums and fifes, and his personal trumpets. They passed several triumphal arches, including one in which clouds opened as the king passed and a voice (of God) declared His love for the king.

One sees the trumpets again in the same year in Paris, when emissaries of Queen Elizabeth of England came to bestow upon Henry the Order of the Garter. An eyewitness saw the king's trumpets,

> in horsemen's coats of greene velvet, and very well mounted; then tooke they place, and sounded oftentimes as they passed.[94]

[92] Quoted in Mahoney, *Royal Cousin*, 40.

[93] Harrison, *The Elizabethan Journals*, 2:142.

[94] John Nichols, ed., *The Progresses and Public Processions of Queen Elizabeth* (London, 1788), vol. 3.

Following his conversion to the catholic faith, the path was clear for Henry to finally schedule his coronation. The ceremony took place at Chartres on 25 February 1594. Trumpets led Henry to the cathedral, but a larger wind band participated in the ceremony within. An early account informs us that after the crown was placed on Henry's head, and the congregation shouted, 'Vive le Roy! Vive le Roy! Vive eternellement le Roy!', then 'hautboys, clarions, trumpets, fifes and drums' sounded.[95]

The musical establishments of the aristocratic courts in France outside of Paris have received little scholarly attention, but Prunières points to large shawm-type bands in the courts at Lorraine and Montpellier.[96] These are all the more interesting as they seem to consist of French players, rather than Italian as in Paris.

[95] Pierre Matthieu, *Histoire de France sous les règnes de Francois I, Henry II, Francois II, Charles IX, Henry III, Henry IV, Louis XIII* (Paris, 1631), 2:170ff.

[96] Prunières, 'La musique de la Chambre et de L'Écurie sous le Regne de Francois Ier,' 240.

3   Court Wind Bands in Spain

Philip I

Philip I of Spain (1504–1506) was first Philip, Duke of Burgundy. This title was given him by his illustrious father, Maximilian I, at the time the latter was elected emperor (1494). Maximilian also arranged Philip's marriage to Juana of Spain, who, if she did not appear entirely normal, brought all of

Philip I of Spain, by Juan de Flandes, 1500

Spain as her dowry. During the marriage ceremony itself a motet was performed by a wind band of three shawms and a 'trompette-saiequeboute.'[1]

For the principals, the future was not so fortunate as the past. Philip, King of Spain at age twenty-six, was dead two years later, while Juana, retreating into madness, locked herself in her room for the next half-century. Their brief marriage, however, produced two children who became emperors—Charles v and Ferdinand I.

Philip, true to his Burgundian heritage, seems to have been a lover of music. For his personal wind players, life during his brief reign consisted of almost constant travel. Late in 1501 he made his first trip to Spain, as king, taking with him various court officials, singers, nine trumpeters[2] (of a very international character), three 'musettes,'[3] two drummers,[4] and four sackbuts, especially hired for the occasion.[5]

The royal party was welcomed upon their arrival in Madrid, on 27 April 1502, and led to their lodging, by the trumpets, drums, and shawm band of Don Diego Hurtado de Mendoca, duc de l'Infantado.[6] On Pentecost Sunday, 15 May 1502, in Toledo, the royal singers of Philip participated in a Mass, which he attended, and one heard the famous cornettist, Augustin, performing in the church with the singers.[7]

After barely a year in Spain, Philip was back in France with his musicians, now apparently having added to them the cornettist, Augustin. One reads of his performing with the royal musicians during a Mass in Lyon, on 2 April 1503;[8] again in Bourg, performing before Philip's sister, Marguerite of Austria;[9] and yet again with Philip's wind band on a visit to Louis XII of France.[10]

Early in 1506, Philip was off to Spain again, this time with twelve trumpets[11] and an ensemble called, 'Joueulx d'Instrumens,' which I believe was his wind band.[12] On this trip the singers seem to have had their own ship, but the various wind players were spread around on various ships, for the enjoyment of the travelers. On their departure, at least, one eyewitness observed, 'it was fine to hear trumpets, drums, and other instruments all around on the ships.'[13]

[1] Rastall, 'Some English Consort-Groupings of the Late Middle Ages,' *Music & Letters* 55, no. 2 (1974): 193, fn. 82.

[2] Edmond Vander Straeten, *La musique aux Pays-Bas avant le XIXe siecle* (Bruxelles, 1885), 7:151–152.

Pierre Nacroix, Cornille de Zellande, Jehan l'Ytalien, Jehan de Merfalys, Augustin de Scarparye, Inocent de Galera, Chrestofle d'Autreye, Antoine Martin Moer, and Jehan Angel.

[3] Bertrand Brouart, Guillaume Terrou, and Matthys de Wildre.

[4] Joachim de Trombslagher and Jehan de Pyffer

[5] Vander Straeten, *La musique aux Pays-Bas avant le XIXe siecle*, 7:149.

Josse Denis, Pierre Jourdan, Jennin de Calus et Michel de Chastreul, sacquebouttes …

[6] Vander Straeten, ibid., 153–154.
Vint ledict duc, sonnant trompettes, tamburins et chalémeux, descendre à court, fist la révérence à mon seigneur et à ma dame; puis remonta a cheval, et les prédicts seigneurs le convoyèrent à son logis.

[7] Ibid.
Les chantres du roy chantèrent une partie de la messe, les chantres de mon seigneur l'autre partie, avoecq les quelz chantres de mon seigneur, jouait du cornet maistre Augustin; ce qui faisoit bon à oyr avoec les chantres.

Charles v

In Charles v, with his lifelong contests with Francis I of France and the popes in Rome, not to mention his role as the defender of the faith against Luther and German Protestantism, we come to one of the major figures of the sixteenth century. He was born in Ghent, in 1500, and thus his native tongue was Flemish, although he learned through necessity German, Spanish, Italian, and French. Perhaps his broad education is reflected in the fact that even as a boy of fifteen he personally hired the leading writer of his day, Erasmus, to adorn his court.

[8] Ibid., 158.
> Monsigneur et sa soeur oyrent la messe, tres solennèlement célébre par le dict évesque, en la chappelle de mon dict signeur, où ses chantres et les chantres du duc chantèrent très-bien les ungs après les autres, et, avoecq les chantres, jouait de son cornet maistre Augustin, lequel faisoit bon à oyr.

[9] Georges Van Doorslaer, *La Chapelle*, 50ff., quoted in Louise Cuyler, *The Emperor Maximilian I and Music* (London: Oxford University Press, 1973), 65.

[10] Ibid. Augustin is identified here (perhaps mistakenly) as the same person as the trumpeter Augustin de Scarparye.

[11] Vander Straeten, *La musique aux Pays-Bas avant le XIXe siecle*, 7:163–164.
> Pierre Nacrois, Cornille de Zeelande, Jehan de Calys, Jehan de Merfalys, Augustin de la Caperie, Innocent Gallera, Phillipe d'Aire, Chrisstoffle d'Autrice, Jehan Angels, Pierquin de Comble, Jehan Baptiste, and Jehan Anthoine.

[12] Ibid.
> Joosse d'Elms, Pierre Jourdan, Hans Nagel, Michel de Chartel, Johan Van der Vincle, Bertrand Brouart, Guillaume Arroul, Mathis de Wildre, Joannin de Tronslagere, and Johan de Phiffere.

[13] Van Doorslaer, *La Chapelle*, 69.

Charles V, by Jakob Seisenegger, 1532

Upon the death of his father, Philip I, in 1506, the six-year-old Charles inherited much of the low countries. At this time he seems to have maintained only a few private musicians for his chapel, in particular the cornettist, Augustin de Verona,[14] and Hans Naghele and Jehan Van Vincle, who were to 'sing and play daily in the divine service.'[15]

At age sixteen, Charles prepared to travel to Spain to assume a further title as Charles I of Spain, Sicily, Sardinia, Naples, and Spanish America. Before his departure there were a number of farewell festivities, including a banquet of the Golden Fleece and a great military pageant in which Charles was a participant. On this occasion, one heard, 'trompettes, tambourins, fiffres et cornets d'Allemaigne.'[16] For the journey itself, Charles took his musicians with him, who, together with a few singers, were the necessary wind players, as one can see in an extant document.[17]

Upon his arrival in Spain, he was the object of many welcoming celebrations. One sees him in Seville (1516) greeted by trumpets, timpani, doucaines, and shawms[18] and in Valladolid

---

[14] José Subirá, *Historia de la Música* (Barcelona: Salvat, 1947), 569.

[15] A document of 1509, quoted in Vander Straeten, *La musique aux Pays-Bas avant le XIXe siecle*, 7:268–269.
   … et Hans Naghele et Jehan Van Vincle, joueurs d'instruments d'icellui sr, la somme de huit cens livres … pour, par ordonnance d'iceulx ars et de madite dame de Savoye, avoir servy continuellement devers mondit sr, en sadite chapelle, en chantant et jouant journellement en discant les heures et service divin.

   Hans Naghele had previously served as a sackbut player under Henry VII of England, but had returned to the continent by 1501, as one can see in a document (Recette générale de Lille) of that date.

   A Hans Haglen et Hans Broen, joueurs de sacqubutes du roy d'Angleterre, trente sept livres dix solz … quant nagaires ils avoient jou' devant mondit sr, pour son plaisir …

[16] Vander Straeten, *La musique aux Pays-Bas avant le XIXe siecle*, 7:284.

[17] Recette générale de Lille, quoted in Vander Straeten, *La musique aux Pays-Bas avant le XIXe siecle*, 7283.
   Innocent de Galata, trompete
   Estienne Du Bois, trompette
   Macabeus Narcroix, trompette
   Corneille de Zeelande, trompete
   Hans Keyzer, fiffer

[18] Nanie Bridgman, 'Charles-Quint et la Musique Espagnole,' *Revue de Musicologie* 43, no. 119 (1959): 46.
   … muchos atabales y trompetas y ducainas y chirimias.

   A miniature from this period, by Remi du Puis, shows 'The Young Charles V,' with three cornets and/or shawms, during such a welcoming procession (Vienna, National Library, MS. 2591).

(1517), where a great tournament was held in his honor. An eyewitness recounts large numbers of wind and percussion instruments taking part in this festivity.

> First were twenty timpani (of the princes and great men of Castille), mounted on mules, making a great noise. Afterward came twenty-eight Spanish trumpets, followed by the twelve trumpets of Charles, all dressed in sleeveless violet tunics covered with little silver and gold letter C's sown on. Later came twelve more timpani and twelve trumpets … (When Charles presented himself in the field), first came thirty tambors on horse and two large tambors. Next came sixty more drums on foot as well as forty trumpets from Castile, Naples, and Aragon, making so much noise you could not have heard the thunder of God. Next came the twelve trumpets of Charles playing in 'bon art et mode.'[19] Finally came ten German tambors on foot, and six fife players of German flutes.[20]

Not content with his many titles, the nineteen-year-old Charles now aspired to be emperor. By supplying greater gifts (bribes) to the imperial electors than his competitors, including among them Francis I of France, Charles was elected. An eyewitness reports many trumpets, drums, and fifes participating in his coronation in Aachen in 1520.[21]

---

[19] Vander Straeten, *La musique aux Pays-Bas avant le XIXe siecle*, 291, says 'bon art et mode' proves the royal trumpets were an organization based on rigorous principles of music.

[20] Quoted in Vander Straeten, ibid., 289-291.

> … premièrement, marchoient devant eulx (les princes et les grands maistres de Castille), XX atabales, montés sur mullets, menant grand bruict; après, marchoient XXVIII trompettes espagnoles, et, après, les XII trompettes du Roy, tous habillés en sayons de velour violet, bordé et semé partout de la lettre C, couronnez les aulchuns d'argent et d'autres d'or … (later) XII atabales et XII trompettes … venue du Roy sur les rengz … Premièrement, marchoient devant le Roy, XXX tambourins à cheval, aveucq chascun deulx grotz tambourins, à dextre et à senestre, qui menoient un grand bruict et retentissement, tous acoustrés à la musique. Après, marchoient LX aultres, telz tambourins, nommés ataballes, et aussi XL trompettes castillans, napolitains et aragonois, menans ung tel son et bruict, que on n'y eult point oy Dieu tonner; et marchoient les XII trompettes du Roy, qui fort bien et gaillardement sonnoient de bon art et mode, tous accoustrés de satin blancq, couvert de satin cramoysi, décopé, et pardessus bordés de deulx larges bordz de drap d'or. Apres, marchoient X tambour ins d'Alemaingne à pied, six fiffres joueurs de leurs fluttes d'Alemaingne bien gaillardement …

[21] *Deutsche Reichstagsakten*, jüngere Reihe, I, Nr. 379.

> … und als solichs usgeruffen wart, haben die drumpeter des pfalzgrafen und des markgrafen von Brandenburg, der ungeverlich umb die 22 gewest sin, in die drumpeten gestossen und gepiffen und die alsbald te deum laudamus gesungen und uf den urgeln geschlagen, und sin die churfursten darnach vor den alter gangen, doselost vor dem hohen alter gestanden in der zile, bis der gesang ungewest ist.

One who knew him at this time reported to Pope Leo X, 'This prince seems to me well endowed with … prudence beyond his years, and to have much more at the back of his head than he carries on his face.'[22] For perhaps increased ceremonial demands, Charles apparently augmented his own personal winds with those of his mother. In one specific case, at least, it is known he borrowed his mother's wind band, her '8 ministriles altos.'[23] In 1530, Charles went to Italy for another coronation, this time by the pope; it was the last time an emperor would be so crowned by a pope. Charles made the trip with ten Spanish 'ministriles,' of whom only one is known by name, 'Juan de Garimendi, ministril de flauta.'[24]

In the years after becoming emperor, Charles V held center stage in the political affairs of Europe, particularly with regard to the growing drama surrounding the Protestant movement. It was Charles and Martin Luther who were the principal antagonists at the famous Diet of Worms in 1521. These constant political demands made Charles one of the most traveled persons of the century. He once recalled that he had made nine trips to Germany, six to Spain, seven to Italy, four to France, and two each to England and Africa! One can imagine the importance of the aristocratic winds during these trips. On one visit to Barcelona, in 1533, the celebrations given for him were of such a scale that no one could remember ever having seen the equal. One eyewitness reported, 'players of both loud and soft instruments, shawms, sackbuts, dulcians (the prototype bassoon), trumpets, timpani, and others.'[25] For Charles' official entry into Valenciennes, in 1540, another eyewitness writes of Charles's nineteen or twenty trumpets playing very melodiously.[26] The potential for the use of winds in aristocratic circles at this time can be seen in the enormous number of winds owned by Charles's sister, Mary of Hungary, upon her death.[27]

By 1555, Charles was prematurely old, suffering from ulcers, gout, asthma, indigestion, stammering, and difficulty in sleeping.[28] He said, in the fall of this year,

> The cares which so great a responsibility involves, the extreme dejection which it causes, my health already ruined—all these leave me no longer the vigor necessary for governing.[29]

And so, in 1556, he began resigning his many titles and entered retirement.

[22] Edward Armstrong, *The Emperor Charles V* (London: Macmillan, 1910), 1:69.

[23] Higino Anglès, 'Die Instrumentalmusik bis zum 16. Jahrhundert in Spanien,' in *Natalicia Musicologica* (Hafniae: Hansen, 1962), 155.

[24] Higino Anglès, *La musica en la Corte de Carlos V* (Barcelona: Consejo superior de investigaciones cientificas, 1944), 40ff.

[25] Quoted in Jenaro Alenda y Mira, *Relaciones de solemnidades y fiestas públicas* (Madrid: Sucesores de Rivadeneyra, 1903), 31ff.

> ministriles altos y baxos, de chirimias e sacabuches e dulcaynas y trompetas y atabales y otros minystriles.

[26] Quoted in Vander Straeten, *La musique aux Pays-Bas avant le XIXe siecle*, 7:381.

> Les trompettes, qui estoient bien XIX ou XX, de la dicte majesté, commencèrent à sonner fort mélodieusement.

[27] See note page 93

[28] Will Durant, *The Reformation* (New York: Simon and Schuster, 1957), 635.

[29] Quoted in James Harvey Robinson, *Readings in European History* (Boston: Ginn & Co., 1906), 317ff.

[27] The inventory (Archives generales de Simancas, *Contaduria mayor*, lego. Nr. 1017, fol. 162ff.), dated 1559, is given as follows:

V violones de arco
VII vihuelas de Harco
VI sacabuches de Laton en sus caxas
VI pifanos de box
IIII cornetas
I corneta de Laton Morisco
I corneta de Marfil
I pedaço de cuerno de Onicornio
VII vihuelas con siete arquillos
VI vihuelas de arco con doz arquillos
IIII flautas metidas cada una en su caxa
XV flautas et quatro pifanos en su caxa
I chirimia metida en su caxa
II chirimias metidas en sus caxas
III chirimias metidas en sus caxas
II chirimias metidas en sus caxas
XI ynstumentos hechos a manera de cornetas
Una caxa y en ella quatro regalos como chirimias
I caxa con seis pifanos de Marfil
I caxa en que avia XV pifanos
I caxa con siete flautas de Alemania
I caxa en que avia otras dichos pifanos
I caxa y en ella ocho cornetas negras
I caxa pequena con seis cornetas
I caxa que tenia dentro VIII cornetas
I caxa con VI cornetas de Madera
I sacabuche engastado de plata
I caxa de cuero negro y dentro della otro sacabuche
I caxa e dentro della VII bordones de musica
I caxa que tenia dentro seys cornetas
I caxa de VIII cornetas
II ynstrumentos de musica en sus caxas
I contravajo grande de chirimia
I fagot contra alt
I contravajo de chirimias
II chirimias pequenas
I caxa de flautas
III clavicordios
I clavicordio
I caxa y dentro della I sacabuche de Laton
I caxa y dentro una dulcayna
I sacabuche de Laton
I caxa de cornetas de Alemania
IIII Laudes

Philip II

Philip inherited great power from Charles V, but it was his unhappy fate to see the beginning of the decline of Spain as a power. After his death an inventory was made of his instrument collection, for tax purposes, and since the great size of this collection seems inconsistent with the few reports of his interest in music, perhaps he inherited most of this collection from Charles V as well.[30]

Although no trumpets and timpani are present in the inventory of Philip's instrument collection, it is known that he maintained ten trumpet and five timpani players during his reign (1556–1598). For a journey through Flanders, Italy, and Germany, in 1548–1550, he had taken, in addition to seventeen

---

[30] The inventory (1607) is quoted in Vander Straeten, *La musique aux Pays-Bas avant le XIXe siecle*, 8:306ff, and lists eleven keyboard, forty-seven lutes and string, and the following wind instruments:

Six ivory fifes, four small and two large
Six box-wood fifes
Six ivory fifes
Seven German fifes of rough wood
Eight German fifes of wood
Fourteen German fifes, of which four are large
Fifes of various dimensions
Seven large German wood flutes
Two large flutes, three small ones, two fifes
A box-wood flute
Four ivory cornetts à b ouquin
Contrabass cornett à bouquin
Four wood German cornetts, two large and two small
Seven wood German cornetts
Six wood German cornetts, to be played with the silver sackbuts
Five wood German cornetts, large and small
Two black cornetts
An ivory cornett
An ivory shawm
A wood German shawm of great dimension
Contrabass shawm
Two small wood German shawms
A wood German shawm, same as the others, known as a 'bajon'
A bassoon of very great dimension, the contrabass of the flutes
A very large box-wood bassoon, contrabass of the flutes
A large bassoon of box-wood
Contralto fagot
A box-wood doucaine
Sixteen wood German cornemuses (crumhorns)
Two bagpipes (tudelos)
Four silver sackbuts, with keys
A silver sackbut of great dimension
A soprano sackbut
A brass sackbut

singers, ten 'ministriles' and two cornettists. One of the singers, Alonso de Morales, is also listed in 1588–1589 as a player of the 'alto de corneta.'[31]

Perhaps it was some of Philip's wind players who welcomed him and his new bride, Isabel, daughter to Henry II of France, at the border. An account speaks of hearing cornetts, shawms, trumpets, and a 'tarbatz,' a Moorish drum.[32]

The reign of Philip II coincides with the struggles of the Dutch Republic against Spain and there are occasional accounts of Spanish wind bands serving in the low countries. In 1567, for example, one reads of a banquet given by the Grand Prior, Don Ferdinando, for which the music was provided by the military band of the Duke of Alva.[33]

The infamous St. Bartholomew's massacre of Protestants in Paris was celebrated by these good catholics, as by catholics everywhere.

> With anthems in Saint Gudule, with bonfires, festive illuminations, roaring artillery, with trumpets also, and with shawms, was the glorious holiday celebrated in court and camp, in honor of the vast murder committed by the Most Christian King upon his Christian subjects.[34]

Philip II, by Sofonisba Anguissola (1530–1625), ca. 1564.

[31] Anglès, 'Die Instrumentalmusik,' 157.

[32] Subirá, *Historia de la Música*, 571.

[33] John Lothrop Motley, *The Rise of the Dutch Republic* (New York, 1864), 2:123. Unfortunately, the instrumentation is not given.

[34] Ibid., 393.

4 *Court Wind Bands in the German-Speaking Countries*

SOME OF THE MOST INTERESTING ACCOUNTS of wind bands, not to mention some of the most colorful personalities, during the sixteenth century come from the German-speaking parts of Europe.

Bavaria, Austria, and the South

In Bavaria, the earliest sixteenth-century accounts of court music in Munich speak mostly of the familiar royal trumpets. An early list of the entire court musical establishment, from 1514, gives ten trumpets, one drummer, three 'instrumentalists,' and six singers.[1]

The trumpet instruments themselves were purchased from the makers in Nürnberg, who were already famous at the end of the fifteenth century. In the Nürnberg civic accounts one reads of Duke Wilhelm of Bavaria sending one of his trumpeters, Jörg Stumpf, to purchase ten new trumpets in 1510.[2] Munich continued to purchase new trumpets from Nürnberg throughout the century, including twelve in 1567, twenty-four in 1590, eighteen in 1592, in addition to two trombones in 1576.[3]

The scope of this court began to grow musically after the appearance of Ludwig Senfl, who had been a court musician under Maximilian I. Now one sees a real wind band, performing a repertoire of both transcribed and original works by the master composers of that era.

> It was the prevailing condition that zinks (cornetts) and trombones took over the performance of the works of Josquin, Issac, Brumel, Mouton, and Willaert. Similar performances of the works of Orlando we can see in Praetorius.[4]

Under the leadership of Lassus, who arrived in Munich ca. 1557 and was appointed Hofkapellmeister in 1563 by Duke Albert V, the Munich court music reached a great and well-documented climax. The richness of the musical life at this time is suggested by an account by one of the court singers,

[1] Martin Ruhnke, *Beiträge zu einer Geschichte der Deutschen Hofmusikkollegien im 16. Jahrhundert* (Berlin: Merseburger, 1963), 251.

[2] *Briefbücher des Nürnberger Rates Auskunft*, Nr. 65, fol. 217; Nr. 66, fol. 124.

[3] Fritz Jahn, 'Die Nürnberger Trompeten- und Posaunenmacher im 16. Jahrhundert,' in *Archiv für Musik-Wissenschaft* 7, no. 1 (1925): 37.

[4] Adolf Sandberger, *Beiträge zur Geschichte der bayerischen Hofkapelle unter Orlando di Lasso* (Leipzig, 1894).

Massimo Troiano, who indicates that even ordinary meals often included a five-member wind ensemble during the first course.

> ... sometimes with corna-muse, sometimes with recorders or with flutes, or cornetts and trombones[5] in French chansons and other light compositions.[6]

Troiano also gives an instrumentation for an eight-member wind band as, 'fagotto, corna-musa, mute cornett, cornett, tenor cornett, flute, dolzaina, and bass trombone.'[7]

For outdoor music, of course, it was the 'loud' instruments, and percussion, which were used. A manuscript plan for a procession, written in 1580 by the court Chancellor, Müller, suggests,

> where the pipe and tabor, dulcin, triangle ... Quintern and ... trombones are also made use of as they used to be in the days of Duke Albert.[8]

After mid-century, both Duke Albert v and his son, William v, maintained musical establishments and as each was married in the same year, 1568, there are extant two extraordinary accounts of their wind bands performing during the resultant festivities.

The first of these weddings was that of Albert to Renate von Lothringen. Albert was one of the great squanderers of the sixteenth century, assembling so costly a collection of treasures, jewels, gold, etc., that when he died he left his son, William v, a debt of more than two million gulden. Perhaps a better example of his extravagance can be seen in his concept of hunting. Between 1555 and 1579, court records indicate he personally slew 4,483 deer, 525 boar, 150 foxes, and 2 bear! In the year 1564, he devoted no fewer than 103 days to hunting.[9]

His wedding banquet, according to Troiano,[10] began with trumpet fanfares followed by the performance of an original wind band composition, a 'Battle-music' by Annibale Padovano. This work, in eight-parts, was performed by cornetts and trombones. During the first course, these same players performed a seven-part motet by Lassus. During the second course, a six-part madrigal by Striggio was performed by six

---

[5] One of the trombonists, Battista Mosto, son of the director of the Udine (Italy) civic wind band, served with his three brothers in this court. (See Grove, 12:615) Also I might note that in 1566 a payment in the court at Innsbruck was made to 'Hieronymus of Udine and his two brothers,' visiting musicians, who are described as 'Welch zink players in the service of Duke Albert of Bavaria.' See Walter Senn, *Musik und Theater am Hof zu Innsbruck* (Innsbruck: Osterreichische Verlaganstalt, 1954), 148.

[6] Quoted in Anthony Baines, *Woodwind Instruments and Their History* (New York: Norton, 1962), 256–257.

[7] Ibid.

[8] Quoted in Wolfgang Boetticher, *Aus Orlando di Lassos Wirkungskreis* (Kassel: Barenreiter, 1963), 98.

> ... do man auch die Tannberin pfeiffen, Dulcin, Driangl ... Quintern vnnd ... Pusaunen widerumb wie es bey Herzog Albrecht Hochseliger dedacht vnnd Zeiten im gebrauch gebe auch gewesen anrichten macht.

[9] Johannes Janssen, *History of the German People After the Close of the Middle Ages*, trans., A. Christie (New York: AMS Press, 1966), 15:207.

[10] Quoted in Otto Kinkeldey, *Orgel und klavier in der musik des 16. Jahrhundert* (Leipzig: Breitkopf and Hartel, 1910).

large (grosse) trombones, the bass of which was reported to have sounded an octave lower than the normal instrument. Yet another composition was performed by a 'soft' wind band, consisting of dolzaina, cornamuse (crumhorn),[11] shawm, and a mute cornett.[12]

[11] The wealth of this court's musical collection of instruments can be seen in a note by Hans Jakob Fugger, artistic advisor and administrator of the court, regarding a case of instruments made by the 'Bassani brothers.' He wrote, 'Item, in the space mentioned there are 12 crumhorns, namely alto, tenor, bass, great bass, and half-bass, all very fine excellent and good instruments, with their keys.' See, Bertha Wallner, 'Ein Instrumentenverzeichnis aus dem 16. Jahrhundert,' in *Festschrift zum 50. Geburtstag Adolf Sandbergers* (Munich: J.J. Lentnersche Hofbuchhandlung, 1918), 277.

> Item an gemelten luckh seind noch 12 khrump Horner, nemblich Discant, Tenor, Bass, Contrabass, und halbe Bass, alles gar schöne herrliche und guette Instrument, mit Ihren clauibus.

[12] Frank Harrison and Joan Rimmer, *European Musical Instruments* (London: Studio Vista, 1964), 25.

Duke Albert V of Bavaria, by Hans Mielich (1516–1573)

Albert's son, William, was known during his lifetime as one of the few nobles who was always sober; indeed he complained in 1587 of the disorderly peasant weddings which resulted in 'hallooing, shouting and yelling, and rioting' in the church.[13] Nevertheless, his own wedding, with Renée of Lorraine, shocked his government when it was revealed to have cost 190,000 gulden.[14] During the banquet more than two

[13] Janssen, *History of the German People After the Close of the Middle Ages*, 404.

[14] Ibid., 326.

hundred different dishes were served! According to Kazdin, a motet by Lassus, 'Providebam dominum,' was performed by cornetts and trombones.[15] At the end of the banquet a work was played in twenty-four parts, by eight viols, eight violas, and eight winds: a curtal, a cornemusa (crumhorn), a mute cornett, an alto cornett, a large 'twisted' cornett (a tenor cornett), a flute, a dolzaina, and a large trombone.[16]

This wedding celebration apparently also included a procession and a contemporary engraving shows a group of six musicians, dressed as satyrs, playing wind instruments.[17] While these instruments cannot be identified specifically, another account of a similar appearance by the Munich court wind band mentions a shawm, two cornetts, two crumhorns, and a curtal.[18]

William's interest in music can be seen in his helping his brother, Duke Ernst of Bavaria, establish his wind band by buying trombones, flutes, and crumhorns for him in Rome, in 1574.[19]

In Austria, to the south, sixteenth-century accounts speak most often only of the aristocratic trumpets; which were found in great numbers. Archduke Karl I, of Graz, for example, had ten trumpets in 1572 and twelve in 1587, although his inventories reveal a much broader use of wind music.[20]

One often sees trumpets 'announcing' a banquet, which one takes as an initial fanfare of some sort, but an extant letter by the duke in Graz, written in 1584, refers to a multi-part performance of perhaps more complicated repertoire. The duke's sister had heard the duke's trumpets at a banquet and wrote asking for a copy of the music. The duke answered that this was impossible, as the music was not notated.[21] It is well-known that the aristocratic trumpet corps of the sixteenth century played memorized repertoire pieces and perhaps the performance heard on this occasion was a work similar to those described by Praetorius.

> The word 'sonata' or *sonada* is also used with reference to music played on trumpets for banquet and dance.[22]

Duke William V of Bavaria

[15] Andrew Kazdin, Notes for 'The Glorious Sound of Brass' (Columbia Recording, MS 6941).

[16] Massimo Trojano, *Discorsi delli triomfi, giostre, apparati, e delle cose piu notabile* (Munich, 1586), 150, fol. 111v, 112r.

[17] Hans Wagner, *Kurtze doch gegründte beschreibung* (Munich, 1568), between 40v and 41r.

[18] See Anthony Baines, 'Crumhorn,' in Grove (Fifth edition, 1954).

[19] Bertha Wallner, *Musikalische Denkmeler der Steinätzkunst* (Munich: J.J. Lentnersche Hofbuchhandlung, 1912).

[20] As for example, 'A case of dolzani, including a bass, two tenors, and an alto'; 'Three large bass dulzani'; and 'A case full of crumhorns containing eight instruments large and small.' See Julius Schlosser, *Die Sammlung alter Musikinstrumente* (Vienna, 1920), 19–20.

[21] Hellmut Federhofer, *Musikpflege und Musiker am Grazer Habsburgerhof* (Mainz: Schott, 1967),29.

> die music wie es meine Trumpetter brauchen, Im fall du das mainst, dann Sy sonst nichts blasen, alls wie man zu tisch Plast, desselbige is nit geschriben, vnd machens nur aus dem Synn …

One sees the Graz court trumpets again in an icon of the funeral procession for Archduke Karl II, in 1590.[23] An eyewitness describes the musicians, who were at the end of this procession; first came the timpani players (Hörpaugger) and then the trumpets, three by three. The timpani, he notes, were covered with black cloth and the trumpets were all using their 'small mouthpieces.'[24] This is certainly an error; no doubt he heard a 'smaller' sound than usual and concluded this was made possible by smaller mouthpieces. What he must have heard was mutes!

Archduke Ferdinand II of Innsbruck (1564–1595) had an ensemble of twelve trumpets, but again an inventory of his instrument collection, made in 1596, reveals a much broader practice. This collection, divided as it is into full consorts of so many kinds of wind instruments, suggests a great tradition of wind band music in this court.[25]

An interesting regulation, dated 1 May 1572, by Archduke Ferdinand II to his personal trumpet players is extant. He seems to imply that if there is any discipline problems, it will be easy to transfer them to another court.

[22] Michael Praetorius, *Syntagma Musicum*, trans., Hans Lampl (1619), 3:48.

[23] Engraving by Georg Peham, copy in Graz Stadtmuseum (Inv.-Nr. M. 48/1–13).

[24] Wallner, 'Ein Instrumentenverzeichnis aus dem 16. Jahrhundert,' 85.

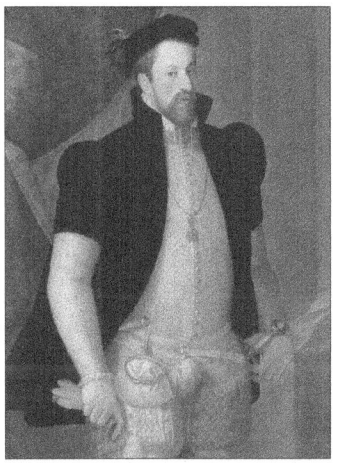

Ferdinand II, by Francesco Terzio, 1557

[25] Senn, *Musik und Theater am Hof zu Innsbruck*, 166–167. The inventory lists 37 violas (da Gamba, mostly), 4 old 'Zitern,' and the following wind instruments:

27 trumpets
20 trombones, including 1 Quart, 6 tenor, and 2 bass
23 cornetts, 8 white and 15 black, including 1 discant, 6 tenor, and 2 bass
5 unidentified bass wind instruments
8 sordune, including discant, tenor and bass
6 crumhorns, including discant, tenor, and bass
17 French fifes, including 4 discant, 5 tenor, 4 bass, 2 great bass, and 2 Zwerchpfeifen 'for concerts'
7 old German fifes, including 1 small discant, 12 discant, 3 tenor, and 2 bass
11 Zwerchpfeifen, including 2 tenor and 2 bass
6 bagpipes, including 1 discant, 3 tenor, 1 bass, and 1 undesignated
6 flutes, including 2 discant, 3 tenor, and 1 bass, 'to be used with the trumpets'
1 great flute, 'to be used in concerts'
6 'Instrument per Concerta,' including 2 large flutes, 2 curtals, and 2 Zwerchpfeifen
12 shawms, including 3 discant, 4 tenor, 2 bass, and 3 great bass
16 curtals, including 4 discant, 8 tenor, and 4 bass
8 'Tolzanae,' including 2 discant, 4 tenors, and 2 bass
1 dulzian
5 'Cabassi,' including 3 tenor and 2 bass
2 small drums
3 pair of timpani

(The trumpet corps) must have diligent attention and must also appear for services on Sundays and holidays. Unless one has a better reason not to appear, he or they will receive serious punishment. According to the circumstances that we use in our trumpet service players from all nations ...[26]

The Emperor, Ferdinand I, succeeded his brother, Charles V, in 1558, establishing his court in both Munich and Vienna. There are several references to his wind players before his coronation as emperor, the first while he was still in Spain. An eyewitness reports seeing his trumpets and timpani, 'which we call great tambors.'[27] A very early reference speaks of Ferdinand's trombone consort performing in the palace of Margaret of Austria, Regent of the Low Countries, on 14 March 1521.[28] An engraving by the anonymous 'F.A.,' called, 'Ballfest in der Wiener Hofburg, 1560,' pictures four royal trumpets leading the dancers on the dance floor, with an eight-member wind band playing from a special box in the foreground.

Emperor Ferdinand I, by Hans Bocksberger, ca. 1550–1555

Ferdinand's coronation as Emperor of the Holy Roman Empire occurred in Frankfurt in 1562. An English eyewitness, if he can be believed, noted no fewer than forty thousand hunting horns participating in the procession, as part of the ceremonial dress.

> ... suche pomp and triumph as ye thought not to have ben done the lyke at any tyme synce the great Charles ... forty thousand ... everi man ... a lyttel bugl horn about his neck hunterlyk.[29]

---

[26] Senn, *Musik und Theater am Hof zu Innsbruck*, 135.
Unser Stallmeister sol auch auf die Trumpeter sein fleissig Aufmerk halten, damit dieselben alle Sunntag und Feyrtag beim Dienst erscheinen, und welcher one sondere ehhafte Ursach ausbleibt, denorder diesel ben darumb mit Ernst strafen. Nachdem wir auch im Gebrauch, under unsern Trompetern mer als ainerlei Nation Personen zu halten, deshalb sich dann zwischen denen leichtlich Widerwillen und Unainigkait begeben mag, als soll unser Stallmeister allen muglichen Fleiss fürwenden und bei inen verfüegen, dass sy mit gleichem Verstand und gueter Ainigkait iren Dienst versehen, und sonst auch aller Widerwillen zwischen inen verhuetet werde.

[27] Vander Streaten, *La musique aux Pays-Bas*, 7:286.
... trompettes de monseigneur l'infant don Fernande ... avec leurs atabales, que nous appelons gros tambourins.

[28] Ibid., 501.

[29] Dorothy Gies McGuigan, *The Habsburgs* (Garden City, NY: Doubleday, 1966), 139.

According to Köchel, the court in Vienna maintained only wind instruments before 1543, the strings appearing for the first time in 1566.[30] We know that Ferdinand employed ten trumpets and four 'trumpet youths' by 1539,[31] and that, as emperor, his trumpeters enjoyed the additional prestige of being entitled to a horse (Yedem ain Pferdt).[32] In addition to their ceremonial duties, these trumpet players also had regular meal performances duties (Die sollen ordenlich all mal zu tasch plasen).[33]

Ferdinand's son, Maximilian II (Emperor, 1564–1576), moved the court to Prague, where it remained for the rest of the sixteenth century. In addition to the listing of two cornett players, his court records begin to distinguish the trumpet players as either 'musical' or 'not musical.'[34] This I take as an indication that some of them were now beginning to read music, rather than performing only a handed-down repertoire of memorized literature. This distinction is continued under the next emperor, Rudolf II, where one reads of one cornett player, sixteen to twenty trumpets (of which twelve are 'musical'), one timpanist, and five to twelve students of trumpet and organ.[35]

Hesse and the West

Duke Ludwig III of Wurttemberg (reigning 1568–1593), of Stuttgart, must have had a great interest in wind music. So, at least, would suggest an inventory of his musical instruments, made in 1589, which includes perhaps the largest number of wind instruments of any court in Europe. One finds, for example, no fewer than two hundred and twenty flutes, forty-eight recorders, one hundred and thirteen cornetts, fourteen crumhorns, etc., as compared with thirty-nine viols.[36] Court records for this same year list eleven instrumentalists, eleven singers, and two trumpet players—although the court usually averaged from five to seven trumpets.[37] An eyewitness speaks of the combination of the singers and wind players during a performance for Ludwig's marriage to Ursula, Duchess of Bavaria, in 1585.[38]

[30] Ludwig Ritter von Köchel, *Die Kaiserliche Hof-Musikkapelle in Wien von 1543–1867* (Hildesheim: G. Olms, 1976), 20.

[31] Wilhelm Ehmann, *Tibilustrium* (Kassel: Barenreiter-Verlag, 1950), 13.

[32] Don Smithers, *The Music and History of the Baroque Trumpet before 1721* (London: Dent, 1973), 167–168.

Kaiser Maximilian II, by Nicolas Neufchâtel (fl. 1539–1567), 1566

[33] Ibid.

[34] Köchel, *Die Kaiserliche Hof-Musikkapelle in Wien von 1543–1867*, 48–49.

[35] Ibid., 52–53.

[36] Bossert, *Württembergisches Vierteljahrheft für Landesgeschichte*, 1912.

[37] Detlef Altenburg, *Untersuchungen zur Geschichte der trumpete im Zeitalter der clarinblaskunst* (Regensburg: G. Bosse, 1973), 1:19.

[38] G. Pietzsch, 'Beschreibungen Deutscher Fürstenhochzeiten von der Mitte des 15. bis zum Beginn des 17. Jahrhunderts als musikgeschichtliche Quellen,' in *Anuario Musical*, vol. 15 (1960): 53.

Philipps von Hessen was another extravagant duke who spent a great part of his life in hunting. In 1559, he wrote to Duke Christopher of Wurttemberg, complaining,

> At this boar-hunt we had fine sport ... and caught over 1,120 boars. We had intended to have 60 more field days, but as we found that the boars had become thin, we did not go on hunting.[39]

[39] Janssen, *History of the German People*, 202.

Any starving peasant caught hunting on Philipps' land was given severe punishment, the *least* of which was having the arms tied behind and being drawn upwards by a rope, pulling the arms backwards over the head, and left hanging.[40]

[40] Ibid., 219.

This Hessian court, like most in Germany, suffered from common drunkenness.[41] At nearby Münster, the Bishop himself used to get so drunk that his trumpets and drums were kept nearby to wake him by their playing.[42]

[41] Ibid., 249.

[42] Ibid., 243. One duke even quoted his pastor, 'after the holy days you are free to drink well and to let the heavenly sackbuts ring on.' (Ibid., 239) This is not quite what Brahms had in mind in his *Begräbnisgesang*, op. 13, for band and chorus, where the text refers to 'God's trombones!'

Philipps von Hessen, when not hunting or drinking, was perhaps dancing. A hint that this was considered too time consuming by his wind band, can be seen in an order given out in 1541 to his cornett and trumpet players. They must have made some complaint, for Philipps orders them henceforth to play for his dances with an attitude that is, 'willing, unquestioning, and untiring!'[43]

A valuable inventory of the instrument collection at the Hessian court at Kassel was made by the Kapellmeister, Johann Heugel, in 1573. Here one finds sixteen string, three keyboard, and sixty-seven wind instruments.[44]

[43] Altenburg, *Untersuchungen zur Geschichte der trumpete im Zeitalter der clarinblaskunst*, 100–101.

> ... mit Plasen, es sey zu Hof, Tantz, Hoffirerey oder wozu er sonst geschickt wird, gutwillig, unweigerlich und unverdrossen brauchen lassen.

[44] Anthony C. Baines, 'Two Cassel Inventories,' *The Galpin Society Journal* 4 (1951): 31–32.
   1 Quart, 3 Second and 3 small trombones
   3 German trumpets and 4 field trumpets
   1 case of flutes with ten instruments
   2 bass flutes
   2 small Tenorpfeiffen
   6 Damerin Pfeiffen
   1 case which should contain 8 box-wood Zwerschpfeiffen, but 3 are missing
   1 case of 4 box-wood cornetts
   1 case of 7 crumhorns
   4 stille cornetts
   4 Bommarts (bass shawms), new
   2 new shawms
   3 new cornetts
   2 new discant shawms
   1 doppelt Zinken
   1 new 'Vagant' (small shawm)

The real growth in the musical activities of this court, however, comes with one of the best-known of sixteenth-century German princes, Moritz, Landgraf of Hesse-Cassel. A visiting contemporary Englishman describes,

> his education prince-like, generally knowen in all things, and excellent in many, seasoning his grave and more important studies for ability in judgment, with studies of pastime for retiring, as in poetrie, musike, and the mathemitikes; and for ornament in discourse in the languages, French, Italian, and English.⁴⁵

This passage no doubt was written under diplomatic necessity for exaggeration, for Moritz was also a drunk, spendthrift, and egotist.⁴⁶ Moritz also considered hunting one of the important uses of his time, as can be seen in the authority given the court official in charge. This Master Huntsman once shot a peasant who had lingered behind in the chase, struck an ear off another who came up late with his hounds, and slashed in two the head of a third. He was only brought to justice when he made the unfortunate mistake of addressing Moritz in an impolite manner.⁴⁷

Moritz maintained a wind band which was described as being eight members when it appeared in 1596, during a procession celebrating the baptism of his daughter, Elizabeth.⁴⁸ A description of the band five years later, seen during the festivities welcoming the arrival of the Ambassador of Queen Elizabeth of England, indicates a somewhat larger band and implies it was a fine ensemble.

Moritz, Landgraf of Hesse-Cassel

⁴⁵ Edward Monings, quoted in Nichols, ed., *The Progresses and Public Processions of Queen Elizabeth* (London, 1805), vol. 3.

⁴⁶ Once during a visit to Berlin he left for Spandau, so drunk 'he could scarcely find the gate of the town.' (Janssen, *History of the German People*, 249) On another visit to Berlin he traveled with a personal escort of three thousand horses. (Ibid., 300)

⁴⁷ Ibid., 212. In an interesting letter written in 1600, Moritz speaks with disparagement of the middle-class tradesmen who populated his domain.

> On work-days the masters and the journey men flock in shoals to christenings, weddings and wine bouts, and when they cannot go to these they drink brandy-punch in the morning and go to beer parties in the taverns in the afternoon; all this time the buyers must wait for the sellers ... until the guild gentlemen have drunk themselves out, and then they must pay for the bespoken goods at whatever rate it pleases the besotted vendors to ask ... the handicraftsman does not provide for his house and his children, but for his own stomach, he invests his coins in liquid wares, and when he cannot wash his mouth with wine, or foreign beer, he must have roast capon ... when Monday comes they haven't a farthing left in their purses; then they lounge about idly in the market-places, stare at the windows, fall to gossiping and chattering, or indulge in idlers' pastimes, which are profitable neither to civic life nor to the art of war, such as target shooting, nine-pins, football and other trumpery, whereby they often commit thefts, murders, and all kinds of misdeeds. (Ibid., 122–123)

⁴⁸ Wilhelm Dilich, *Historische Beschreibung der Fürstlichen Kindtauff Fräwlein Elizabethen zu Hessen* (Cassel, 1598), 51.

⁴⁹ Nichols, *The Progresses and Public Processions of Queen Elizabeth*, vol. 3.

At the tilt-field, various games such as running at the rings. The challengers enter with six trumpets. Then a pageant 'Seaven deadlie Sinnes' ... but of all, the Unknown Knight came in like a Prince, with his musicke of sackbotes and cornets clade in greene tafetie to the ground, six before and six behind, with the most harmonious noyse that could be, answering one another like an eccho. This kind of musicke had a princely ayre ... After supper, as in the manner of a triumph, ... and so the rest of the lordes and ladies in their order, with drum and trumpet for their musick.[49]

The importance of court music under Moritz is reflected in the great growth of the court instrument collection, as compared to the previous inventory. Now one finds forty-four string, ten keyboard, and one hundred and forty-two wind instruments. The winds reflect the wind band preferences of the sixteenth century, in their organization into consorts and their strong emphasis on the lower family members.[50] It is no surprise that trumpets are missing from this residential collection, but it is known that Moritz maintained at least five trumpeters continuously from 1538 to the end of the century.[51]

[50] Baines, 'Two Cassel Inventories,' 32–33.

    1 consort of great 'Bombartten', 1 bass, 3 tenor, and 3 soprano
    2 great 'Fagott octaf,' one in C, one in Bb
    1 small Fagott in C
    1 still smaller Fagott
    4 Schriari, basset, tenor, alto, soprano
    1 consort of Bassanelli, 1 bass, 3 tenor, 1 alto, and 4 soprano
    1 consort of 14 flöten, 1 bass, 4 tenro, 4 alto, 3 soprano, and 4 'still higher' soprano
    2 Schalmeyen and 3 pommern
    1 case of Zwerchflöten, 1 basset and 5 others
    1 case of Zwerchpfeiffen, 1 bass and 5 others
    1 case of larger Zwerchpfeiffen than the above, with 4 similar Zwerchpfeiffen therein
    2 cases of white stillen Zincken, 6 in each, of like size and pitch
    1 case of 6 white Stillen Zincken a tone higher
    1 case of 6 white Stillen Zincken a fourth higher than the preceeding
    1 case of loud black curved Zincken or Cornetti, 6 therein
    5 great black curved basszincken
    1 Krumbhorn case with 8 Krumbhörner of different sizes
    1 long straight instrument, basset to the Krumbhörner
    2 white curved ivory loud Zincken
    8 Racqueten in a small chest, 2 bass, 2 tenor, and 3 soprano
    3 Zwerchpfeiffe without case
    2 old Zwerchpfeiffe
    1 small bassflöte to the above
    7 black curved loud Zincken
    1 great posaune
    1 bad posaune
    4 tenor and alto posaune
    2 small alto or soprano posaune
    1 Quart posaune
    1 Drumscheit

Brandenburg and the North

An early account of the great wind instrument activity in the Brandenburg court is found relative to the wedding festivities of the Margrave Casimir of Brandenburg (d. 1527) and Dorothea Pfalzgrafin bei Rhein, in 1518. It was reported that the ceremony was held in great solemnity and elegence, 'especially through the triumphant performance of the Margrave's singers, organists, (and band of) trombone and cornett players.'[52]

When Joachim II of Brandenburg was married to Hedwig, daughter to Sigismund, in Krakau, in 1533, he seems to have paid all the personal wind bands of all the visiting aristocrats to perform, for one finds one of the largest gatherings of wind players in the sixteenth century. An eyewitness reports no fewer than one hundred and fifty-six trumpets, twenty-eight timpani, and fifteen shawms participating![53] It seems that this extravagance was typical of Joachim for by 1540 he had spent so much coin of the realm[54] that, in a desperate attempt to balance his books, he hired ten different alchemists during the following decade in hope that they could make gold for him. This is not to say, of course, that his abundance extended to his citizens. He gave out one order aimed at poachers which said anyone taking a deer or pig from his forest would have both eyes put out; anyone taking a rabbit would have a hare branded on his cheek!

In Duke Albert of Prussia, who made his court residence in Konigsberg, one finds not only a duke who was very interested in wind music, but a very significant extant band repertoire. The rise of this wind band covers the period 1525–1578 and from 1540 the size ranged from twelve to seventeen members; after 1578 only nine trumpeters and a timpanist are mentioned.[55]

The most frequently mentioned instruments in the court records are trumpets, timpani, and trombones, but the extant correspondence between Albert and various instrument makers reveal a much more extensive instrumentation. In an extant letter to Sebald von Thyll in Nürnberg, dated 3 September 1541, the duke ordered a consort of Rauschpfeifen and also some of,

> the large loud instruments of Rauschpfeifen which can be played in six or more parts.[56]

[51] Altenburg, *Untersuchungen zur Geschichte der trumpete im Zeitalter der clarinblaskunst*, 16.

[52] Tomaso Garzoni, *Allgemeiner Schauplatz aller Kunst, Professionen und Handwerker* (Franckfurt am Mayn, 1659).

[53] Adolf Aber, *Die Pflege der Musik unter den Wettinern und Wettinischen Ernestinern* (Leipzig: Siegel, 1921), 109, and Ehmann, *Tibilustrium*, 13. Krakau itself not only had a rich tradition in its civic wind band music at this time (see Grove, 20:217), but saw the development of the court musical establishment beginning with Alexander (1501–1506), who had six singers and nineteen instrumentalists. An icon of Alexander's coronation shows three visible trumpeters, dressed in red uniforms, playing in the upper left balcony (Kraków, Muzeum Narodowe, Biblioteka Czartoryskich, MS. 1212, fol. 35). Under Sigismund I (1506–1548) the court musicians increased to more than sixty, not counting the young singers (MGG, VII, 1693). A poem celebrating the return of Sigismund and his new bride, Bona Sforza, in 1518, noted, 'brass instruments sound, "litui" buzz and drums are repeatedly beaten, the joyful noise of trumpets rises to the stars.' (M. Brahmer, 'La Cour et la Campagne dans les Fêtes Nuptiales en Pologne au XVIe siècle,' in Jacquot, ed., *Les Fêtes de la Renaissance* (Paris: Centre National de la Recherche Scientifique, 1975), 3:343.

[54] In 1540 his Councilor, Eustachius von Schlieben, wrote to him, 'this country has lost all faith in your Electoral Grace; securities are not to be obtained.' (Janssen, *History of the German People*, XV)

[55] Maria Federmann, *Musik und Musikpflege zur Zeit Herzog Albrechts* (Kassel: Barenreiter-Verlag, 1932), 7, 47.

In December of the same year, the duke made an extensive purchase of additional instruments from the same dealer, including twelve German trumpets, twelve 'Welch' [Italian] trumpets, a tenor and bass pomhart, two Welch cornetts, six cornetts voiced together [a consort], and mouthpieces for his trombones.[57]

In 1571, the duke purchased additional instruments from Antwerp, including a case of German 'Pfeiffen' and '2 Engelische Cornethen.'[58] Additional evidence regarding the instrumentation of the duke's wind band can be seen in court records for repairs, as for example in a document of 1537.

> Veit the trumpeter has received 4 Marks for sackbuts, Rauschpfeifen, and shawms sent to Danzig for repairs.[59]

Finally, there are interesting offers of instruments made by dealers to Duke Albert, which may be taken as hints of his instrumentation in so far as we can assume the dealers were familiar with his preferences. A very interesting document of this kind is a letter from the Nürnberg instrument maker, Georg Neuschel. The evidence is that Duke Albert knew his instruments and was a tough bargainer when it came to prices. Thus in an attempt to settle a dispute over prices in 1541, Neuschel writes that he has some less expensive instruments which he has acquired in Lyons and Venice, including a

[56] Quoted in Robert Eitner, 'Briefe von Jorg Neuschel in Nürnberg, nebst einigen anderen,' in *Monatshefte für Musikgeschichte* vol. II (Leipzig, 1877), 149.

---

[57] Federmann, *Musik und Musikpflege zur Zeit Herzog Albrechts*, 58.
  Item 12 deutzsche trommethen sampt mundstucken vnd claret stucken
  Item 4 mund stuck zu mittel bosaunen
  Item ein tenor bomhart sampt einem bass bumhart mit etzlichen roren
  Item 2 welsche krumme zincken vberzogen
  Item 12 welsche trumethen
  Item 6 Zincken die zusamen stimmen
  Item 2 welsche krumme zincken vbertzogen
  Item 1 par bogen ahn die quart posaun

[58] Ibid., 65.

[59] Ibid., 54.
  4 M. Für pusaunen, Rhauschpfeiffen, vnd Schalmeien zuzerichten geben Nach Danzik hatt Veitt Trumpetter empfangen.

silver trombone, four ivory Zwergpfeiffen, five ivory cornetts, and some 'schreyendt peiffen, which are much louder than the pumhart.'[60]

Another interesting letter from the same maker, dated 3 September 1542, offers a great case of crumhorns.

> In addition I have a fine case of crumhorns, ten in all; the tenors also have keys and are made like the large (perhaps great bass) which is blown with a brass tube.[61]

The repertoire of Duke Albert's wind band consisted of both original works and the usual practice of performing instrumental transcriptions of multi-part vocal music. A very interesting example of the latter is the massive seven-part 'Erzürne dich nicht,'[62] by Thomas Stoltzer, a court composer in Hungary. Stoltzer sent the work to Duke Albert in a version specifically arranged so that it could also be performed by the court wind band, as one can see in a letter he attached to the manuscript.

> It occurred to me in this work to specially serve your Lordship, to whom I owe all I have, and so I have thought of crumhorns and thus have set the psalm so that it completely suits them, which is not the case with every composition and especially those with many voices. However I have written the extra discant in the last section with some notes which do not suit. This part can be omitted or played with another instrument or the human voice ... Since, your Lordship, I have thought to arrange the first part so that it suits crumhorns and lest I appear wanting, I am also sending your Lordship a Latin psalm, 'Exultabo te.'[63]

---

[60] Ibid., 57.
 Eyn Silbern pussanen mit 4 Zugen gehort zue dem gesang vnd Instramenten wie hernach folgent.
 Item 4 helffenbaine Zwergpfeiffen seindt beschlagen mit sylber vnd verguldt.
 Item 5 helffenbayne Zinken seindt auch also beschlagen.
 Item ein Instrumente darauff man schlegt stett auch darzue.
 Item ein Zypressene lauten stett auch darzue.
 Item ettlich schreyendt peiffen seindt vill lauter denn die pumhart.

[61] Eitner, 'Briefe von Jorg Neuschel in Nürnberg, nebst einigen anderen,' 152.

[62] Gustave Reese, in *Music in the Renaissance* (New York: Norton, 1959), 725, calls this work, 'the earliest preserved example of a cycle of instrumental pieces in the literature of music.'

Additional choral works which must have been performed by this wind band as well include the compositions by the court wind players themselves, as for example Paul Kugelmann's *Etliche Teutsche Liedlein* (1558–1560) and Johann Kugelmann's (who calls himself here, 'tubicinae symphoniarum') *Concentus novi* (ca. 1540).[64]

Beyond the extant manuscript wind band music of this court, I might mention here a lost set of five part-books for the shawm players mentioned in a document of 1569.[65]

By far the most significant surviving repertoire of Duke Albert's wind band, and one of the most important sources of sixteenth-century wind band literature in general, is the set of part-books now in Copenhagen.[66] This set of seven part-books, ca. 1541–1543, contains one hundred and forty-nine compositions, most of which are assumed to represent the literature of the duke's wind band. The part-books were compiled by Duke Albert's trumpeter, Jörgen Heyde, who later transferred to the court of Christian III in Denmark. The transfer of these part-books to Copenhagen is further explained by the fact that Christian III was a brother-in-law to Duke Albert.[67]

Unfortunately there is one part-book missing from this historic collection. One wonders if the lost part-book was the one which Duke Albert accused Wolf Metzsch, one of his court trumpeters, of taking in 1527. In a letter of that year, the duke requests the Danzig town council to arrest the trumpeter.[68]

It is in this North German–Copenhagen connection that we also have a very rare and valuable insight into the quasi-secret art of the aristocratic trumpeter, this in the form of two manuscript notebooks of their music, dated 1598.[69] These manuscript books, prepared by the court trumpeters, Hendrich Lübeck and Magnus Thomsen, are thought to have been done in order to help players memorize their literature. One sees here an early form of all the basic international military signals ('le boute selle,' 'à cheval,' 'la charge,' etc.), in a version played by the North German players.

Of special interest are a number of 'concert' works, called 'Sonaten,' 'Aufzüge,' 'Sersseneden,' and 'Tokkaten.' One, for example, is the familiar 'In dulci jubilo!,' here, 'In dultzi gubilo.' These are examples of the kind of literature these trumpet corps played at banquets, as the reader has so often seen in these pages.

Panoff, quoting a contemporary, W. Dilich, writes that in the military one found at least one trumpet for each two hundred soldiers.[70] Another valuable insight into the art of the field trumpeter is found in a publication (1555) by Lienhart Fronsperger. On the duties of the field trumpeter, he writes,

> Each squadron should have at least one trumpeter serving under his captain and he should be found day and night by his captain's tent ... He should know and be able to variously blow: when one mounts, when one eats, when one dismounts or sets out; also when the enemy is

---

[63] Thomas Stoltzer, 'Erzürne dich nicht,' in *Das Chorwerk*, ed. Otto Gombosi, nr. 6 (Wolfenbüttel: Moseler Verlag, 1930).

> Ist mir in dem eingefallen, in desser arbeit E.F.G., der ich alles was ich vermag schuldig bin, sunderlich zu dienen, Hab an die Khrumphörner gedacht und den psalm also gesetzt, das er gantz darauff gerecht ist, Wann sunst nitt ain jeder gesang darauff bekqwem ist und sunderlich vil stimmen. Jedoch der ander Discant des letzten tails erst danach nitt von notten gemacht etwas sich in disse sach nitt schikt. Mag man den selben wol auss lassen oder in ander Instrument oder menschlich stimmen darzu prauchen ... Hab ich dannoch gedacht E.F.G. des ersten pars hal ben zu unterrichten darumb, das er auff Khrumphörner gestimpt sey und damit ich nitt so gar lär kwäm, schick ich E.F.G. einen Lateinischen psalm Exultabo te.

[64] See Volume 6 in this series.

[65] Federmann, *Musik und Musikpflege zur Zeit Herzog Albrechts*, 64.

[66] Denmark, Kobenhavn, Det kongelige Bibliotek (MS. Gamle kongelige Samling, 1872/4).

[67] See Henrik Glahn, ed., *Music from the Time of Christian III: Selected Compositions from the Part Books of the Royal Chapel (1541)* (Denmark: Edn Egtved, 1978). It was under Christian III (1534–1559) that the court wind music in Copenhagen first began to fully develop. The royal library there also includes works associated with the wind band of Frederik II (1559–1588). The coronation of Christian IV (1588–1648) in 1596 included twenty-three of his own trumpeters and timpani players together with another thirty-one visiting trumpeter. (Altenburg, *Untersuchungen zur Geschichte der trumpete im Zeitalter der clarinblaskunst*, 139) His own trumpeters performed regularly, three times a day, at meals. (Niels Friis, *Det kongelige kapel* (Copenhagen: Hasse, 1948), 30). This Christian once issued an order to his subjects on German soil informing them that they had no rights whatever, that they should appear before his throne humbly with gifts and offerings, and that he would impose taxes as he chose, making account to no one! (Janssen, *History of the German People*, 9.)

[68] Federmann, *Musik und Musikpflege zur Zeit Herzog Albrechts*, 70.

[69] Denmark, Kobenhavn, Det kongelige Bibliotek (Gl. Kgl. Smlg. 1874/1875/4). For a detailed study of these works see Georg Schünemann, 'Sonaten und Feldstücke der Hoftrompeter,' in *Zeitschrift für Musikwissenschaft*, vol. 17 (Leipzig, 1935).

[70] Peter Panoff, *Militärmusik in Geschichte und Gegenwart* (Berlin: K. Siegismund, 1944), 54.

present, alarms, or when one should attack the enemy ... a trumpeter should be bold, manly, intelligent, and honorable, as he may have to serve as an ambassador to the enemy.[71]

In Berlin, the court musical establishment begins its period of major growth under the Elector Johann Georg (1571–1598), a period, by the way, when string instruments are introduced into this court for the first time.[72] An inventory of the instrument collection in this court, made in 1582, lists five new viols and 'some old ones,' fourteen keyboard and fifty-one wind instruments.[73]

---

[71] Leonhart Fronsperger, *Fünff Bücher von Kriegsregiment* (Frankfurt, 1555).

Under jedem geschwader Reutter soll zum wenigsten ein Trommeter sein der wart auff sein Hauptman unnd soll sich tag unnd nacht bey seins Hauptmans Zellt oder Losament finden lassen damit was sich zutragt jne der Hauptman bey der hand habe. Am ziehen zeucht er allzeyt vor den Reuttern und dem Hauptman her. Er soll wissen und konden sein underschidlich blasen also wann man Sattlern wann man essen wann man auffsitzen unnd anziehen soll auch so feynd vorhanden. Lärmen oder so man mit den feynden trauffhawen und treffen soll hatt alles sein underschid am Trommeten darnach sich auch die Reutter wissen zuuerrichten. Ein Trommeter soll keck und mannlich sein auch verstanden geschicht und aussrichtig darumb so man an feynden ist soll er allzeit sich hierfur zum Fanen halten geschickt und aussrichtig, darumm so man jne als offt geschicht etwann mit feinds brieffen oder gefangnen oder etwann besatzungen anff znfordern oder in andern geschaefften unnd bottschafften zun feinden geschickt er die sachen wihss geschicklich aufzurichten zureden und schweigen was unnd wann sich zimpt. Sein Hauptman nimpt gepürliche pflicht in deren er jne einbindt was jne für gut und not ansicht von jne. Es wird jne doppelsold gegeben unnd sunst mit und ern zehen pferdten ein Reihswagen zugeordnet. Wa ettwann Fürsten Herrn oder ander Pottentaten in ein Feldtzug wern so pflegt man jnen etwann ein Herrbaucker zuhalten dess beueich ist wie des Trometers wart staetigs auff sein Obersten Herrn sein besoldung wirt gestelt zum N. Herren.

[72] Grove, 2:566.

[73] Curt Sachs, *Musik und Oper am kurbrandenburgischen Hofe* (Berlin: J. Bard, 1910), 205.
3 trombones
7 crumhorns, bass, 2 tenor, 2 alto, 2 soprano
2 Bombardte
1 discant Schalmey
7 recorders (Handt-flöten), bass, 2 tenor, 2 alto, and soprano
1 tabor-pipe
8 recorders (Brauhne-flöten), 2 bass, 3 tenor, 2 alto, and soprano
9 flutes (Querpfeifen) 2 bass, 4 tenor, 2 alto, and 3 soprano
4 cornetts, two with keys
1 tenor cornett, with key
7 Schreipfeifen, bass, 3 tenor, 2 alto, soprano
1 Dulzan

Saxony and the East

An early sixteenth-century account of the wedding of Duke Johann to Sofia of Mecklenburg, in Torgau, contains a very interesting account of a royal wind band, divided into two ensembles, participating during the Mass.

> On the Tuesday after Quinquagesima (March 1, 1500), the bride and bridegroom together with the other princes and princesses heard Mass in the castle chapel; the singers belonging to my Most Gracious and Noble Lord sang two masses with the help of the organ, three sackbuts and a cornett, and also four crumhorns with the positive organ which were almost joyful to hear.[74]

At the court in Dresden the first permanent body of musicians were the wind bands under Duke Moritz (1541–1553) and the Elector August (1553–1586).[75] Each of these dukes also maintained nine or ten trumpets and court records speak of regular meal duty for these players.[76]

A very interesting letter is extant, written by the Elector August to Duke Albert of Bavaria, dated 13 May 1563. Duke Albert had apparently written inquiring about the crumhorns he had heard in the wind band of August, when it performed at a meeting of the Electors, in Frankfurt, in 1562. August answered,

> When Your Lordship kindly asked us in an enclosed note to inform you where the crumhorns can be obtained, such as you heard in our band in Frankfurt, our instrumentalists and other servants have reported that some time ago our dear late brother Elector Moritz ... bought these crumhorns from a merchant in Nürnberg and that they are said to have

---

[74] Adolf Aber, *Die Pflege der Musik unter den Wettinern und wettinischen Ernestinern Von den Anfängen bis zur Auflösung der Weimarer Hofkapelle 1662* (Bückeburg: Siegel, 1921), 82.

> Dinstag nach 'esto mihi' had der brewtigam und die Brawt sampt andern fursten und fürstinnen In der Capeln auf dem Slosse messe gehoret, haben die genannten synger meiner gnedigsten und gnedigen Hern zwue messen gesungen mit Hulf der orgall, dreyer posaun und eins zincken, desgleichen vier Cromhorner zum positief fast lustig zu horen.

> Otto Kinkeldy, *Orgel und klavier in der musik des 16. Jahrhunderts* (Leipzig: Breitkopf and Hartel, 1910), 192, gives 'Bromhorner' for 'Cromhorner.'

[75] Grove, 5:616.

[76] Altenburg, *Untersuchungen zur geschichte der trumpete im zeitalter der clarinblaskunst*, 13, 107–108.

been made in Memmingen ... Our instrumentalists have no other information except that the Cardinal of Trent also has a case full of crumhorns of this type which are supposed to be better than ours.[77]

For the marriage of Christian I, in 1582, a great allegorical pageant was held during which all the members of the court appeared in disguise. Some of the musicians appeared as 'nymph-musicians, ' swimming in a reservoir.[78] An engraving of a carnival procession organized by Christian I in 1584 pictures his wind band as a group of eight playing sackbuts, cornetts, tenor shawm and bass recorder.[79]

Icon of a wedding procession for the marriage of Christian I of Saxony, a symbolic representation of Bacchus amid a band of 2 trombones, cornett, and tenor shawm, 1582.

[77] Reinhard Kade, 'Antonius Scandellus (1517–1580). Ein Beitrag zur geschichte der Dresdener hofkapelle,' *Sammelbande der Internationalen Musikgesellschaft* (1914), XV, 554.

... alss unss dan E. L. durch einen ingelegten zeddel freundlich bittend diesselbig zu verstendigen, wo die Krumbhörner, so sie in unser musica zu frankfurt gehort, zu bekommen. Darauff haben unss unsere instrumentisten und andere unsere diener berichtet, dass weiland unser geliebter bruder Churf. Moritz ... dieselbigen Kromphörner von einem Kauffman zu Nurenberg kauffen lassen und dass dieselbigen zu Memmingen gemacht sein solten ... Er wissen auch unsere instrumentisten anders nit, dan der Cardinal zu Trent habe dieser sort Krumphörner, die besser als unsere sein sollen, auch ein futteral voll.

[78] Janssen, *History of the German People*, 265.

[79] This has been reproduced in W. Schrammek and V. Herre, *Museum Musicum: Historische Musikinstrumente* (Leipzig: Musikinstrumenten-Museum der Karl-Marx-Univ., 1976).

Christian 1, like many of his contemporaries, spent enormous time at hunting and drinking. On a single hunt, on 4 October 1562, according to his own statement, he killed '539 wild swine.' In 1563 the hunt yielded 1,116 animals and in 1565 he personally killed 330 deer. To put the starving poacher at a disadvantage, he ordered that all dogs belonging to the peasants who entered his fields must first have a forefoot cut off! A famous drinker, Christian once wrote to Prince Hans George of Anhalt,

> The reason why this letter is so stupid and badly written is that I have not yet altogether got over that last splendid orgy, and my hands tremble so that I can scarcely hold my pen.[80]

An inventory of the instruments in this court's collection made in 1593 reveals more than one hundred and twenty wind instruments at the disposal of the wind band.[81]

We gain a view of the Saxon court at Leipzig in the marriage celebrations of the Princess Anna of Saxony and the Prince of Orange in 1561. The ceremony, in the Lutheran tradition at that time, was held not in the church but in the palace. There was a formal procession from the great hall to a ceremonial bed where drinks and confections were served. A contemporary account mentions the royal trumpeters participating in this procession and also mentions that the banquet music was 'the merriest and most ingenious.'[82] The following morning the newly married couple and the entire court made a procession to the church of St. Nicholas for a final benediction, accompanied by 'fifers, drummers, and trumpeters.'[83]

[80] Janssen, *History of the German People*, 198, 217, 233.

[81] Quoted in Panoff, *Militärmusik in Geschichte und Gegenwart*, 74.

2 new small Posaunen
11 Quartposaunen
11 straight H8rner
8 Krummhllrner
9 small and large shawms
11 great flute
6 recorders
17 Querpfeifen
5 Flaten mit drei L8chern
2 timpani
10 straight cornetts
1 great curved cornett
5 Sordun
7 additional shawms
8 Dolzom (Dulziane)

[82] 'Acta des Printzen tzu Uranieun und Frawlein Annen tzu Saxen Beylager, 1561.' (Dresden, Royal Archives)

[83] John Motley, *The Rise of the Dutch Republic* (New York, 1864), 317.

5   Court Wind Bands in Italy

FOLLOWING THE GREAT CULTURAL ACCOMPLISHMENTS of the fifteenth century, Italy begins in the sixteenth century a long period of political strife, countless wars, and domination by foreign lords. This made for a hostile environment for art and music, but art and music did not disappear. On the contrary, arts sometime take on new importance during such periods, as for example in the case of the great celebrations by the dukes in sixteenth-century Italy. Their ceremonies were even more lavish in the hope of masking their lost independence and in holding out hope for the future.

Furthermore, the great flow of visitors through Italy in that century included artists and musicians and this contributed to the further unification of Western European culture. To cite an example, relative to the subject of this volume, a visitor passing through Piacenza, in October 1581, reports hearing a Spanish wind band, Piacenza then being under Spanish control. Both morning and evening, he said, they gave an hour concert with shawms.[1]

The great political disruptions of the sixteenth century, however, resulted in many destroyed documents and records, making the story of the Italian wind bands very difficult to piece together.

The Papacy

Rodrigo Borgia, elected pope in 1492 at age sixty-one, named himself Alexander VI, not for a previous pope by this name, but for Alexander the Great. Perhaps the worlds he sought to conquer were the Papal States themselves, which had fallen under the control of local dictators. One means of achieving this end was the politically expedient marriages of his children. His son, Cesare, was sent to marry the sister to the King of Navarre in order to form an alliance with Louis XII of France, but this was to have adverse consequences for both Italy and the papacy.

---

[1] Allessandro d'Ancona, ed., 'Giornale del viaggio di Michele de Montaigne in Italia nel 1580 e 1581,' in *L'Italia alla fine del secolo XVI.* (Citta di Castello: Lapi, 1889), 545.

> Viddi il Castello il quale è nelle mani del Re Filippo, il quale ci ha guardia di 300 spagnuoli mal pagati a quel ch'io intesi d'essi. La diana la mattina e la sera si sona con quelli instrumenti che noi chiamiamo hautbois, et essi fiffari e si sona una ora.

An eyewitness describes Cesare Borgia as he joins Louis XII at the French encampment at Chignon in 1499 as dressed like a potentate, in red satin and cloth of gold covered with pearls and diamonds. His many followers included, 'kettledrums, the trumpeters, and minstrels carrying instruments of silver slung on chains of gold.'[2]

One sees him again after his capture of the city of Pesaro in 1500, entering the Sforza palace as the twelve resident Sforza trumpeters proclaimed the new lord from the castle battlements.[3]

It is, however, the pope's daughter, Lucrezia Borgia (1480–1519), who is more familiar to the modern reader. Her marriage to Alfonso, of the House of Este, was intended by Alexander VI to reclaim Ferrara, long a papal fief, and indeed in 1598 it again returned to this status.

The party which left Ferrara in December 1501, to bring the lady back for the wedding, included some four thousand men, not to mention five hundred and eighty horses and fifty wagons for baggage.[4] The musicians traveling with the party consisted of thirteen trumpeters and an eight-member wind band, the piffari.[5]

The arrival of this Ferrara party in Rome was met by the Governor and senators of Rome, preceded by trumpets and drums and followed by another two thousand persons.[6] After a preliminary ceremony, the bridegroom, dressed in a silk tunic with golden belt, upon a charger with harness completely covered with gold and pearls, rode to the principal gate of the city where he was greeted by nineteen cardinals, each attended by two hundred followers. Here a two-hour speech was endured.

Finally, 'to the din of trumpets, fifes, and horns,' the cavalcade set out over the Corso toward the Vatican.[7] Arriving at the apartment of Lucrezia, they found her dressed in a mulberry colored gown, embroidered with gold and ermine, with a head-dress trimmed with gold and pearls.

Although the marriage had already been performed *vis volo* in Ferrara, Alexander insisted on a repetition of the ceremony in St. Peter's. A group of musicians played on the steps of the cathedral as Lucrezia arrived—probably they were the pope's wind band.[8] A week of entertainment followed the wedding in

[2] John Fyvie, *The Story of the Borgias* (New York: Putnam, 1913), 138.

[3] Pietro Marzetti, 'Memorie di Pesaro', (MS., Bibl. Oliveriana, Pesaro).

[4] Fyvie, *The Story of the Borgias*, 165.

[5] Ferdinand Gregorovius, *Lucretia Borgia*, trans., John L. Garner (New York: Appleton, 1904), 208, gives 'fifes' for piffari, a frequent mistranslation into English.

[6] Fyvie, *The Story of the Borgias*, 166.

[7] Gregorovius, *Lucretia Borgia*, 211.

[8] Ibid., 216.

Rome, including stage plays, dances, ballets, bull-fights, pageants, and banquets. One finds the usual trumpets announcing each event.

The procession of the bride and groom on to Ferrara now included eighty-six mules bearing the trousseau and jewels of Lucrezia. As they arrived in Ferrara they were joined in a great procession through the city by fourteen floats (beautiful local ladies) and eighty trumpeters together with a 'number of fifes.'[9] Here another week of celebration included allegorical depictions of the Triumph of Virtue, the Triumph of Agriculture, and the Victory of Love and Music over the Rude and Savage Natures. For the banquets, the host, Duke Ercole, had been preparing for weeks, accumulating three hundred oxen, fifteen thousand head of poultry, and great quantities of food of all kind in similar proportion.[10]

The popes themselves, of course, were not to be surpassed by such munificence. When Erasmus visited Rome in 1513, he was so shocked by the extravagance that he wrote a little satire in which Julius II, on having been excluded from heaven, is trying to impress Saint Peter of his significance.

> You should see the Pope carried in his golden chair by his soldiers with the crowds adoring as he waves his hand. Hear the boom of the cannon, the notes of the clarion, the beating of the drums ... What spectacles! Chariots, horses, troops, comely boys ... trumpets blaring, coins tossed to the crowds, and me as well nigh a god, the author and head of it all.[11]

This description reads very much like the entry of Pope Leo X into Florence in 1515. An eyewitness speaks of 'trompettes et des pifferi,'[12] the throwing of coins, and the largest crowd ever seen in Florence. The preparations, he says, required several thousand men laboring for more than a month.[13]

Leo had an artificial salt-water lake constructed near Ostia to satisfy an occasional urge to fish. For hunting pheasants and partridges he would visit Cardinal Farnese's estate at Viterbo, where he could bag them by the thousands, but it was hunting larger game at his Villa Magliana that this rugged outdoorsman loved best. It was accomplished as follows: first all the

[9] Ibid., 241.

[10] Fyvie, *The Story of the Borgias*, 177.

[11] Quoted in Charles L. Mee, *Daily Life in Renaissance Italy* (New York: American Heritage, 1975), 111.

[12] Luca Landucci, quoted in Nanie Bridgeman, 'Fêtes Italiennes de plein air au quattrocento,' in *Hans Albrecht in Memoriam*, ed. Wilfred Brennecke and Hans Haase (Kassel: Barenreiter, 1962), 36.

[13] Luca Landucci, *A Florentine Diary from 1450 to 1516*, trans., Alice de Rosen Jervis (London: Dent, 1927), 280.

game was collected and penned within an enclosure sealed off by tough sail-cloth, the pope would give a signal, a horn would sound, and then,

> the keepers, shouting, blowing trumpets and exploding charges of gunpowder, entered the pen and began to drive the game toward a gap in the canvas screen. Soon a torrent of animals came rushing out into the open, stags and boars, hares and rabbits, wolves, goats and porcupines. The waiting sportsmen would then eagerly fall upon their chosen target with spear or sword, axe or halberd.[14]

But to be fair, this was only one facet of a very interesting man. He had been groomed for an ecclesiastical–political career since birth by his father, Lorenzo de' Medici, who had suffered at the hands of Sixtus IV and thus hoped to build guarantees against the future. Everyone was surprised when the thirty-seven year old Giovanni de' Medici was elected pope, especially as he was not yet a priest!

Having been born a Medici, he received the finest possible education, not the least of which was his musical education under the great Issac.[15] He had a good ear, a fine voice and composed rather well. He was particularly interested in the development of the Vatican choir and it is appropriate that, in his portrait by Raphel, he is pictured reading a volume of sacred music.

Leo X also maintained a wind band, as one must assume from the fragmentary evidence. This band even participated in the services of the Sistine Chapel, according to the diary of the papal Master of Ceremonies, Paris de Grassis.[16]

Leo's interest in his wind band is evidenced in the international character of the players and their instruments; he must have constantly been on the search for its improvement. Much of his court musical establishment was influenced by Franco–Flemish ideas, and indeed we know he employed, in 1519–1521, two Flemish shawm players, named Bartholo and Bartholomeo.[17] Yet, one of his most popular ensembles was an Italian shawm band, his 'quattro sonatori di pifferi milanesi.'[18] Finally, Leo called the famous Hans Neuschel of Nürnberg to Rome and rewarded him for the silver trombones which he had commissioned.[19]

[14] Christopher Hibbert, *The House of Medici* (New York: Morrow, 1975), 230–231.

[15] Issac's *Optime pastor* was composed for the coronation of Leo, in 1513.

[16] Dr. John Shearman, 'Leo X and the Sistine Chapel,' London: BBC Radio 3, August 20, 1971.

[17] Vander Straeten, *La musique aux Pays-Bas*, 6:432–433.

[18] H. Frey, *Regesten zur päpstlichen Kapelle unter Leo X und zu seiner Privatkapelle*, quoted in Dietrich Kämper, *Studien zur Instrumentalen Ensemblemusik des 16. Jahrhunderts in Italien* (Köln, 1970), 51.

[19] Reese, *Music in the Renaissance*, 656.

Another important Medici pope of this century, Clement VII (1523–1534), was also reared as a son to Lorenzo, although he was actually an illegitimate son of Giuliano de' Medici. This pope was perhaps too intellectually inclined, for his thought processes tended to prevent action when needed. Caught between the great struggle of Francis I and Charles V, Clement delayed so long his decision of whom to support that when he finally backed Francis it was only days before his historic defeat. The result was to bring the full wrath of Charles V upon him and, in 1527, the infamous 'Sack of Rome.'

> The wall and the ramparts taken, the Romans began to flee, and save themselves. The Imperial armies of Charles followed their victory with such fury, that, as the Spanish say, 'the devils were all there.' One could not have heard the thunder in the sky, because of the noise of the muskets, the cries of the wounded and dying, the clashing of weapons, the sounds of the trumpets, and the clamor of drums, which animated the soldiers greatly.[20]

This great political disaster, and others such as the loss to the Church of England and Henry VIII, in 1531, is offset to some degree, in our perspective of four centuries later, by his support of the arts in Rome, foremost of which was his patient encouragement of Michelangelo.

Clement VII was also trained in music; indeed some believe that it was to distinguish himself from this pope that Jacobus Clemens took the sobriquet, 'Clemens non Papa.' We have an extraordinary account of Clement's wind band in one of the masterpieces of sixteenth-century literature, the *Autobiography* by Benvenuto Cellini. Because the passage in question is so rich in detail, including a very rare glimpse of the rehearsal process, it must be quoted in full.

> It happened that at that time that one Giagiacomo, wind player (piffero, probably shawm) from Cesena, who is now in this capacity with the Pope, a very excellent performer (sonatore), sent word through Lorenzo, trombonist from Lucca, who is now in the service of our Duke (Cosmo I), to inquire whether I was inclined to help them at the Pope's celebration of the Ferragosto,[21] playing soprano with my cornett in some motets of great beauty selected by them for that occasion. Although I had the greatest desire to finish the vase I had begun, yet, since music has a wondrous charm of its own, and also because I wished to please my old father, I consented to join them. During the eight days before

[20] Brantôme, *Vie du connétable de Bourbon*, VII.

> La muraille et les remparts gaignés, les Romains commencèrent à fuyr, et sauve qui peut. Les Impériaux poursuivent leur victoire de telle furie, qu'on disoit que tous les diables estoient là tous assemblés, comme disent les Espagnols en leur langue, car les arquebusades, les crys des blesses et mourans, le battement des armes, le son des trompettes, la rumeur des tambours, qui animoient d'autant plus les soldats au combat, et les coups de piques faisoient un tel bruit, qu'on n'eust ouy tonner le ciel quand il eust tonné.

[21] A festival on 1 August.

the festival we practiced two hours a day together; then on the first of August we went to the courtyard of the Vatican Palace (the Belvedere), and while Pope Clement was at his banquet, we played those carefully rehearsed (disciplinati) motets so well that his Holiness protested he had never heard music more sweetly executed or with better ensemble (unita). He sent for Giangiacomo, and asked him where and how he had procured so excellent a cornett for soprano, and inquired particularly who I was. Giangiacomo told him my name in full. Whereupon the Pope said: 'So, then, he is the son of Maestro Giovanni?' On being assured I was, the Pope expressed his wish to have me in his service with the other musicians. Giangiacomo replied: 'Most blessed Father, I cannot pretend for certain that you will get him, for his profession, to which he devotes himself assiduously, is that of a goldsmith, and he works in it miraculously well, and earns by it far more than he could do by playing.' To this the Pope added: 'I am the better inclined to him now that I find him possessor of a talent more than I expected. See that he obtains the same salary as the rest of you; and tell him from me to join my service, and that I will find work enough by the day for him to do in his other trade.' Then stretching out his hand, he gave him a hundred golden crowns of the Camera in a handkerchief, and said: 'Divide these so that he may take his share.' When Giangiacomo left the Pope, he came to us, and related ... all that the Pope had said.[22]

[22] Benvenuto Cellini, 'La Vita,' in *Opere* (Milano, 1968), 94–95. Translation by the present author.

This passage tells us many things, first that the ensemble had eight-members. All evidence from the first half of the sixteenth century would lead one to suppose it was a wind band and this seems to be confirmed in the mention of a shawm, trombone, and a cornett playing the uppermost voice.

The performance of motets by a wind band was also, as we have seen, a normal practice. Here we find the repertoire was carefully chosen and carefully rehearsed. Certainly musicians holding so important a position would have been fully capable of performing motets at sight from part-books, especially considering that the performance took place while the pope was at a banquet. But no, they rehearsed two hours per day for eight days! The 'carefully rehearsed' performance and the terms (via the Pope), 'sweetly executed' and 'better ensemble,' I take to mean these musicians probably rehearsed exactly as we would today: adding the articulations which are not to be found on the page, listening for balance, precision, etc. It reminds one how nearly related we really are.

This passage, in my opinion, is also a clear testimonial to a concept which seems difficult for most scholars to accept: that such performances were far more than 'dinner music,' as we think of it. Not only the description of the careful rehearsals, but the remarks of the principal listener, the pope, prove the music was in fact listened to at some point during the banquet. I believe we must begin to think of such performances as one of the kinds of *concerts* found in earlier centuries.

Such banquets, as part of festive celebrations, were common in sixteenth-century Rome, held not only by the pope, but by cardinals and the princes of the noble families in the city. One of the greatest feasts was held in 1534 to celebrate the election of Paul III. Perhaps because the 'Sack of Rome' was still so recent in the minds of all Romans and because the coronation reminded everyone of the continuity of the 'Roman Family,' this feast became for a time an annual one, held in early November. Extant records reveal payments to both papal and military wind bands performing for this celebration.[23]

It is for the period of Paul III that one begins to find extant documentation relative to the papal wind bands, of which there were several. First there was the 'i musici di Castel Sant'Angelo,' a band for which all early documents were destroyed in the 'Sack of Rome,' but which is described from 1578 to ca. 1700 as 'piffari,' or a shawm band.[24] Near the end of the seventeenth century the name of the band was changed to 'musici del concerto di Campidoglio,' and shortly thereafter is referred to as 'Concerto de' tromboni e cornetti del Senato et inclito Popolo Romano.'[25] In a document of 1706, there is an indication that it was an eight-member trombone ensemble.[26] This band was led by a 'Priore,' who could levy fines and make payments to players. Their regular duties included performing in any procession which passed by the castle and in all papal coronations and celebrations by the princes. When Paul III went to Lucca to meet with Charles V, in October 1541, to discuss the treaty between France and Spain, these musicians were given extra money to buy horses to make the trip.[27] Two years later they were again given money to buy horses to travel with the pope to Bologna.[28]

Vessella cites a number of sixteenth-century documents relative to this wind band, including attempts to gain retroactive pay in 1531 (here, 'biffari') and 1558 ('pifferi e tromboni') and relative to housing privileges in the Campidoglio in 1566 ('pifferi').[29]

[23] Regio Archivio di Stato di Roma, Archivio Camerale 1540, 1543, Nr. 2044; 1541–1544, Nr. 2045, including the 'trombetti et piffari di Campidoglio,' 'trombetti della guardia,' 'tamburini et piffari della guardia,' 'trombetta del signor duca Di Castro,' and 'Pifferi di Castello.'

[24] Alessandro Vessella, *La Banda* (Milano: Insituto editoriale nazionale, 1935), 103.

[25] Ibid.

[26] Biblioteca Vaticana, Cod. Barberini Lat. 5153, fols. 9, 17v. See also, Emmanuel Rodocanachi, *Le Château Saint-Ange* (Paris: Hachette & cie, 1909).

[27] Rodocanachi, *Le Château Saint-Ange*, and Antonio Bertolotti, 'Speserie segrete e pubbliche di Paolo III,' in *Atti e Memorie delle RR. Deputazioni di Storia Patria, per le provincie dell'Emilia*, Nuova serie, III, ia, 181.

[28] Vessella, *La Banda*, 102.

[29] Ibid., 105–106.

Next there was a trumpet ensemble called 'i trombetti del Popolo Romano,' a self-contained consort ('concerto') with its own constitution, regulations, etc., and documents of the sixteenth century already speak of older, lost, constitutions. As in the case of the first band I have discussed, the principal members of the trumpet band were called 'trombetti di numero,' with adjunct members called 'coadiutori' and 'sopranumerari.' During the sixteenth century it seems these players also had to double, as needed, on timpani; a position for a timpani players first appears in 1734.[30]

There was also an ensemble of drum players, who seem to have been paid less and were perhaps not as appreciated, musically.

Finally, the pope also had his own militia and here one also finds wind and percussion players. Until 1552, the cavalry of the pope had six trumpet players, whom Vessella says played not only the usual signals, but also for the enjoyment of the troops.[31] In the organization of the pope's Swiss Guards, each unit of two hundred men had two timpani or tamburi and two 'pifferi.' These players were organized under a head drummer (Capo tambruo), who in addition to knowing all the military signals ('sonerie,' in Italian), had to know the various papal regulations concerning the ceremonies in which they appeared. These players also seem, by the nature of the restrictions upon them, to have enjoyed the least respect within the many divisions of papal music. They alone could not accept outside performance for extra money and they had additional non-musical jobs to perform, which included the cleaning of lamps and fireplaces.[32]

Given this extensive organization of the papal wind bands, it comes as no surprise that when Paul III visited Francis I in Paris, in 1538, he was accompanied by no fewer than four separate wind bands! Two were composed of shawms, and two of trumpets.[33]

[30] Ibid., 113–114.

[31] Vessella, *La Banda*, 123.

[32] Ibid., 124.

[33] Henri Prunières, 'La musique de la Chambre et de L'Écurie so us le Regne de François Ier,' *L'Année Musicale* (Paris, 1911): 238.

(Payment to) Jean Jacques et ses compaignons, joueurs de hautbois du pape, con de 45 livres … A Francisque de Mante et ses compaignons, autres joueurs de haulxbois, don de 45 livres … A Angelo Félice et autres trompetes du Pape et du Marquis del Guasto. A Pierre de Mantoue et ses compaignons, autres trompêtes de la Cour du Pape.

Ferrara

I have mentioned above the participation of the court wind band players of Ferrara, in connection with the wedding of Lucrezia Borgia. The next reference to this band is found in a discussion of the marriage of Ercole d'Este (later Ercole II) and the Princess Renée of France in 1529. Although tiny, somber and deformed, the political significance of the marriage entitled Renée to a sumptuous wedding celebration.

The first official banquet, called 'The Banquet of Meat,' was held on 24 January 1529 and followed a performance of Ariosto's *Cassaria*. As was often the case, this banquet consisted of many courses, each introduced by trumpets and then accompanied by a variety of musical performances. It is clear that during the sixteenth century the custom was to vary the instrumentation with each composition, thus accomplishing the tonal variety we achieve today through 'orchestration.' We are fortunate, in this case, to have an eyewitness who gives a detailed description of an example of this practice.[34]

During the first course, one heard a composition by Alphonso dalla Vivola, performed by voices, accompanied by five viols, keyboard, lute, and large and medium size flutes. The second course was accompanied by sung madrigals and the third course with Dialoghi, for two choirs of voices, accompanied by flute, sackbut, lute and viol. During the fourth course another work by dalla Vivola, with singers, viols, a contrabass viol, a dolzaina, a crumhorn 'played by M. Giovambattista Leone without windcap,' an organ, two medium size recorders, and mute cornett.[35]

A pure wind ensemble accompanied the fifth course, consisting of five sackbuts and a cornett. Then a choral work, followed by another wind ensemble during the seventh course—now two dolzaine, crumhorn, large cornett and sackbut. For the desert course another large mixed consort performed.

These celebrations continued throughout the spring, and in May, another banquet, 'Banquet of Fish,' was given. Again each course was accompanied by a different kind of ensemble, two of which were wind ensembles.

[34] Christoforo Messisburgo, *Banchetti, compositioni di vivande, et apparecchio generale* (Ferrara, 1549).

[35] According to Vessella, *La Banda*, 84, Duke Ercole himself was infatuated with the flute and studied the instrument with dalla Vivola.

> And as this course was on the table, a dolzaina, a sackbut and a flute played ... And suddenly as this course was laid on the table the musicians began to play these instruments: three recorders, three cornamuse (crumhorns), and a great bass viol.[36]

As in many parts of Italy, German musicians were popular. In 1534 a shawm band (piffari todeschi) accompanied a German noble to Venice to attend one of the celebrations for the wedding of one of the Ferrara princesses.[37] In 1566, Ferdinand of Bavaria visited the Ferrara court and during the banquet one heard a 'concert' by twenty-six singers and a mixed consort of strings and winds.[38]

During this visit, one performance by a band of cornetts and sackbuts was given in an adjoining room. Some scholars point to this as an example of the growing preference for *gli strumenti delicati*, but it may instead only reflect the preference of some nobles to eat apart from their guests.

According to Bottrigari,[39] the Duke of Ferrara maintained a large collection of instruments, including strings, keyboards, and 'cornetts, sackbuts, dolzaine, and shawms.' These instruments, he goes on to say, were 'always in playing condition and tuned, ready to be picked up and played on the spur of the moment.'

The Duke also maintained a famous ensemble of twenty-three nuns of Saint Vito, who were also described by Bottrigari.

> You would see them betake themselves in Indian file to a long table, upon one end of which a large harpsichord is laid. Silently they entered, each one with her instrument, be it a stringed or a wind instrument ... and gathered around the table without the slightest noise, some sitting down, some standing, according to the nature of their instruments. At last, the conductress (la Madre Maestra) faced the table from the other end and, after having made sure that the other sisters were ready, gave them noiselessly the sign to begin with a long, slender, well polished baton.[40]

Vessella adds that this ensemble was 'suave of harmony, angelic of voice, and very fine instrumentalists.' He notes that each played several instruments, 'and not just cornetts and trombones.'[41]

---

[36] Messisburgo, quoted in J. Llorens, 'Estudio de los instrumentos musicales·que aparecen descritos en la relación de dos festives celebrados el año 1529 en la corte de Ferrara,' in *Anuario-Musical* 25 (1970): 22-24.

[37] Kämper, *Studien zur Instrumentalen Ensemblemusik des 16. Jahrhunderts in Italien*, 50.

[38] Emilie Elsner, *Untersuchung der instrumenta1en Besetzungspraxis der weltichen Musik im 16. Jahrhundert in Italien* (Berlin, 1935), 53.

[39] Hercole Bottrigari, *Il Desiderio* (Venice, 1594; reprinted in Berlin, 1924), trans., C. MacClintock (American Institute of Musicology, 1962), 40.

[40] Translation by Curt Sachs, *Our Musical Heritage* (New Jersey: Prentice-Hall, 1948), 160.

[41] Vessella, *La Banda*, 85.

Florence

After the death of Lorenzo, Florence passed through various unusual and short-lived experiments in government, one a democracy and another under the gloomy cleric, Savonarola. By 1512 the Medicean family was in control again, but, excepting those members who became pope, the family had no great leaders left. The remaining dukes tried whenever possible to recapture the grandeur of the past by staging great regal celebrations, in particular for family marriages.

The first of these was the wedding of Lorenzo de' Medici (not *il magnifico*) with Madeleine de la Tour d'Auvergne in 1518. The festivities included a performance of Lorenzo Strozzi's *Commedia in versi*, with five intermezzi. Although the music has not survived, the only contemporary description of this event tells us that before the first act a wind band of trumpets, crumhorns,[42] and shawms (*pifferi*) performed. During the final act another composition was performed by four sackbuts.[43]

Cosimo I, upon becoming Lord of Florence at age eighteen, wanted to marry the daughter to the Emperor, Charles V, as a means of renewing the power and glory of his city-state, but Charles V had other plans and Cosimo had to settle for

Musicians, by Giorgio Vasari, 1545. This fresco was possibly made in Naples for Tommaso Cambi, a merchant and collector originally from Florence.

Eleanore of Toledo. An eyewitness account[44] of the wedding celebrations provides an excellent view of the use of wind instruments in this court before mid-century and a rare bonus is that, with the exception of the composition for Apollo and the nine Muses, the music is extant.[45]

The bride arrived with her party in seven galleys in June 1539, and was greeted by a chorus standing at the foot of a great triumphal arch representing Fertility, Security, and Eternity. Here a performance of Francesco Corteccia's 'Ingredere felicissimis auspiciis urbem tuam Helionora,' was accompanied by a wind band of four cornets and four sackbuts from an arch over the great door leading to the prato.

Following the wedding banquet, an allegorical pageant appeared before the tables representing Apollo and the Nine Muses, performing a canzona, 'Sacro et Santo Hymeneo.' The instruments carried by the muses can perhaps be taken as representative of the instruments used in the court of Cosimo.

The Muse, Thalia, wore a bright blue silk costume with a girdle of olive branches, with ornamental bees fastened to her hair. Across her breast was a panther skin and each foot was dressed in catskin, ornamented by a crab. She carried a sackbut.

---

[42] In the original account (see following footnote), 'cornamuse' is given. It seems clear that this term, in the sixteenth century, was used at times to mean the bagpipe and at other times to mean a family of wind instruments very similar to the crumhorn, an instrument first described in detail by Praetorius, in *Syntagma Musicum*, vol. 2. Howard M. Brown, in *Sixteenth-Century Instrumentation: The Music for the Florentine Intermedii* (Dallas: American Institute of Musicology, 1973), 87, translates this as bagpipe. Other modern scholars assume the crumhorn-type is intended; see Barra Boydell, *The Crumhorn and other Renaissance Windcap Instruments* (Buren: Knuf, 1982), who gives an extensive discussion, 304ff.; David Munrow, *Instruments of the Middle Ages and Renaissance* (London: Oxford Univeristy Press, 1976), 49; and Anthony Baines, *European and American Musical Instruments* (London: Batsford, 1966), 97. Baines cites, as an example of the Italian practice at this time, a letter by Vincenzo Parabosco, dated 28 January 1546, Brescia, which recommends instruments for the court musical establishment then forming in Parma.

> First, of the types of trumpet, one should play the trombeta; then six shawms (pifari), then six cornetts, then six cornemuse, then six recorders (flauti), then six German piferi, then six violas da braccio.

The implication is that a consort of six family members, while typical of a crumhorn-type instrument, would be most unlikely for the bagpipe.

[43] Pietro Stromboli, ed., *Le vite degli uomini illustri della Casa Strozzi, commentario di Lorenzo di Filippo Strozzi ora intieramente pubblicato con un ragionamento inedito di Francesco Zeffi sopra la vita dell'autore* (Florence, 1892).

[44] Pierfrancesco Giambullari, *Apparato et feste nelle nozze del Illustrissimo Signor Duca di Firenze, et della Duchessa sua consorte, con le sue Stanze, Madriali, Comedia, et Intermedii, in quelle recitati* (Florence, 1539).

[45] Andrew Minor and Bonner Mitchell, *A Renaissance Entertainment* (Columbia: University of Missouri Press, 1968).

Euterpe, Muse of Music, wore a yellow-green dress with a hyena skin across the breast and with shoes of monkey skin. Her hair was filled with flowers and a winged hat set with semi-precious stones. This muse carried the proto-type bassoon, the dolcian.

Erato, Muse of Love Poetry, was more voluptuously dressed and heavily perfumed. With a billy-goat skin over breast and shoes of rabbit skin, she carried a violone.

Melpomene, Muse of Tragic Poetry, wore a costume of gold and silk, with a lion skin over the breast. The robe was embroidered with musical instruments and the headpiece was in the form of five rows of organ pipes. She carried a shawm.

Clio, Muse of History, carried a flute and a broom. She wore a leopard skin with wolf skin shoes and a headpiece in the form of a woodpecker.

Terpsichore, Muse of Dance, was dressed in yellow silk, with deer skin across the shoulders and shoes of white lamb skin. She carried a lute, with two partridges and ears of corn.

Polyhymnia, Muse of Sacred Poetry, carried a crumhorn (sorta) in her left hand and pine boughs in her right hand. She was dressed in black silk with a hareskin over her breast.

Urania, Muse of Astronomy, carried a cornett and wore a blue taffeta gown covered with gold stars and constellations.

Calliope, Muse of Epic Poetry, carried a small rebec and wore a white linen robe covered with cabalistic signs.

Three days later, on 9 July 1539, a performance of Antonio Landi's comedy, *Il Commodo*, was given. The intermezzi given between the acts included the court wind band performing music by Corteccia. After the first act, twelve musicians, dressed as rustic shepherds, appeared in pairs to perform, 'Guardane almo pastore,' with a cornett, panpipes, and crumhorns. The work was then repeated with singers and the same instruments.

> (One of the first pair) carried in his hand a piece of fresh, leafy cane—or so it seemed from the outside, for inside was a sorta ... (one of the second pair) carried a broken-off branch from a chesnut tree, with chestnuts and leaves. Hidden in it was a sorta, as above ... (one of the third pair carried a cornett and) the first member of the fourth couple was playing another sorta with all the apparatus of a bagpipe ... (one of the

fifth pair) had in his hand two goat horns joined together, with a sorta hidden between them ... (one of the final pair) was playing that instrument of seven reeds carried by the God of the Countryside.

At the conclusion of the play, the character, Night, sang an aria, 'Vienten' almo riposo: ecco ch'io torno,' accompanied by four sackbuts. This was followed by a dance, with bacchantes and satyrs, a four-part instrumental work performed by two cornetts, two crumhorns, a coiled trumpet (tromba torta), pipe and tabor, rebec and harp.

The son of Cosimo I, Francesco de' Medici, was married to Johanna of Austria during the Christmas season of 1565–1566 and another round of extraordinary entertainments was given.[46] The bride entered Florence in a great procession on 16 December 1565, the wedding following two days later.

One of the many German guests present was Duke Ferdinand of Bavaria, who heard the Florentine court wind band in a performance at a breakfast the morning of the first procession.

> At the breakfast ... music was played with cornetts, trombones, also with crumhorns; but they only played 'Welsche' dances which in my opinion were nothing special.[47]

On 25 December, a performance of Francesco d'Ambra's comedy, *La Cofanaria* was given, with intermezzi which included the court wind band. The first intermezzo presented the characters, Venus, the three Graces, the Four Seasons, and somewhat later, Cupid and the Four Passions—Hope, Fear, Joy, and Pain. The second intermezzo consisted of the performance of two compositions by Alessandro Striggio, played by a mixed consort; here Cupid serenaded Psyche.

The third intermezzo shows Cupid so taken by love for Psyche that he has neglected mortals, resulting in the appearance of characters representing Frauds and Deceptions. Here a madrigal, 'S'amor vinto, e prigion posto in oblio,' by Corteccia, was performed by eight singers, five crumhorns, and a mute cornett.

[46] The primary source is Domenico Mellini's *Descrizione Dell' Apparato Della Comedia Et Intermedii D'essa Recitata in Firenze il giorno di S. Stefano l'anno 1565 ...* (Florence, 1565).

[47] Quoted in Adolf Sandberger, *Beiträge zur Geschichte der bayerischen Hofkapelle unter Orlando di Lasso* (Leipzig, 1895), 3:351.

> ... beim Morgenmal ... hat man Musica gehallten, mit Zinckhen und Pusaunen. Dergleichen mit khrumb Hörnern, aber alles nur Welsche Dannz, so meines erachtens auch nur gemain Ding gewest.

The fourth intermezzo presented various characters representing Discord, Ire, and Cruelty—the result of love having died among mankind. Musically, this was another madrigal, accompanied by two trombones, dolzaina, three cornetts (one, a tenor cornett), and two tamburi.

This tale finally ends with a sixth intermezzo, set at the foot of Mount Helicon. The eyewitness, Mellini, describes the ensemble performing here as a large mixed consort of two mute cornetts, two trombones, dolzaina, crumhorn, lirone, rebec, and two lutes. Our other eyewitness, Duke Ferdinand, however, describes only the court wind band.

> After the Fifth Act … came twelve naked nymphs and as many satyrs who sang and played on large curved pipes (crumhorns?) with which harmonized cornetts and trombones.[48]

The wedding entertainments continued into February 1566, with an allegorical parade called, 'Trionfo de' Sogni,' on the second day of the month; a siege of a fortress by eleven hundred knights on the seventeenth; and on the twenty-first, another allegorical parade. This final procession began with eight trumpeters dressed in women's clothing!

Another series of festivities was held in 1568, to celebrate the baptism of Francesco's daughter, Leonora. On 2 February, a group of maskers disguised as hunters roamed the city, accompanied by singers who performed two canzoni, 'Noi siam Donne Caccia,' and 'Cacciator Donne scorriamo,' accompanied by two cornetts, two crumhorns, and two trombones. On 23 February, a similar group of maskers sang a canzona by Allessandro Striggio, 'Scorte dal chiaro lume,' first a cappella and then accompanied by cornetts and trombones.[49]

On 26 February, a procession through Florence included a float in the form of a ship (the Triumph of Fortune) filled with singers, two cornetts, three trombones, a flute and a lira. They performed Stefano Rossetto's canzona, 'Donne poscia ch'a voi son fatte ancelle.' The wind band also performed more functional roles, such as mounted trumpeters in this procession and a group of shawms and drums during a joust in the Piazza Santa Croce on 9 February. The actual baptism began with a procession into the church by trumpets and drums.

[48] Quoted in Sandberger, *Beiträge zur Geschichte der bayerischen Hofkapelle unter Orlando di Lasso*, 353.

… nach dem fünfften Act … khomen 12 Nackent Nimphe vnd souil Satirj, die haben aber gesungen vnd mit grossen khrumben Pfeiffen, darein Zincken vnd Pusaunen gestimbt gewest …

[49] Alessandro Ceccherelli, *Descrizione di tutte le feste e mascherate fatte in Firenze per il carnovale, questo anno 1567* … (Florence, 1567).

Another comedy, Lotto Del Mazzo's, *I Fabii*, was given with intermezzi. These included Striggio's 'D'ogn' altra furia, è peste,' sung by the characters, Calumny, Ignorance, and Fear, and accompanied by bass crumhorn, two trombones, and two mute cornetts. Another intermezzi was Striggio's 'O che non sol pur guerra,' sung by Love, Fear, Glory, and Honor, accompanied by two trombones and three recorders.

Three months later a folk pageant was given in the Piazza Santa Croce which, being another allegory, included in the cast a buffalo, the Seven Deadly Sins, and the Furies, etc. Two choral compositions were performed: a chorus of 'hunters,' accompanied by two cornetts, two crumhorns, and two trombones , and a chorus of 'butterflies,' sung a capella, and then repeated with cornetts and trombones.[50]

A later marriage of Francesco, to Bianca Cappello, in 1579, included performances by shawms and tamburi, in mostly functional music.[51]

Medici festivities after this date seem to have used mixed consorts, although they are often primarily of winds. An exception is an intermezzo to Girolamo Bargagli's, *La Pellegrina*, performed as part of the 1589 wedding celebration of Ferdinand I and Christine of Lorraine.[52] This composition, 'Lieti solcando il mare,' was sung by a group of sailors and accompanied by trombones, cornetts, dolzaini, and bassoons (fagotti).[53]

Mantua

In the first volume of this series, I have described the development of the court wind band in Mantua under the influence of Isabella, one of the great women of the Renaissance, and this development continues during the sixteenth century. According to Fenlon, 'Francesco's attentions appear to have been directed towards the traditional band of pifferi,'[54] and Vessella points out that in Mantua the entire century is filled with references to 'trombetti, tromboni e pifferi.'[55]

An insight into the instrumentation of this court band can be found in 1505, when the trombonist, Giovanni Aloize, in Venice, was commissioned to arrange music for cornetts, trombones, and shawms for Isabella.[56] Vessella writes that

[50] Thurston Dart, *The Interpretation of Music* (New York: Harper & Row, 1963), 141.

[51] Jean Jacquot, ed., *Les Fêtes de la Renaissance*, 1:116.

[52] Bastiano de' Rossi, *Descrizione dell'apparato, e degl'intermedi ...* (Florence, 1589). An inventory of the instrument collection of Ferdinand, made in 1599, included many wind instruments.

    6 cornetts
    a consort of 8 flutes
    a consort of 13 flutes
    3 wood flutes and a 'flauto di tararuga'

(Archivio di Stato di Firenze, Guardaroba Nr. 225, Ruolo della famiglia di Sua Altezza, Carte 11).

[53] Brown, *Sixteenth-Century Instrumentation*, 126.

[54] Iain Fenlon, *Music and Patronage in Sixteenth-Century Mantua* (Cambridge: Cambridge University Press, 1980), 22.

[55] Vessella, *La Banda*, 86.

[56] Ibid.

Isabella was so interested in the flute and trombone that, in the privacy of her apartments, she had her own children study these instruments.[57]

During mid-century, the wind band continues under Ercole, as we can see in a payment of 1537 to the court trombone and piffero players to perform in the bishop's palace.[58] Indeed, other than one singer and one lute player, the wind band seems to have been the only regular musicians on the court payroll.[59]

This band provided the music for all the court ceremonies, as for example the wedding of Guglielmo to Eleonora of Austria in 1561.[60] When Duke Friedrich of Bavaria visited the court in 1565 he reported hearing a band of four shawms, cornetts, and 'Pomhart' performing during dinner.[61]

Near the end of the century, one finds the court wind band performing in San Pietro's Cathedral, as part of the coronation ceremonies of Vincenzo Gonzaga in 1587. An eyewitness describes a band of cornetts and trombones performing before and after the wedding Mass.[62]

Finally, there is a rare reference to lady wind players during this period. It seems one, Antonio Pellizzari, an official of the Accademia Olimpica, had two daughters (or perhaps sisters) who were performers on cornett and trombone. A record of 1585 speaks in admiration of their performance[63] in the incidental music to Sophocles' *Oedipus Rex*, composed by Andrea Gabrieli.[64] Fenlon believes that these ladies were among those heard in Ferrara, when Vincenzo and his retinue visited in 1589. An eyewitness recalled,

> For entertainments (there) were … hours of exquisite music-making … with the Duke of Mantua came four ladies from Vicenza who sing very well and play the cornetto and other instruments.[65]

[57] Ibid.

[58] Fenlon, *Music and Patronage in Sixteenth-Century Mantua*, 65. Duke Ercole was also Bishop of Mantua.

[59] Ibid., 68.

[60] Ibid., 84.

[61] Quoted in Sandberger, *Beiträge zur Geschichte der bayerischen Hofkapelle unter Orlando di Lasso*, 3:350.

> … Weil die Malzeit gewertt Vnd ain guete Weil daruor seindt 4 schalmeier sambt ainem Pomhart vnnd Zingkhen Plasser oben auf ainem Camin gesessen, die haben Welsche Tanz Pfiffen.

[62] Follino, *Descrittione dell'infirmita*, quoted in Fenlon, *Music and Patronage in Sixteenth-Century Mantua*, 121.

> … Preparate dunque tutte queste cose, posti all'ordine gli cantori con suoi concerti di tromboni, cornette & voci … Finita la messa, la quale fu di musica perfettissima, composta per questo effetto, dell'eccellentiss. musico & mastro di capella di S. A. il Sig. Giachtes Vuert, huomo per l'eccellenza dell'opre sue, assai famoso al mondo: & spediti i concerti d'organo, voci, cornette, e tromboni, si cominciarono tutti ad incominare per una sbarra …

[63] Quoted in Fenlon, Music and Patronage in Sixteenth-Century Mantua, 128.

> Ebbe massima parte nell'apprestamento degli abiti Giambattista Maganza, nelle musiche M. Pordenone, nei cori M. Andrea Gabrieli organista di S. Marco. Fecero specialmente attoniti gli ascoltanti col suono del cornetto e del trombone due giovinette figlie del Pellizzari custode dell'Accademia.

[64] This music is extant, in Gabrieli's *Chori*.

[65] Quoted in Fenlon, *Music and Patronage in Sixteenth-Century Mantua*, 132.

Verona

Verona itself was not a great center of culture, but during the sixteenth century does seem to have specialized in the development of wind players, especially those of the cornett. Castellani observes that this preference for the cornett gave rise to the appearance of numerous virtuosi who were 'exported' from Italy.[66]

One palace central to this activity was that of Count Mario Bevilacqua, a widely known connoisseur of music. His private concerts featured vocal music accompanied by instruments 'capable of blending with the voices, such as recorders and cornetts.'[67] The inventory made of his personal instrument collection, upon his death in 1593, included four keyboard, twenty-two string, and fifty-two wind instruments.[68]

Venice

Although the famous Bellini painting of 1496 shows ten members of the Doge's wind band, the regular number of players for the sixteenth century seems to have been six. One authority tells us that this wind band performed an hour-long concert in the Piazza each day.[69]

A clue to the instruments used by this band may perhaps be found in the instance, cited above, of the music sent to Manuta arranged for 'cornetti, tromboni e pifferi.' Another clue is found in Sylvestro Ganassi's *Fontegara* (1535), the first recorder tutor to be published. Here one finds a plate showing a consort of four recorder players. Ganassi, himself, was a member of the Doge's wind band.

Two sixteenth-century icons picture the Doge's wind band as well. 'The Procession of the Doge in Venice,' ca. 1520, by Jost Amman, shows five trumpeters in uniform.[70] A similar work, ca. 1559, by Matteo Pagani, shows six players with straight trumpets so long they are supported by children.[71] (see images pages 138–141)

Another great procession which survives in iconographic form was one celebrating the Victory of Lepanto, in 1571. According to Chambers, 'triumphal music,' which must certainly have meant the wind band, performed a work by Gabrieli on this occasion.[72]

---

[66] Marcello Castellani, 'A 1593 Veronese Inventory,' in *The Galpin Society Journal* 26 (May 1, 1973): 23.

[67] Ibid.

[68] Ibid.

16 recorders
6 transverse flutes
6 Bassanelli
6 curtale
4 cornamuse (crumhorns)
1 fagotto
11 cornetts
2 trombones

These instruments were still probably consorts of several family members. The Bassanelli are thought to have been a double reed, played without cap, with a tone not as strong as the bassoon or bombard.

[69] Eleanor Selfridge-Field, *Venetian Instrumental Music from Gabrieli to Vivaldi* (New York: Praeger, 1975), 14.

[70] Jost Amman, woodcut, in Coburg, Kunstsammlungen (Inv.-Nr. I/330/2616).

[71] Matteo Pagani, woodcut, Venice Museo Correr.

[72] David S. Chambers, *The Imperial Age of Venice* (New York: Harcourt Brace Jovanovich, 1971), 192.

Fontegara, by Sylvestro Ganassi, 1535

Siena

In Siena, the court wind band, called the 'Concerto di Palazzo,' continued despite the fall of the republic in 1559. This body of players consisted of shawms, cornetts, trombones, and twelve trumpets, organized under a leader who was usually a cornett or trombone player. We know the name of one of the most highly respected trombonists, from near the end of the century, one Giovanni Francesco.[73]

[73] Vessella, *La Banda*, 95–96.

136 The Renaissance Wind Band and Wind Ensemble

Procession of the Doge of Venice, by Matteo Pagani, ca. 1559

138 The Renaissance Wind Band and Wind Ensemble

Procession of the Doge of Venice, by Matteo Pagani, ca. 1559

PART 2
Civic Wind Bands

Civic Wind Bands

THE READER HAS SEEN, IN THE FIRST VOLUME OF THIS SERIES, the development of the European civic wind bands from purely functional roles, such as 'watch' duty, to the beginnings of more musical appearances during the fifteenth century. During the sixteenth century the civic wind band is seen not only in a much broader range of official civic appearances, but now also in music for the stage and the church. The tradition of public concerts, which were begun during the fifteenth century and represent the first real concerts of Western art music in the modern definition, are also more frequently found.

Many testimonials to the quality of these wind bands point to a real climax in most countries for this medium during the sixteenth century, Germany being somewhat of an exception as it continues to develop and reaches its climax in the seventeenth century.

In their literature the civic wind bands follow the lead of the court wind bands and for the first time we have substantial bodies of extant literature, especially from France and the low countries.

With regard to instrumentation, the civic wind bands also follow their court counterparts, reflecting the new and improved instruments made possible by the advances in wood working during the sixteenth century and adopting the fashionable consort principle. This wider availability of instruments brings a new demand: now the civic wind band member must be a musician capable of performing on a large number of instruments and, as the century continues, even on string instruments and in some cases must sing. Thus already in 1502 one reads of two tower musicians in Hall (Tyrol) who were fired by the town because they were not sufficiently qualified in playing 'all the winds.'[1] Similarily, three musicians applied, unsuccessfully I might add, in 1540 for membership in the civic band of Rothenburg an der Tauber, in Germany, promising that they were proficient on,

> trombones, cornetts, flutes, schreyerpfeifen, pipe and tabor, crumhorns, shawms, recorders, string instruments, organ and lutes.[2]

[1] Walter Salmen, *Musikleben im 16. Jahrhundert* (Leipzig, 1976), 15. (allein pfeiffen und nit [trompete] plasen haben können)

[2] Georg Reichert, *Erasmus Widmann (1572–1634)* (Stuttgart: Kohlhammer, 1951), 44.

> Pusaunen, zinckhen, zwerchpfeuffen, schreypfeuffen, thrumel und pfeuffen, krumbhörner, Pommert, fletten, uff saytten spilenn, Orgeln, Lautten schlahen, darein zu blasen.

As I have pointed out above, the purpose for this broad proficiency was to enable a small number of musicians to provide sufficient variety in instrumental texture during, for example, a long civic banquet. It follows that many towns assembled large collections of instruments for this purpose. Nürnberg, for example, which maintained only four or at most five civic musicians during the sixteenth century, had ninety instruments in 1575 in its Ratsmusik Musikkammer.[3] Some civic musicians, perhaps unwilling to trust the town to have the necessary instruments available and in good repair, owned large personal collections of all the instruments they might need. For example, upon the death (1613) of a town musician named Wolf Hueber, from Freistadt, in Austria, it was found that he owned three trombones, four trumpets, five cornetts, a shawm, nine 'Querpfeifen,' eight violins and a zither![4]

With established court and civic wind bands in even the smallest courts and towns of Europe, the wandering minstrel now becomes increasingly unwelcome. The civic musicians guilds[5] devoted considerable effort during the sixteenth century in attempting to prevent his playing for money in their individual towns. He continued to exist, but his day was distinctly past.[6]

Finally, a new form of 'civic' wind band music begins to appear during the sixteenth century: private wind bands supported by wealthy merchants, who are clearly trying to emulate the aristocracy. One example, perhaps, was the Krakow merchant, Jacobus Ellendus Augustanus, who died in 1577. He maintained a number of consorts of cornetts and crumhorns, in the latter case a consort of seven and another of eight instruments.[7] Another private citizen with an enormous collection of wind instruments was Raimund Fugger of Augsburg. His inventory, made in 1566, revealed eighty-two cornetts, fifty-nine recorders, forty-seven flutes, thirteen fagotti, two Doltzana, nine shawms, and eight crumhorns.[8]

The suggestion that persons with such large collections of instruments either maintained their own bands, or hired them for private performances, can be seen in the case of an English merchant, Thomas Kytson, of Hengrave, Suffolk. Here a surviving household account lists a payment in 1574 which reads, 'For seven cornetts bought for the musicians.'[9] Upon his death, in 1603, again a large collection of instruments was found,

3 Salmen, *Musikleben im 16. Jahrhundert*, 16.

4 Ibid., 15.

5 A few interesting new guilds appeared during the sixteenth century, such as the 'Juden Spielleutezunft' in Prague. (Salmen, *Musikleben im 16. Jahrhundert*, 14) In some places the guilds seem to have become more specialized during the sixteenth century. Kastner, in his *Manuel général de musique militaire* (Paris, 1848), 126, indicates that in Lisbon one found a separate shawm guild, with twenty members; one of singers, with one hundred and fifty members; one of twenty keyboard members; and one of twelve trumpet and timpani players.

6 A wood-cut in Olaus Magnus' *Historia de gentibus septentrionalibus* (Rome, 1555) shows three minstrels of the trumpet and a pipe and tabor man playing for dancing bears. (Example in Kiel, Universitätsbibliothek)

7 Adolf Chybiński, 'Polnische Musik und Musikkultur der 16. Jahrhunderts in ihren Beziehungen zu Deutschland,' in *Sammelbände der Internationalen Musikgesellschaft* 13 (1912): 465. Poland may have been a center for wind instrument manufacture serving the Eastern nations, for an extant letter, dated 1544, refers to a musician from Bracov (Roumania) who traveled there to purchase '1 sackbut, 1 great bass pommer, 1 alto shawm, 1 Korner, and 1 cornett.' See, Viorel Cosma, 'La Culture Musicale Roumaine à l'Époque de la Renaissance,' *Musica Antiqua-Acta Scientifica* (Bydgoszoz, 1969), 224.

8 Richard Schaal, 'Die Musikinstrumenten-Sammlung von Raimund Fugger d.J.,' *Archiv für Musikwissenschaft* 21, no. 4 (1964): 212ff. The collection also included one hundred and forty lutes.

9 Woodfill, *Musicians in English Society*, 263.

including large numbers of keyboard instruments and several consorts of strings. Among the wind instruments, there is a curious reference to 'one wind instrument like a virginal' and,

> One case (consort) of recorders, in number seven. Four cornutes, one being a mute cornute ... Two sackbuts ... Three hoeboys, a curtall and a lysarden. Two flutes ...[10]

[10] Ibid.

6   *Civic Wind Bands in England*

OFFICIAL CIVIC MUSIC IN ENGLAND reached its greatest period of development as a purely wind instrument medium during the sixteenth century. The proliferation of these wind bands, called 'waits,' continued throughout England. London, in addition to its official wait band, had at this time additional wait bands in all the major wards of the city, in Finsbury, Southwark, Blackfriars, Tower Hamlets, and the City of Westminster.

Although the official size of these bands may have been four or five players, often the performing ensemble was larger. This was made possible by yet another stratagem on the part of the musicians to increase their income by taking on official or unofficial apprentices. In London the members of the wait band were restricted to one apprentice each beginning in 1502, but increased to two in 1548. Therefore the actual performing band was at times as large as twelve before mid-century and eighteen for the second-half of the century.[1]

In addition to these 'official' civic wind bands, London was one of the few cities in sixteenth-century Europe which was large enough[2] to support independent wind minstrels, that is, there was still work available beyond that filled by the official civic bands and the court wind band. These resident minstrels led a constant fight to preserve their identity and to prevent the wandering minstrel from seeking work. The restrictions they sought were all the more difficult because London had a great number of members of other guilds, some of whom were also musicians, who were entitled, as freemen, to engage in any form of employment in the city.

These independent minstrels applied for and received a charter in 1500 as a Guild of Minstrels, claiming authority over even the city waits. They took as their patron saint, St. Anthony, swore to guard against unfitting language, and complained,

> The continual recourse of foreign minstrels, daily resorting to this City out of all the countries of England and enjoying more freedom than the freemen, causes the Minstrels of the City to be brought to such

[1] Woodfill, *Musicians in English Society from Elizabeth to Charles I*, 33.

[2] At the beginning of the sixteenth century seventy-five per cent of the people were farmers and did not live in towns and villages, thus most towns were relatively small. In fact only five cities in the Western world (Paris, Constantinople, Venice, Naples, and Milan) had more than 100,000 inhabitants; Leipzig, in 1585, had a population of 30,000. (Salmen, *Musikleben im 16. Jahrhundert*, 6)

poverty and decay that they are not able to pay 'lot and scot' and do their duty as other freemen do, since their living is taken from them by these foreigners.[3]

[3] Henry Alastair Ferguson Crewdson, *The Worshipful Company of Musicians* (London: Knight, 1971), 28.

They accused the 'foreign' (or, wandering) musicians of outrageous behaviour, appearing,

uninvited, sometimes as many as five or six at a time crowding to the end of the tables, playing without skill and causing great pain and displeasure to the Citizens and to their honest friends and neighbors.[4]

[4] Ibid.

It was of these 'foreign' musicians that Alexander Barclay, in his *Ship of Fools* (1508), wrote,

That by no means can they abide or dwell
Within their houses, but out they need must go
More wildly wandering than either buck or doe,
Some with their harps, another with his lute,
Another with his bagpipe or a foolish flute.[5]

[5] Quoted in Lyndesay Graham Langwill, *Waits, Wind Band, Horn* (London: Hinrichsen, 1952), 173.

When Henry VIII came to power, the minstrel guild renewed its charter, at the same time attempting to strengthen its position. Now it said no member could appear in a court without first appearing before the Master and the Wardens of the guild; it limited the appearances of apprentices (they had to pass a proficiency examination before playing in taverns, hostelries, or alehouses); and warned members not to take jobs away from each other.

It shall not be liefull to eny Mynstrell ffreman of the said ffelishp to supplante hire or gete out another mynstrell ffreman of the same ffelishp beyng hire or spoken to ffor to sue (serve) at eny Tryumphes, Ffeests, Dyns, Sowps, Mariags, Gilds or Brotherhede or eny such other doynge whereby eny such mynstrell shuld have perte of his lyvyng under the payn to eny such Supplanter ... of 40 shillings.[6]

[6] Crewdson, *The Worshipful Company of Musicians*, 34.

It seemed necessary, at this time, to specify even more clearly the proper respect due fellow members. Should a member be so misadvised as to rebuke, revile 'with unfitting language' or smite another freeman in the presence of the officers of the guild, he would be fined, 'regardaunt to the qualitye and quantitie of said misbehaviour.'[7]

[7] Ibid., 33.

The pressure of competition sent the Minstrel Guild[8] back to court in 1554, winning new regulations from the City Corporation against foreign competition. Noting that the competition was causing 'hindraunce of the gaines and profits of the poore minstrels being freemen of the Cytie,' the ordinances now forbid the foreigners to sing or play in public halls, taverns, etc., or to take on apprentices. Only the city waits could perform in the streets between ten o'clock in the evening and five o'clock in the morning and no minstrel, freeman, or 'foreign musicion,' could teach any form of dancing.[9] Because freemen of other professions, who enjoyed appearing as musicians during their free time, were now also representing serious competition to the 'official' minstrels, the 1554 ordinances observe that these part-time musicians,

> leaving the use of their crafts and manual occupations and giving themselves wholly to wandering abroad riot vice and idleness do commonly use nowadays to sing songs called 'Three Men's Songs' in taverns, at weddings, etc … to the great loss of the poor fellowship of minstrels, it is enacted that such conduct is to cease.[10]

During the sixteenth century, even the smaller towns in England were passing similar ordinances. A civic code in Beverley, passed in 1555, aimed at the 'part-time' musician, forbids any 'miller, shepherd, or husbandman playing on pipe or other instrument should perform without authority at any wedding or merry-making, outside his own parish.'[11] In York,[12] one finds a 1561 ordinance concerning the non-resident minstrel, specifying that 'no manner of foreigner' be allowed to practice any form of minstrelsy,

> singing or playing upon any instrument within any parish within this city or franchise thereof upon any church holidays or dedication days hallowed or kept within the same parish, or any brotherhood's or freeman's dinner or dinners.[13]

These various ordinances in England which are directed toward the wandering minstrel reflect in part a growing concern of civic authorities for all kinds of beggars, peddlers, vagabonds, and rogues; civilization was beginning to think of itself as civilized. A national law passed in 1547 defined a vagabond as any able-bodied person without an income suf-

---

[8] By the end of the sixteenth century the fortunes of this guild of independent minstrels seem to have reached a low ebb, for one finds such references as 'the poore decayed company.' They appear at this time to have given up all attempts at controlling the competition, from any quarter, and petitions to the Corporation deal mostly with the teaching and taking on of apprentices.

[9] Crewdson, *The Worshipful Company of Musicians*, 36–37.

[10] Ibid.

[11] Duncan, *The Story of Minstrelsy*, 217. This same ordinance names a guild leader, Alderman of the Minstrels, with stewards and deputies authorized to control membership and collect dues (customable duties).

[12] Another interesting ordinance in York deals with apprentices, stating that the members should instruct the apprentice in the art of conversation, in addition to just music, so that 'he may be well thought (of, if he serves) a nobleman or man of worship.' (Woodfill, *Musicians in English Society from Elizabeth to Charles I*, 111)

[13] Ibid., 112.

ficient to support him who was found 'either like a seving man wanting a master or like a beggar,' wandering and 'not applying himself to some honest and legal art, science, service or labor ... for three days or more.'[14] A justice of the peace was empowered to decide, in the case of an independent minstrel for example, if he were following an 'allowed art,' or a vagabond. The penal ties were rather serious: branding with a 'V,' enslaving for two years, whipping until bloody, or the loss of ears, to name a few!

An ordinance of 1572 specifically mentions musicians as potential vagabonds and attempts to restrict their travels. Now, traveling without a patron or proper traveling papers could result in his being 'grievously whipped, and burnt through the gristle of the right ear with a hot iron of the compass of an inch about' on first conviction and death on the third conviction![15] A similar ordinance in 1597 requires all traveling musicians to wear the uniform of their employers.

Returning now to the organization of the official civic wind bands in England, one finds numerous records which demonstrate they were acquiring the broad range of new instruments which the sixteenth century produced. An eyewitness who heard the Exeter civic band in 1575, describes their instruments as,

> a Doble Curtall, a Lyserden (tenor cornett?), Two tenor Hoyboyes, a Treble Hoyboyes, a Cornet, a sett or case (or consort) of ffower Recorders.[16]

In 1572, the instruments in 'Custodye' of the well-known Norwich Waits were,

> ij Trompettes; iiij Sacquebuttes; iij haukboyes; v Recorders beeying a Whoall noyse;[17] and one old Lyzardyne.[18]

This same band sought funds from the city in 1583 for expanding their collection of instruments, 'they bee at greatter chardges then heretofor by providing of sondry sorts of Instruments which heretofore haue not been by them vsed.'

The minutes of the Court of Common Council gives the instrumentation of the London Waits in 1553 as trumpets, shawms, sackbuts, fife, drums and cymbal for 'loud music,'

[14] Ibid., 56.

[15] Ibid., 57.

[16] John Hooker, 'Description of the Citie of Exeter,' unpublished manuscript, quoted in Langwill, *Waits, Wind Band, Horn*, 176.

[17] A 'Whoall noyse' (whole noise) being a consort.

[18] Fox, *Instruments of Processional Music*, 26.

and flutes and a lute for 'soft music.'[19] Soon they too were enlarging their collection, the records of the Court of Aldermen of London listing the purchase in 1559 of a new sackbut, a consort of recorders and six cornetts in 1569, and in 1597,

[19] Rachel and Allen Percival, *The Court of Elizabeth the First* (London: Stainer and Bell, 1976), 15.

> The Chamberlain shall presently buy and provide the several instruments called a double saggbutt, a single saggbutt and a curtal for the musicians at the charge of the city.[20]

[20] Langwill, *Waits, Wind Band, Horn*, 177.

The ever expanding forms of entertainment offered by the waits are demonstrated by the fact that the London Waits even had begun to sing on occasion after 1555. The most far reaching development in instrumentation, however, came at the end of the sixteenth century with the incorporation of string instruments, for this sounded the death-knell for the golden age of the civic wind band in England. During the seventeenth century the mixed consort would become more popular for indoor music, with the pure wind band appearing only in outdoor ceremonial functions. For the civic bands mentioned above, one can document the arrival of strings in Norwich in 1585 and in Exeter in 1602.

The change in instrumentation of the London Wait Band can be seen in the publication by Thomas Morely of his famous *First Booke of Consort Lessons* (1599). This collection of twenty-five compositions by unnamed composers is dedicated to the Waits of London, yet recommends performance by 'Treble Lute, Pandora, Cittern, Base-violl, Flute, and Treble-Violl.'[21] To encourage wider sales, as was often the case, the editor, Morley, suggests other instruments may be substituted, 'to the ende that whose skill or liking regardeth not the one, may attempt some other.'

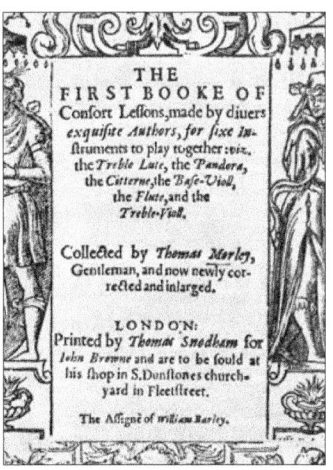

The dedication to the waits is interesting as it contains a tribute to their skill, in drawing a distinction with the common musicians of the street.

> ... for I desire no to satisfe bablers, which are baser than brute beasts in reprouing excellencie, neuer attaine to the first degree of any commendable Science or misterie. But as the ancient custome is of this most honorable and renowned Cittie hath beene euer, to retaine and maintane excellent and expert Musitians, to adorne your Honors fauors, Feasts and solemne meetings: to those your Lordships Waits ... I recommend the same to your seruants carefull and skilfull handling.[22]

[21] A reproduction of the first edition title and dedication page, together with suggested composers, can be found in the modern edition by Sydney Beck (New York: Peters, 1959).

[22] Quoted in Beck, ibid., ix.

Even though this collection is recommended for basically a string ensemble, two important points must be made. First, this ensemble was a new one and only the rarest references to it can be found before the final decade of the sixteenth century.[23] Second, as this collection is only an arrangement of earlier wait literature, much of this music may have been originally performed by the waits in their earlier wind band instrumentation.[24]

The introduction of strings into other civic bands in England by the final decade of the sixteenth century is suggested by a 1590 document from Chester which deals with the question of ownership of shawms, cornetts, recorders and 'violens' used by a deceased member of that town's band.[25]

The expanding demands and, as we shall see below, the quarrelsome nature of the musicians, gave the city fathers special concern in the appointment of leaders for the wind bands. York, in 1567, elected one, Robert Hewet, 'a quiet and meet man to be the chief wait.'[26] The London civic government sought, in 1570, outside the country and brought to town a Dutchman, Segar van Pelkam, to lead the London Waits. He remained until 1581 when he returned home with a gift from the city of ten pounds.[27]

[23] Beck, ibid., 15ff, in stating, 'That broken music had a strong attraction for the nobility is vividly set forth in eye-witness accounts of the entertainments prepared for the Queen during her Progresses' is quite misleading. In fact, the eyewitnesses mention either 'broken consorts' or the instrumentation of the Morley work, in only two or three places, whereas wind bands and ensembles are frequently mentioned. There are many references to 'consort,' but nothing to suggest that they were string consorts or mixed consorts—indeed when there is a following reference it is almost invariably reflected to have been a wind consort. There is nothing, for example, to suggest, as Beck does, that the 'Consort of Musicke' within the dolphin's belly during the entertainments of 1575 at Kenilworth was a 'broken consort.' No eyewitness called it that and, as I have indicated in my discussion of this event above, one eyewitness used the frequent synonym for the wind band, 'Noise.' In any case, the ensemble was hidden from the view of all observers and all descriptions were of the ear, and not the eye. It is my belief that the few references to 'broken consorts' before 1590 appear not because they were describing the familiar, but because they were describing something new. The contemporaries were drawing a clear distinction, I believe, with the more familiar consort of winds in specifying a 'broken consort.' The seventeenth century, of course, was another story.

[24] Percival, *The Court of Elizabeth the First*, 83, 'These "lessons" were in fact arrangements of tunes played by the City Waits.'

[25] Joseph Bridge, 'Town Waits and their Tunes,' *Proceedings of the Musical Association* 54 (1928): 79. William Massie, Mayor. At which day matter was in question between Ales Williams, late wife of Thomas Williams, late one of the Waytsmen of the Cittie on the one part, and Christopher Burton and William Maddock the other Waitman of the said Cittie, for and concerning their instruments of music, viz. the howboies, the Recorders, the Cornets, and violens whereof the said Ales claymeth a part as to her said late husband in his lief tyme belonginge, which they deny to yeld unto; but are contented and soe are now agreed and it is now fully ordered by assent, that the said instruments shall from hensfforth for ever remayne continue and bee the survivors of them … or else to remayne forever to the said Citie.

[26] Woodfill, *Musicians in English Society from Elizabeth to Charles I*, 87.

[27] Unsigned article included in Crewdson, *The Worshipful Company of Musicians*, 170.

The civic wait bands continued to take great pride in their official civic uniforms. The Leicester Waits wore scarlet gowns, edged with gold; London Waits now had two sets of gowns, one for summer and another for winter.

The pay which the members of the town bands received continued to be meager, Cambridge, for example, fixed the wages at two pounds per year. Sometimes the pay was fixed in the form of money and goods, and so in Lincoln, in 1599, one reads of a raise in wages of one hundred shillings and also the provision of 'four coats yearly at Christmas over and besides the coats they have now.'[28]

Many towns made direct tax assessments on the citizens for the support of the waits. A typical new tax was announced by Leicester, in 1581, as follows:

> It is agreed that every Inhabitant or housekeeper in Leicester (being of reasonable ability) shall be taxed (at the discretion of Mr. Mayor) what they shall quarterly give to the Waytes towards the amending of their living. In consideration whereof the said Waytes shall keep the town, and to play every night and morning orderly, both winter and summer, and not to go forth of the town to play except to fairs and weddings, and then by licence of Mr. Mayor. Item, that no strangers, viz. Waytes, minstrels or other musicians whatsoever be suffered to play within this town, neither at weddings nor fair times or any other times whatsoever.[29]

This general taxation apparently was not generously received by the public for the following year a new system was tried, now the mayor selected only leading citizens to support the waits.

> It is agreed that the twenty-four (leading men of the town) shall give twelve pence per quarter and forty-eight sixpence per quarter for Wayts wages and the other inhabitants to be taxed by the Mayor from time to time.[30]

As during the fifteenth century, wait bands were able to augment their income by appearances in other towns, where they were invariably rewarded by the host town. To allow their own waits to travel, therefore, was an easy way for a town to help provide for the financial support of their musicians. Nottingham, in 1617, even granted an increase in the wages of their

[28] Woodfill, *Musicians in English Society from Elizabeth to Charles I*, 93ff., summarizes the wages for several English town wait bands.

[29] Bridge, 'Town Waits and their Tunes,' 80.

[30] Ibid.

waits, observing that 'their gratuities abroad in their travels are not so beneficial as heretofore they have been.'[31] An indication of how wide spread this practice was can be seen in the case of Nottingham itself, which in the single year, 1571–1572, rewarded visiting wait bands from Wakefield, Derby, Newark, Barton upon Humber, Leicester, Chesterfield, Ledes, Oxford, Ratford, and Grantham.[32]

Sometimes, of course, the travels were of a partly ceremonial or official character. In 1577 one reads of the London Waits traveling to Sir Nicholas Bacon's house in Gorambury 'in a wagon with four horses' to perform before the Queen who was visiting there.[33]

On even more rare occasions, waits must have had the opportunity to travel abroad. In 1589, the famous Sir Francis Drake was preparing to sail to Portugal, 'to singe the King of Spain's beard,' and made a request to the Norwich Corporation for the loan of their wait band to accompany him at sea.

> This day was redd in the Court, a letter sent to Master Mair and his brethern from Sir Francis Drake, wherebye he desyreth that the Waytes of this Citie may be sent to hym, to go the new intended voyage; whereunto the Waytes being here called do all assent, whereupon it is agreed that they should have vi cloaks of stemell cloth made them redy before they go; and that a wagon shall be provided to carry them and their instruments, and that they shall have iiiilb to buye them, three new howboyes and one treble recorder, and xlb to bear their chargys; and that the Citie shall hyre the wagon and paye for it. Also that the Chamberlyn shall pay Peter Spratt xs.3d. for a saquebut case; and the Waytes to delyver to the Chamberlyn before they go the citie's cheanes.[34]

This particular adventure of Sir Francis was a military failure and many lives were lost; of the six Norwich waits who made the voyage, only two returned.

The personal misfortune suffered by those four waits reminds one that these early wind players must be thought of as humans, and not mere historical characters. No doubt among them were representatives of the best men of their times, and also those who failed to achieve so high a standard. It is clear from the surviving records that the city governments moved swiftly if their character threatened to bring discredit to the town. One, Thomas a Wait, was warned in 1561 by the York city officials that he must,

---

[31] Woodfill, *Musicians in English Society from Elizabeth to Charles I*, 103–106.

[32] Ibid., 288.

[33] Crewdson, *The Worshipful Company of Musicians*, 32.

[34] Bridge, 'Town Waits and their Tunes,' 84–85. Upon his death, the ship of Sir Francis was found to contain a 'chest of instrumentes of musicke,' and the inventory listed 'a lute, hobboyes, sagbutes, cornettes & orphorions, bandora & suche like.' (Carl Bridenbaugh, *Vexed and Troubled Englishmen* (New York: Oxford University Press, 1968),348).

respite to learne and applie himself in the instruments and songs belonging to the sayd wayts, and to leave his unthrifty gamyng upon payne to be putte forth of that office.[35]

The same officials in 1584 dismissed two waits, charging,

their evil and disorderly behavior, to the discredit of this city. Viz. for that they have gone abroad, in the country, in very evil apparel, with their hose forth at their heels, also for that they are common drunkards and cannot so cunningly play on their instruments as they ought.[36]

A fellow member of the York Wait Band testified against one of those dismissed in 1584.

He is become so disordered and distempered and such a person as will be oft drunk and is at diverse times troubled with the falling sickness and his hearing imperfect or almost deaf as that he is not sufficient to serve in his place, And that diverse times he hath so disordered himself in the exercise of his place in playing before. The magistrates of this city and others as that he hath made the rest of them by his playing forth of tune and time to be ashamed of themselves and they to be thereby thought of the hearers to have no such skill as is requisite for their places to their great discredit.[37]

While this last testimony sounds perhaps exaggerated, it does suggest that the possible failings of a musician then read much as they might today. As a matter of fact, the entire York band was dismissed in 1566 and again in 1572, as were those in Nottingham in 1578, Ipswich in 1597, and Leicester in 1563. The dismissal order in the case of the Leicester Waits read,

The Waits because they cannot agree together are therefore now dismissed from being the Town Waits from henceforth.[38]

During the sixteenth century the waits, in many towns, continued their traditional and original function as watchmen against fire and theft, although this was a tradition beginning to die. In Coventry they divided the city into quarters and alternated during the year, although some evenings still had the midnight to four o'clock shift. In Ipswich an order in 1587 states that the Waits shall walk about the town,

[35] Ibid., 72.

[36] Woodfill, *Musicians in English Society from Elizabeth to Charles I*, 88.

[37] Ibid.

[38] Bridge, 'Town Waits and their Tunes,' 73.

from Michaelmas until our Lady-day … (and) shall go thereabout nightly from two of the clock until they have gone throughout the town.[39]

39 Woodfill, *Musicians in English Society from Elizabeth to Charles I*, 75.

Leicester in 1582 ordered the waits to play 'about the town both evening and morning, continually and orderly at reasonable and seasonable times.'[40] A London order in 1553 forbidding anyone to play any instrument in the open streets between ten o'clock at night and five o'clock in the morning suggests that at least this city still considered the night watch of some importance.

40 Ibid., 77.

From a musical standpoint, it was probably the great civic celebrations which allowed the wait bands to present themselves at their best. In London the annual highpoint of civic ceremony was the Lord Mayor's Procession by water to Westminster. An eyewitness account of this procession in 1553, by Henry Machyn, a member of the Merchant Tailors Guild, gives us the character of this event.

> On 20 October the new Lord Mayor, Sir Thomas White, went toward Westmynster, craftes of London in their best levery … with trumpets blohyng and the whets (waits) playing … a goodly fuyst (galley) trimmed with banners and guns … And then came trumpeters blohyng, and then came those in gownes, and capes and hosse and blue sylke slevys … and then came a duiflill (devil) and after that cam all the bachelors all in a leaveray, and skarlett hods; and then cam the pageant of Saint John Baptist gorgeously with goodly speeches; and then cam all the kynges trumpeters blowhyng, and every trumpeter having skarlet capes, and the wetes capes and godly banars, and then the craftes and then the wettes playhyng, and then my lord mayrs offesers, and then my lord mayre.[41]

41 Warwick, *A Noise of Music*, 23.

In 1556, besides the waits who played when the Mayor took his oath and 'at other accustomed times,' there were twenty-four royal trumpeters and various other winds and percussion. In 1561 there were again the waits, five harps, and,

> There was also a grett shutyng of gunnes and trumpettes and blohyng … and so to Powlles (St. Paul's) chyrche-yarde, and ther met ym a pagantt gorgyously mad, with chylderyn, with dyvers instrumentes playing and syngyng.[42]

42 Ibid.

The procession of 1575 began with 'devils' who cleared the route of march, then the city flags, drums, and a fife. A London haberdasher, William Smythe, described the London Wait Band.

> Then a set of hautboys playing … certain wifflers (young men with staves) in velvet coats, and chains of gold … then the pageant of Triumph richly decked … sixteen trumpeters … the drum and fife of the city … and after, the waits of the city in blue gowns, red sleeves and caps, everyone having his silver collar about his neck.[43]

[43] Woodfill, *Musicians in English Society from Elizabeth to Charles I*, 48.

There were similar ceremonial appearances for the installation of mayors in other cities, as well as numerous other civic occasions. There was the aldermen's 'beef breakfast' in York, the Mayor's dinner in Nottingham, and in Liverpool performances before the door of every former civic official.

News of military victories was always a source for celebration as well. When the English forces took possession of Edinburgh in 1544, the Cambridge Waits joined in the procession which celebrated the occasion.

> Payd to the wayts for goyng abowte the Towne with Mr. Mayor when Edenboroughe in Scotland was wonne, iijs. iiijd.[44]

[44] Langwill, *Waits, Wind Band, Horn*, 174.

For towns by the sea, the arrival of ships was always an important occasion. There are accounts of wait bands in Whitehaven welcoming the seafaring men from their voyages. In Liverpool the tradition was to wait until the day after their arrival, before the band appeared at the door of the homes of the sailors and their families.[45]

[45] Bridge, 'Town Waits and their Tunes,' 66, 84–85.

Civic welcomes were never more important nor festive than when the visiting party was a member of the royal family. For such a visit in 1549 not only the London Waits were heard in performance, but also another eight wait bands formed from the Minstrels Company.

The London Waits, of course, had their part to fill in coronation processions, such as that of Elizabeth I in 1558. An eyewitness was impressed by the quality of their performance.

> Uppon the porche of Saint Peters church dore, stode the waites of the citie, which did geve a pleasant noyse with their instrumentes as the Quenes majestie did passe by.[46]

[46] John Nichols, ed., *The Progresses and Public Processions of Queen Elizabeth* (London, 1788), vol. 1.

The City of London gave the queen a special entertainment on 1–2 July 1559, called a 'muster,' which included a parade by fourteen hundred men, mock battles, and wind music.

> … and to set the two battles in array to skirmish before the Queen; then came the trumpets to blow on each part, the drums beating, and the flutes (fifes?) playing.[47]

[47] Ibid.

When the queen visited Norwich, in 1578, the Norwich Waits greeted her arrival by a performance at the city gate.

> The waites of the citie were placed with loude musicke, who cheerefully and melodiously welcomed hyr Majestie into the citie.[48]

[48] Ibid., vol. 2, quoting an account by 'Ber. Gar.,' published in London in 1578.

Tradition has it that the queen was so pleased with this particular performance that she gave each of the five waits a new instrument and a house on King Street as well![49]

[49] Bridge, 'Town Waits and their Tunes,' 83.

During the sixteenth century one also finds the local civic waits performing for university ceremonies. The Oxford Waits, for example, performed in 1583 as part of ceremonies welcoming a 'noble and learned' Polish person to the university. He was met by the Oxford officials, given gloves, presented with a Latin oration, and,

> which being done a consort of musicians, that stood over the East Gate, played on their wind-music till they were gone into the City.[50]

[50] Quoted in Nan Cooke Carpenter, *Music in the Medieval and Renaissance Universities* (Norman: University of Oklahoma Press, 1958), 176.

Carpenter believes that references to trumpets may even be references to university employees. She cites their appearance in a pageant in 1556, 'Item. a show in trinite college in ther courte of the wynninge of an holde and takinge of prisoners, with wytes, trumpettes, gonnes, and squybbes,' and a similar appearance on the occasion of a visit by Queen Elizabeth to Cambridge in 1564, 'Then came the Trumpetters and by solemn blast, declared her Majesty to approach.'[51]

[51] Ibid., 195.

Another sphere of major activity by the wait bands was their participation in the performances of the great body of dramatic literature of the Elizabethan theatre. This association had its roots in the traditional relationship of both the dramatic literature and the waits with the church. For example, early in the century one reads of a minstrel and three waits from Cambridge assisting with a play, *The Holy Martyr St. George* at Basingbourne[52] and in 1517 the household book of the Hickling Priory contains an entry, 'Regiis histrionibus vocatis waytes.'[53]

An account from the city of York, dated 1561, indicates that the waits in this city were given a fundamental responsibility for producing these great civic–church dramas. The Guild of Minstrels, including the Waits of York, were instructed at their own charge,

> to bring forth and cawese to be plaied the pageant of Corpus Christi, viz. Herold and Messenger enquiringe the Thre Kyngs of the Child Jesu, sometime accustomed to be brought forth at the charg of the late Masons of this Cittye on Corpus Christi Day.[54]

On some occasions, the waits—versatile entertainers as they were—apparently took a speaking part on the stage. An account from Norwich, in 1550, suggests as much.

> This Paggeante was done by the wagghts of the Cytte of Norwich. There was a Skaffoold made at Sancte Peters of Houndegate Church. Styelle rounde like a Pavyllion: Richele adorned, full of targetts, with a Morien on the topp standing naked, with a target and a great Darte in his hand; within which stood an Auncyente personage who represented Tyme, hauing the speeche to the Mayor as he came forby, following the procession.[55]

In the city of Lincoln, in 1565, the city fathers had the waits dress as senators and address the public with warnings about the proper observation of Christmas. The speeches made by the waits in this instance, are extant.[56]

FIRST SENATOR
The Aungells with myrthe the schepperdes did obey;
When they sang *Gloria in Excelsis* in tunes mysticall;
The byrdes with solemnyte sang on every spray,
And the beastes for joye made reverence in every stall.

SECOND SENATOR
Therefore with a contrite hart let us be merye all
Havyng a stedfst faith and a love most amyable,
Disdayning no man of power greate or small
For a crewell oppressor is nothyng commendable.

[52] Langwill, *Waits, Wind Band, Horn*, 173.

[53] Bridge, 'Town Waits and their Tunes,' 81.

[54] Ibid.

[55] Ibid.

[56] Ibid., 82.

THIRD SENATOR
That is the chiefe cause hither we were sent,
To gyve the people warning to have all things perfitly,
For they that do not, breaketh Mr. Mayor's commandement
And according to the order, punysshed must they be.

As one nears, chronologically, the period of Elizabethan theatre, one sees the waits beginning to assume the role of musicians again, rather than actual speaking roles. In 1567, in Newcastle for example, one reads of the performance of a miracle play on Corpus Christi Day for which the Corporation paid two shillings, 'to the waites, for playeinge befor the players.'[57] The Norwich Waits, in 1570, went to court to obtain the privilege of playing regularly in the theaters.

> The whole company of waytes of this Citie did come into this Court and craved that they might have leve to play comodies and Interludes and other such pieces and Tragedes which shall seem to them meete; which petition is granted, they not playing in the Tyme of Divine Service and Sermons.[58]

On one occasion in 1562, a Chelmsford dramatic performance included not only the Bristol Waits, but forty other minstrels.[59]

By the end of the sixteenth century the participation of the various wait bands seems clear from occasional stage directions:

Anonymous, *Sir Thomas More* (ca. 1596),
  'the waytes playe.'

Heywood, *If you know not me, you know nobody* (1605), II,
  'Enter Sir Thomas Ramsie, the 2 Lords, My Lady Ramsie, the Waits in Sergeants' gowns ...'

Heming, *The Fatal Contract* (ca. 1635),
  'Enter the Eunuch, whilst the waits play softely.'

Who played the music for Shakespeare? Some of it was no doubt provided by the Southwark Waits, as Shakespeare's Globe Theater was in their district. This was one of the best known wait bands of this period and in one play, *The Knight of the Burning Pestle*, they are actually mentioned in the dialog.[60]

[57] Langwill, *Waits, Wind Band, Horn*, 173.

[58] Bridge. 'Town Waits and their Tunes,' 81.

[59] Chambers, *The Elizabethan Stage*, 2:140.

[60] Quoted in Hartnoll, ed., *Shakespeare in Music*, 25.

CITIZEN: What stately music have you? You have Shawms?
SPEAKER OF THE PROLOGUE: Shawms! no.
CITIZEN: No! I'm a thief, if my mind did not give me so. Ralph plays a stately part, and he must needs have shawms: I'll be at the charge of them myself, rather than we'll be without them.
SPEAKER OF THE PROLOGUE: So you are like to be.
CITIZEN: Why, and so I will be: there's two schillings,—let's have the waits of Southwark; they are as rare fellows as any are in England; and that will fetch them all o'er the water with a vengeance, as if they were mad.
SPEAKER OF THE PROLOGUE: So you shall have them.

There is evidence that the wait bands played real public concerts during the sixteenth century. A description of the concerts played at mid-century by the Norwich Wait Band is found in a notice by the Mayor's Court in 1553, ruling,

> that the waits of the City shall have liberty and license every Sunday at night and other holidays at night betwixt this and Michaelmas next coming to come to the guildhall, and upon the nether leads of the same hall next the council house shall betwixt the hours of seven and eight of the clock at night blow and play upon their instruments the space of half an hour to the rejoicing and comfort of the hearers thereof.[61]

[61] Woodfill, *Musicians in English Society from Elizabeth to Charles I*, 81–82.

These concerts continued until at least 1570 and the instrumentation of this band is perhaps suggested by that known for 1572: two trumpets, four sackbuts, three hautboys, and five recorders.[62]

[62] Grove, 13:329.

In London in 1571, the year after the construction of the Royal Exchange Building, the waits began giving an hour-long concert from the turret of the building every Sunday and Holy Day evening, from 25 March until Michaelmas. This tradition continued until 1642 when a more puritan feeling prevented Sunday concerts.

Yet another performance opportunity for wind bands in sixteenth-century London was the celebrations of the lawyers. These celebrations were held at the Temple (between Temple Bar and the River Thames), center then, as now, of legal training. The lawyers held an annual 'Revel' at Christmas focusing on the honorary court of an honored 'Constable.'

There is an unusually complete account of one of these Revels, held in 1562, honoring Lord Robert Dudley, who was styled, 'Palaphilos, Constable of the Inn.' The festivities lasted from Chrismas Eve until the Twelfth Night, consisting of a series of banquets. Everything was organized with the highest of protocol, beginning with the first call for dinner.

> We entred the Prince his hall, where anon we heard the noise of drum and fyfe. 'What meaneth this drum?' said I. Quoth he, 'This is to warn gentlemen of the household to repair to the dresser.'

The food entered the hall with a great musical announcement.

> The Prince so served with tender meats, sweet fruits, and dainty delicates ... and at every course the trumpetters blew the couragious blast of deadly war, with noise of drum and fyfe, with the sweet harmony of violins, sackbutts, recorders, and cornetts, with other instruments of musick, as it seemed Apollo's harp had tuned their stroke.
>
> ...
>
> At the first course the minstrels must sound their instruments, and go before (the food) ... all which time the musick must stand right above the herth side, with the noise of their musick; and faces direct toward the highest table: and that done, to return into the buttery, with their musick sounding. At the second course every table is to be served, as at the first course, in every respect; which performed, the servitors and musicians are to resort to the place assigned for them to dine at; which is the Valects or Yeoman's table, beneath the skreen. Dinner ended, the musicians prepare to sing a song, at the highest table.

On the following day, Christmas Day, another great meal was served.

> At the first course is served in a fair and large bore's-head, upon a silver platter, with minstralsye. Two gentlemen in gownes are to attend at supper, and to bear two fair torches of wax, next before the musicians and trumpetters, and stand above the fire with the musick, till the first course be served-in through the hall. Which performed, they, with the musick are to return to the buttery.

Another banquet, held on St. Stephen's Day, featured a pageant with a more rustic theme, the hunt. Lord Dudley, dressed in a costume appropriate to the theme, entered the hall, arrayed with a fair, rich, compleat harness, white and bright, and gilt, with a next of fethers of all colours upon his crest or helm, and a gilt pole-axe in his hand: to whom his associate the Lieutenant of the Tower, armed with a fair white armour, next of fethers in his helm, and a like pole-axe in his hand; and with them sixteen trumpetters; four drums, and fifes going in rank before them: with them attendeth four men in white harness … halberds in their hands … with the drums, trumpets, and musick, go three times about the fire. Then cometh in the Master of the Game, apparelled in green velvet: and the Ranger of the Forest also … with either of them a hunting-horn about their necks: blowing together three blasts of venery, they pace round about the fire three times … a huntsman cometh into the hall, with a fox and a purse-net; with a cat, both bound at the end of a staff; and with them nine or ten couple of hounds, with the blowing of hunting-hornes. And the fox and cat are by the hounds set upon, and killed beneath the fire.[63]

[63] These descriptions taken from Dugdale's 'Origines Juridiciales,' quoted in Nichols, *The Progresses and Public Processions of Queen Elizabeth*, vol. 1.

After the fox and cat were torn into a thousand bloody gobbets, amid cheers, dinner was served.

Perhaps it was the use of music for such purposes that caused the Rev. John Northbrooke to write,

> YOUTH. What say you to music and playing upon instruments, is not that a good exercise?
> AGE. Music is very good, if it be lawfully used, and not unlawfully abused.[64]

[64] Rev. John Northbrooke, *Spiritus est vicarius Christi in terra. A treatise wherein dicing, dauncing, vaine apaies or enterludes with other idle pastimes, etc. commonly used on the Sabboth day, are reprooved* (London, 1579).

7 Civic Wind Bands in the Low Countries

ALL EVIDENCE POINTS TO THE CIVIC WIND BANDS of the Low Countries as being distinguished musical organizations during the first half of the sixteenth century. This seems clear from the extant literature composed for them to play and from the fact that players from this area were imported to courts and towns all over Europe. Even a city so relatively distant as Lisbon used only musicians from Flanders in their civic band from 1495–1521.[1]

During the sixteenth century the more prosperous towns had five and sometimes six wind players, but even the smallest towns had four players.[2] The actual size of the ensemble often fluctuated with the economic conditions in the particular city.

Thus, in Ghent, the 'extra' fifth player in the civic wind band appears and disappears in the civic records between 1486–1535,[3] although on at least one occasion in 1521 there were not only six members in the band, but also an ensemble of civic trumpet players. The band in this instance is given as six shawms and sackbuts, who were paid for performing before the Regent of the Low Countries, Margaret of Austria.[4]

After 1535 six players seems to have been the standard number, although on occasion the civic records mention only four.[5] Several documents give the instrumentation of the six-member wind band at this time as pairs of discant and tenor shawms and sackbuts.

> Item, paid to Pieter de Coninc, Goldsmith ... for two silver sackbuts, two discant and two tenor shawms ... to be delivered to the six shawms of the city.[6]

In 1542 Ghent hired Cornelis Van Winckle, a 'shawmist who plays the sackbut,'[7] who appears in 1552 as being in possession of the city's 'excellent' bombard,[8] demonstrating once again the ability of these players to play several instruments. This same player requested in 1551, and received, from the city

---

[1] Grove, 11:25.

[2] Keith Polk, 'Ensemble Instrumental Music in Flanders: 1450–1550,' an unpublished paper from which much of this information is taken with gratitude to this distinguished scholar.

[3] Ghent, *Stads Rekeningen* (this, and similar references, now in the Belgian State Archives, Brussels), 1485–1486, fol. 85; 1486–1487, fol. 210v; 1513, fol. 115; 1518, fol. 81; 1529, fol. 67; 1534–1535, fol. 67.

[4] Quoted in Vander Straeten, *La Musique aux Pays-Bas*, 4:123.

> A vj joueurs de hautbois et sacquebutes de la ville de Gand, le xx juillet, v philippus d'or.
> ......
> Aux trompettes de la ville de Gand, le xxj juillet xve xxj, la somme de vj florins d'or de xxviij patars.

[5] Ghent, *Stads Rekeningen*, 1545–1546, fol. 224.

[6] Ibid., 1540–1541, fol. 246v.

> Item betaelt Peter de Coninc goudsmet ... van twee selveren Zackbouten twee bovenzanghen ende twee teneuren scalmeye ... ghelevert te werdene den zes scalmeyers deser stede.

See also, Vander Straeten, 4:125.

> Nous savons, qu'en 1540, les six ménestrels étaient divisés ainsi: deux saquebutes, deux dessus de *scalmeye* et deux ténors du même instrument.

[7] Ghent, *Stads Rekeningen*, 1542–1543, fol. 294v.

[8] Ghent, *Stads Rekeningen, Jaarenregister*, 1551–1552 (exselent bombaerde).

a double bombard and two 'bassets.' At the same time, the city judged two of the sackbuts to be unfit for service and used them to acquire two shawms.[9]

The civic wind band which interests us the most today is the one which represented Antwerp, this because one of its members was the famous Tielman Susato. He was a member of this band from 1529 to 1549 and the music he composed for it is one of the crown jewels of Renasissance music.[10]

This wind band seems to have been five members from about 1529 and a document of 1532 reveals, as was often the case, that these *stad pijpers* had access to an extensive instrument collection, which included twenty-eight flutes, nineteen crumhorns, and two soprano and two tenor shawms.[11] This document also speaks of 'ii trompetten ende een velt trompet,' used by these players. The latter seems clearly to be a 'field trumpet,' however Polk believes, in view of the confusion of terminology at this time, that the first instruments were slide-trumpets, if not trombones. This view is strengthened by a later document (1542) in which Susato purchased two additional 'trompetten' for use in the church.[12]

In addition, we know the names of at least two other members of this band, Jan de Brasser and the famous Hans Nagel.[13] The city also supplied uniforms for the regularly employed members.[14]

---

[9] Ibid., 1551, fol. 215v.

Betaelt Cornelis Vander Winckele de somme van xx s. gro., ter causen van ghelycker somme dyer noch ghebreect over't voldoen van neghen ponden gr. daervooren hy met ten anderen zynnen medeghesellen scalmeyers deser stede ghecocht heeft drie instrumenten omme der stede daermede te dienene, ghenaempt eene dobbele bombaerde ende twee bassetten accorderende met de huerlieder scalmeypypen, van welcken coope de resterende acht ponden gro. hy bewesen es te betalene, aen Dewez, goudsmet, van den overghescotte vanden zelvere ghecommen van twee zelveren zackbouten, de welcke als niet bequame gheweest om spelen, ghedaen breken zyn ende dan of ghemaect twee zelveren hecsels of teekenen voor de twee scalmeyers die gheen hecsel en hadden, naer 'tverclaers vander ordonnancie, xx s. gr.

[10] Polk, 'Ensemble Instrumental Music in Flanders,' 3, 6. Susato may have joined earlier; civic financial accounts are not extant before 1529.

[11] Antwerp, *Stads Rekeningen*, 1530–1531, fol. 15.

[12] Ibid., 1541–1542, fol. 88.

[13] Nagel was widely traveled, having played in the English court at the turn of the century, then in the Spanish court of Philip the Fair, and finally with the Mechelen civic wind band from 1508–1518.

[14] Polk, 'Ensemble Instrumental Music in Flanders,' 18, 27.

Little documentation exists for the Brussels civic wind band because a late seventeenth century fire destroyed almost all civic records from this period. However, it can be seen in the records of appearances of this band in other towns that it had four members by 1530, increasing to five or six during the next twenty years.[15]

In some towns the decision to enlarge the band appears to have been a hard fought one. In Bruges, for example, the fifth player is listed only as an 'expectant' musician, even though the city provided five uniforms between 1521 and 1550.[16] In 1550, however, the council finally decided to support only four members in the civic band, 'that is, a sackbut and three shawms.'[17]

Another document relative to this band demonstrates that these players read and performed from music during the sixteenth century. Here, in 1552, a payment was made to Jan Leunis for preparing 'songbooks' for the city band. Two years earlier a member, Maarten Rooryck, resigned and was told he must return his songbook.[18]

The Mechelen civic wind band consisted of four players in the beginning of the century, became five with the addition of Hans Nagel in 1509–1518, returned to four, and then again increased to five after 1545.[19]

This band seems to have profited from at least partial financial support from Margaret of Austria, Regent of the Low Countries, who resided in this town. Perhaps this accounts for the numerous purchases of entire consorts of new instruments during the first half of the sixteenth century. There were purchases of consorts (*coker*, case) of flutes in 1502 and in 1532 and no fewer than nine cornetts in 1530.[20] Additional purchases included a case of four crumhorns in 1527, another case of seven in 1543, and between 1534 and 1538, 'leather cases, reeds, keys or metal trimmings for the crumhorns, recorders, shawms, etc.'[21]

The presence of the court of Margaret of Austria accounts for numerous visiting wind bands in the city and no doubt for the rather international experience of some of the members of its own civic wind band. I have mentioned Nagel; in addition Jan van Winckle also had previously played for Philip the Fair, then left the Mechelen band in 1516 to go to the court of Henry VIII.[22] Of three of Nagel's colleagues in 1508, two seem

[15] Dendermonde, *Stads Rekeningen*, 1528–1529, fol. 70v.; 1531–1532, fol. 65v.; 1539–1540, fol. 52; Mechelen, *Stads Rekeningen*, 1550–1551, fol. 230, 'the six shawmpipers of Brussels.'

[16] Bruges, *Resolutieboec*, 1545–1552, fol. 144. (Bruges City Archive)

[17] Polk, 'Ensemble Instrumental Music in Flanders,' 4.

[18] Louis Gilliodts-Van Severen, 'Les ménestrels de Bruges,' in *Essais d'Archéologie Brugeoise* (Bruges, 1912), 2:100, 103.

[19] Mechelen, *Stads Rekeningen*, 1549–1550, fol. 161.

[20] Raymond Joseph Justin Van Aerde, *Ménestrels Communaux … à Malines, de 1312 a 1790* (Mechelen, 1911), 29–31.

[21] Ibid.

[22] Polk, 'Ensemble Instrumental Music in Flanders,' 18, 27; Maarten Albert Vente, *Bouwstenen voor een geschiedenis der toonkunst in de Nederlanden* (Utrecht: Vereniging voor nederlandse muziekgeschiedenis, 1965), 1:222; and Van Aerde, *Ménestrels Communaux*, 72.

to be of the same family, Giellis and Jan Conijn.[23] This specialization of families in various guilds was, of course, not unusual and sometimes continued for several generations, as we can see in the Case of Anthony van Kinckom who joined the Mechelen band in 1520. His father, Jan, had been a member of the same wind band as had his grandfather (before 1485).[24]

Even small towns during the sixteenth century tried to maintain at least four members in the civic wind band. The salary for the players must have been a major budget expense, as is suggested in the Case of Mons which, when it needed to strengthen its fortifications, abolished the town wind band in order to divert those funds toward defense.[25]

The most frequent references, even in the smallest towns, to the basic instrumentation speak of shawms and sackbuts. One finds two documents in Aalst, for example, which suggest this consistency. The first, from 1507–1508, reads,

> Paid to Willem, Gillese and Gillekene Reygermans, minstrels of the city of long standing, two playing shawms and the third playing sackbut.[26]

A later document, dated 1532, now refers to a four-man band, but still shawms and sackbut.[27]

Beyond this 'standard' instrumentation, however, one again finds even the small towns adding consorts of the new sixteenth-century instruments. Dendermonde, for example, purchased consorts of crumhorns in 1543 and again in 1559.[28]

For Oudenaarde there are several such references, first a document regarding the purchase of instruments in 1531.

> Paid to the shawm players of this town in respect of a German case of recorders and a bass for their crumhorns which they have had made, which must always belong to the town, the sum of XVIII lib.par.[29]

The town purchased another consort of flutes in 1536,[30] and another case of crumhorns in 1539.

> Paid to Arent van Curtenbosch because, on orders from the council of this town, he bought in Antwerp on behalf of this town a fine case of crumhorns which belongs to the same town, in all the sum of 80 lib. par.[31]

---

[23] Van Aerde, *Ménestrels Communaux*. The third member was Cornelis Matthys.

[24] Brussels, *Stads Rekeningen*, 1500–1501, fol. 55; 1484–1485, fol. 116; and Van Aerde, *Ménestrels Communaux*, 70, 72.

[25] Leopold Devillers, *Essai sur l'histoire de la musique à Mons* (Mons, 1868), 16–17.

[26] Aalst, *Stads Rekeningen*, 1507–1508, fol. 21.
Willem, Gillese ende Gillekene Reygermans menesteurs vander stede die touderen tijden angenomen zijn gheweest omme de twee te spelene met scalmeyen ende de derde met ten trompe sacqueboutte.

[27] Ibid., 1531–1532, fol. 25v.

[28] Dendermonde, *Stads Rekeningen*, 1542–1543, fol. 78v; 1558–1559, fol. 52v.
Betaelt den vier scalmeyersdeser stede van zeker cromhoorens.

[29] Vander Straeten, *La Musique aux Pays-Bas*, 4:144.
Betaelt den schalmeyers dezer stede, thulpe van eenen duutsche cokere fluyten, ende eenen bascontre van hueren cromhoorenen die zy hebben doen maken, de welcke eeuwelic der stede bliven moeten, de somme van XVIII lib.par.

[30] Ibid.
Betaelt de scalmeyers deser stede, voor een cokere fluuten ende nyeuwe instrumenten.

[31] Ibid., 145.
Betaelt Arent Van Curtenbosch, van dat hy, by ordonnantie van scepenen deser stede, ontrent Sacramentsdach laetsleden, tot behoeve deser stede, gecocht heeft t'Antwerpen, eenen schoonen cokere cromhoorens, die der selver stede toebehoort, tsamen de somme van lxxx lib. par.

A final interesting reference to this town suggests that one of the town players borrowed two consorts of instruments to use for an outside performance opportunity in 1567.

> Master Paul Maes has, with the consent of the town council, taken a set of eight recorders, one of which was slightly split, with their case; together with these also the set of eight crumhorns with the case which serves for them, promising to return the same, as required by law.[32]

One finds these same kinds of civic wind bands in the northern provinces, although in Utrecht, Leiden, and Amsterdam they often went under the name of 'trompers' (trombones?).[33] In Amsterdam, for example, the civic records of 1541 and 1542 speak of four *trompers*, whereas in the following year they are given the more familiar designation of shawm players.[34]

There is an extant icon showing the Leiden civic band in 1575 in a procession celebrating the opening of the University of Leiden. They appear here playing two trumpet-types, a cornett, and a shawm.[35]

A bill for repairs to instrument cases, reveals a portion of the instruments belonging to the Utrecht band in 1554.

> Item one pound four shillings to Floris Lubbertzs, scabbard maker, for completely repairing and recovering in leather the crumhorn case for the town 'trompers,' and also for repairing and recovering the recorder case.[36]

Six years later one finds an account of the purchase of a very broad range of instruments, including five violins, a bombard, two 'cors de basset,' a shawm, and a crumhorn.[37]

One can suppose that the broad range of functions these wind bands performed for the various cities were similar in nature. No doubt a contract for the city wind band in Mechelen, dated 1505, describes the kinds of performances they were all expected to provide. It says they were to play on cornetts and other instruments during solemn masses celebrated by order of the magistrates; they were to play at the town hall, 'met shalmijen, trompetten ende andere instrumenten,' late mornings, every Saturday, Sunday, holiday and days preceding public festivities; in the course of banquets organized by the town, they were to entertain on stringed instruments[38] and flutes; they could not refuse to participate in any service

32 Ibid., 151.
> Meester Pauwels Maes, heeft, by consente van scepenen deser stede, ghelicht een accord handfleuten van achten, metter custode, van de welke de eene wat ghespleten was; metgaders ooc den accord cromhoornen van achte, metter custode daertoe dienende, belovende de zelve weder te keeren ter vermaenynghe van der wet.

33 Vente, *Bouwstenen voor een geschiedenis der toonkunst in de Nederlanden*, 1:222; Leiden, *Stads Rekeningen*, 1483–1485, under, 'dienars loen.' In general one finds a great number of names given the civic wind bands in the low countries, including *menestreux, ministrelen, speelieden, stadtspijpers,* and *schalmeypijpers*.

34 Amsterdam, *Stads Rekeningen*, 1540–1541, fol. 43v; 1542–1543, fol. 40v; and 1531, vol. 24v.

35 *Illustrum Hollandiae et Westfrisiae Ordinum alma Academia Leidensis*, 1614.

36 F.C. Kist and J. van Flensburg, 'De Geschiedenis der Musijk te Utrecht van het Jaar 1400 tot op onzer tijd,' in *Caecilia-Algemeen Musikaal Tijdschrift van Nederland*, 1848, 5:89.
> Item Floris Lubbertsz, sceymaker, 1 l. 4 sc. wt sake hy voor de stads trompers die coecker v.d. cromhoorn geheel verstelt ende up nyws geleert, mitsgaders decsels van de handpypen oeck vernywet heeft ende verleert.

37 Vander Straeten, *La Musique aux Pays-Bas*, 229.

required by the town; in order to maintain a desirable standard of performance, they were ordered to rehearse together at least twice weekly and to obey a leader.[39]

The most commonly mentioned civic–religious ceremony during the sixteenth century remained the *ommegang*, a part-sacred, part-secular procession which now began to emphasize more allegorical themes than in the fifteenth century. Thus the one held in Antwerp in 1559 celebrated 'the return of peace and abundance'; in 1561, 'the vicissitudes of all things mortal in war and peace and richness and poverty'; in 1562, 'the Ages of Man, Time and Eternity'; and in 1564, the good and the evil use of wealth.[40]

An eyewitness account of one of the ommegangs in Antwerp exists in the hand of a famous artist, Albrecht Dürer. In his diary for 19 August 1520, he speaks of observing this procession and seems to have found particular interest in the 'ancient French long silver trumpets' and 'many German fife and drum players.'[41]

As during the fifteenth century, the most famous of these processions was held in Termonde. An account of this celebration in 1519 mentions the civic wind bands (scalmeyers en andere pypers) from Ghent, Brussels, Aelst, Stekene, and Moerbeke and is particularly interesting in demonstrating, in the case of the last two, that even the smallest villages had civic bands.[42]

In 1522 more musicians participated, with civic wind bands from Brussels, Ghent, Mechelen, Antwerp, and Aelst; civic trumpet ensembles from Moerbeke, Ghent, Werveke, and Stekene; and a large number of bagpipes and percussion.[43] The procession in Teremonde in 1551 is unusual in the appearance for the first time in this town of two civic violinists from Brussels.[44]

Processions of a more political nature occurred with the arrival of any important visitor and the civic wind band was an inseparable part of these festivities as well. An excellent example of these events is the welcome given Prince Francis, Duke of Brabant and Anjou, when he arrived in Antwerp in 1581.[45]

An eyewitness observed that while the pageants and displays were not particularly unusual, what was notable was the great number of knights, some twenty thousand in number, in the procession and in particular the quiet and orderly manner of

[38] If this quotation is accurate (the author gives no source) it is very unusual in its mention of strings in the civic band at so early a date. In general they are not found until mid-century, as for example in Antwerp after 1548. Indeed, as Polk points out, 'The strength of the shawm band tradition is nowhere more evident than in its resistance to the intrusion of the stringed instruments.' ('Ensemble Instrumental Music in Flanders,' 19)

[39] Robert Wangermée, *Flemish Music and Society in the Fifteenth and Sixteenth Centuries* (New York: Praeger, 1968), 180.

[40] Ibid., 179.

[41] Quoted in Walter Salmen, *Musikleben im 16. Jahrhundert* (Leipzig: Deutscher Verlag fur Musik, 1976), 198.

> … von unser lieben Frauen Kirchen zu Antorff, do die ganze Stadt versammlet was von allen Handwerken und Ständen, ein Jeglicher nach sein Stand auf das Köstlichs bekleidet. Es hätt auch ein jeglicher Stand und Zunft ihr Zeichen, darbei man sie können möcht. Da waren auch in den Unterschieden getragen gross köstlich Stangen kerzen und ihr altfränkisch lang silbern Posaunen. Do waren auch auf teutsch viel Pfeifer und Trummelschlager. Das ward alls hart geblasen und rumorisch gebrauchet.

[42] Vander Straeten, *La Musique aux Pays-Bas*, 4:201.

their participation. 'Why,' he maintained, 'they made so little noise that if it had not been for the thundering of the cannons, the sounding of trumpets, clarions, halboies (shawms), and other instruments, there was no more noise than is among a councell of grave men.' The procession included civic trumpeters, trumpeters from nearby states, and the 'Swissers with their drums and fiffes.'

The first great pageant the procession passed was the Maiden of Antwerp, surrounded by allegorical figures including, 'Concord, Wisedome, and Defense' (a pelican killing herself for her young birds) and 'Offense' (a hen brooding over her chicks).

At St. Katharins bridge was a triumphal arch of white stone, 'cunninglie painted, garnished with His Highnesses armes, and with torches and cressets, and with musick of holboies and clarions.' Above was written, 'To the happie comming hither of Francis.' Here also were torches constructed of barrels of pitch on poles 'five stories high' and a great 'giant' (legendary founder of Antwerp), constructed in such a way that he turned his head toward the royal guest and moved his arms in greetings.

43 Ibid., 202–203.

Achtervolgens der ouden costwnen, so quam en heir ten ommeganghe diversche trompers en scalmeyers, ende andere pipers van Ghendt ende Brussele, also hier naer. volghen sal:
Speelieden van Ghendt: Joos Soeren, Clays de Tolleneire, Lieven De Vos, Joorys Soetinc …
Speelieden van Mechelen: Adriaen Cools, Cornelis Mathys. Anthonys van K … and Robbrecht Vanden Broucke …
Speelieden van Antwerpen: Jan Conyn. Gillis Conyn. France Conyn …
Speelieden van Aelst: Laurens Vanden Houte, Joos Vanden Houte, Pauwels Van Halsberghe …
Trompetters van Moerbeke: Gillis Willems, Gillis Willems fs Pieters, Pieter Willems, Gillys Willems fs Pieters …
Trompetters van Ghendt: Jean De Vos, Vincent De Keysere, Heyndric Diericx …
Trompetters van Werveke: Daniel Lammens, Andries Lammens, Mieux De Meuleneere. Michel Van Werveke …
Trompetters van Stekene: Mathijs Dalsgart, Pieter Van den Velde, Andries Van den Velde, Gillys Mey, Willem Thybaert …
Trompetters van Gendt: Melchoir De Brouwere, Lyon Ghys, Joorys Denys, Lieven Van den Houte, Boudwin De Keysere …
Andere speelieden, als mouselen, quenen, trommelslagers, velen en de tambouryns: Rogier De Wilde, met eene quene, die speelde voor den Reuse … Jacob De Wilde, met een quene voor't ros Beyaert … Jan Sas, die speelde voor den hellewaghen met eenquene …
Bouwen Van der Eertbrugghe, Jacob Boccaert, Joos Scoutheeten, Joos De Blauwere, Jan Pieron, Govaert Sterrinc, Gillis Pieters, Joos Van Waterschilt, Jan De Pau, Michel Maes, Zanken Van Aelst, Berthel Cooreman, Joos Van den Doore, Willem Tabouryn, Jan Maes, Gheert Maes, Cornelis Sterrinc, Willem De Leghe, Cornel is Meskens, Jan Betten …

44 Ibid.

Betaelt Jan ende Pieter Bert, violons der stadt van Bruessele.

45 The account of these festivities is found in John Nichols, ed., *The Progresses and Public Processions of Queen Elizabeth* (London, 1788).

The Antwerp civic wind band was seen next, situated on another triumphal arch. Here the Goddesses Flora, Ceres, and Pomona, together with the 'helhounds, Discord, Violence and Tyrannie,' stood below the arch, 'furnished with diverse instruments of musicke, and the musicians themselves were clad in colours of that citie.'

Later in the week another pageant was given, representing the Nine Muses, 'playing on diverse kinds of instruments, and a sweet singer.' Across from them was a 'cave verie hideous, darke, and drierie to behold,' in which lurked the three 'hellhounds,' 'Discord, Violence and Tyranie.' These three would come sneaking to the mouth of the cave only to hear the music, which caused them to scamper back into the cave. The point of this was to instruct all observers that as long as the realm was interested in the arts, it would not be disturbed by discord, violence, and tyranny!

At the end of this week of festivities, 'drums and trumpets were sounded everie where, and manie instruments of musike were plaied upon, as had beene doone afore at his first arrivall.'

A similar series of celebrations was given in 1578 in Brussels, upon the arrival of Archduke Matthias for his inauguration as Governor-General. One who heard the Brussels civic wind band on this occasion was very impressed with their performance.

> Orpheus had never played so melodiously on his harp nor Apollo on his lyre, nor Pan on his flute, as the city waits then performed.[46]

Finally, there is an account of the entertainments given the English Earl of Leicester during his visit to the Low Countries in January 1586.[47] In Amsterdam, where a thousand ships lay in the harbor, he was greeted by 'sundry great (mechanical) whales and other fishes of hugeness,' carrying the mayor and other officials who read Latin orations. Traveling to Utrecht, he was greeted by the civic 'trumpeters in scarlet and silver, barons, knights, and great officers, in cloth of gold and silks of all colours.' Here he was given a great banquet with course after course of meats cut in the shape of lions, tigers, dragons, and leopards, etc., and music by 'sonorous metal blowing meanwhile the most triumphant airs.'

[46] Jan Baptist Houwaert, *Sommare Beschryvinghe van den triumphelijcke Incomst van den door luchtigen Aertshoge Matthias binnen die Princelijcke Stadt van Brussele* (Antwerp, 1579).

[47] Described in John Motley, *History of the United Netherlands* (New York, 1861), 1:15ff.

These civic bands also played for the citizens, foremost among such occasions were public concerts. I have mentioned above the Mechelen civic band contract of 1505, which spoke of late morning concerts on weekends, holidays, and on the days preceding public festivities. Similarly, when a new band was hired in Mons, in 1532, their contract demanded they play for the citizens twice a day, at eleven o'clock in the morning and at six o'clock in the evening.[48] A contract for the civic wind band in Bruges, drawn in 1585, required them to perform each Sunday at eleven o'clock in the square in front of the city hall and in the St. Donaes Church after the evening prayer.[49] The contract also observes that this was an old tradition by this time. The band was also to perform every day, in the morning, in September and October and from April through August, and at other times as required by the officials. The repertoire was to be sacred and devotional. A similar contract in 1568 in Mechelen called for concerts on Sundays, Holy Days, and feast days.[50]

In Antwerp the civic band played morning concerts as the delegates of the Hanseatic League walked from their factory to the Bourse,[51] and during the annual fair they played evening concerts before the town hall.[52]

As elsewhere, these civic wind bands formed themselves into guilds, modeled after those of the other crafts. While they had their religious facet, each with a patron saint, and their charitable considerations for members in need, they were for the most part concerned with the control of the performance of their craft.

The by-laws for the Bruges guild in 1534 restricted membership to those who were residents of the town and who could demonstrate their ability before the officers of the guild. Any member who stole a performance opportunity from a brother member,[53] or who criticized a brother's talent, was fined three pounds. One who has a debt to the guild, or is fined, must pay or give a security pledge at the risk of being forbidden to perform. If one accepts a wedding or feast performance, one can not withdraw to take a job which might pay more without the written permission of the first client.[54]

One finds a similar code in Antwerp in 1541, where the guild leaders had to swear before a magistrate to use their talents for the well-being of the community, to play and accept

[48] Devillers, *Essai sur l'histoire de la musique à Mons*, 16.

[49] Gilliodts, 'Les ménestrels de Bruges,' 134.
Aladan was ooc ghevensalviert anderwarf stads dienst te onthouden de vijf stads speellieden ende ten ghecostumerden pensioene van xxvj lb. gr. tsiaers, wel verstaende met last van alle sondaghe naar de elf hueren in den thuyn voor de halle te spelene naer oude costume in de twee burgghemaercten, jn de kerche Sinte Donaes savonds naer het avond ghebet; ende voorts jn de maenden van september ende october metsgaders april, mey, juli ende ougst alle daghe smorghens te vergaderen van college voor de halle in den thuyn als vooren, ende hendelick tallen tyden als zy dies by scepenen versocht wordern, ende dit al ghestichttelyc met lydekens van danckségghinghe ende andere goddelick ende stichtelicke musycke.

[50] Van Aerde, *Ménestrels Communaux*, 39–40.

[51] John Joseph Murray, *Antwerp in the Age of Plantin and Brueghel* (Norman: University of Oklahoma Press, 1970), 143.

[52] Ibid., 45.

[53] A sackbut player, Jan Leunis, who called himself, 'Apollo,' was called before the magistrates of Bruges in 1552 by an official of the guild for illicitly playing engagements. (Polk, 'Ensemble Instrumental Music in Flanders,' 20)

[54] Vander Straeten, *La Musique aux Pays-Bas*, 4:96.

engagements whenever they had openings, not to make double bookings or cut short performances, to instruct apprentices in all the instruments 'expected of them by the laws of the town,' and to teach dancing.[55]

In Mons, in 1588, a candidate for the guild had to perform before the assembly of 'masters,' following an apprenticeship of two years. To become a 'master,' he had to be able to play, 'two pieces of music on each of said instruments (shawm, cornett, recorder, and violin), such songs as the masters see fit to choose.'[56]

Finally, one can see in the 1555 guild by-laws for the Antwerp Guild of Saint Job and Mary Magdalen that, as in England, the apprentices were permitted to join with the regular members in performance, thus forming larger wind bands. This charter says that the master and his apprentices could perform together at banquets and other public occasions as frequently as,

> he with his band or company, being of a reasonable number as stated above, and his boarding pupils will be able to serve decently.[57]

[55] Murray, *Antwerp in the Age of Plantin and Brueghel*, 143–144.

[56] Quoted in Wangermée, *Flemish Music and Society in the Fifteenth and Sixteenth Centuries*, 182.

[57] Grove, 6:10.

Notes on the Repertoire

The surviving repertoire of the civic wind bands of the Low Countries during the sixteenth century centers on one of the most important figures in the early history of the wind band—Tielman Susato, one of the leaders of the Antwerp wind band. Standard biographies always list 1529 as the date Susato appears in Antwerp (he was born in Köln), but Polk points out that this is only the date from which complete civic records can be found in Antwerp.[58] In any case, according to one writer, during 1529–1531, soon after he joined the Antwerp band, Susato himself transcribed thirty-three volumes of six-part music, running to about four hundred folio pages![59] Where is this music? If these volumes are found, one will surely find a treasure in early wind band literature!

One testimonial to this man's ingenuity is the fact that he published the very first collection of music in Flemish, the native tongue of his country, in 1551. Since even he considered this so unusual, Susato attached a very interesting 'apology,' which I quote for it also gives us an insight into this important figure in the story of the sixteenth-century civic wind band.

> Music is a remarkable gift, instituted by order of God and offered to man to be used not for dishonest or thoughtless ends but, above all, to render thanks and praise to the Lord, to shun idleness and make good use of his time, to drive out melancholy and dark thoughts, and in order to restore joy to hearts sorely tried. And wherefore then should this not be done henceforth in our own mother tongue with the same skill and the same harmony as, until now, have been lavished on Latin, French and Italian? Our art and our harmony being the equal of those others, for what reason should one language be scorned to the profit of another?

This collection appears shortly after Susato's departure from membership in the Antwerp civic wind band. Since it stands to reason that his first venture as a publisher of music would be in using music he himself was familiar with, it seems reasonable to assume that this collection of Flemish chansons included those played in instrumental versions by the band of which he was a member. This contention is strengthened by the title-page, which invites instrumental performance.

[58] Polk, 'Ensemble Instrumental Music in Flanders,' 3. It is most unusual that there is an extant icon picturing this man, a woodcut (now in West Berlin, Staatsbibliothek) showing Susato presenting music to Maria of Hungary. This interesting woodcut has been reproduced in Wangermée, *Flemish Music and Society in the Fifteenth and Sixteenth Centuries*, 256.

[59] Murray, *Antwerp in the Age of Plantin and Brueghel*, 147.

Tielman Susato

The first music books in four parts, including twenty-six new love songs in our Low German tongue, composed by diverse composers, most pleasant to sing and play on all musical instruments.[60]

It is, however, a following publication which claims our greater interest. His famous collection of instrumental dances, published in four part-books (1551), is almost certainly taken directly from the repertoire of the Antwerp wind band.

Het derde musyck boexken begre PEN INT GHET AL VAN ONSER neder duytscher spraken, daer inne begrepen syn alderhande danserye, te vuetens Basse dansen, Ronden, Allemain gien, Pavanen ende meer andere, mits oeck vyfthien nieuwe gaillarden, zeer lustich ende bequaem om spelen op alle musicale Instrumenten, Ghecom poneert ende near dinstrumenten ghestelt duer Tielman Susato, Int iaer ons herren, M.D.L.I. ... Ghedruckt Tantwerpen by Tielman Susato wonende voer die niewe waghe In den Cromhorn.

[60] The original:

> Het ierste musyck boexken met vier part yen daer inne begrepen zijn XXVI nieuwe amoreuse liedekens in onser nederduytscher talen, gecomponeert by diversche componisten, zeer lustich om singen ende spelen op alle musicale instrumenten.

A woodcut showing Susato presenting music to Maria of Hungary.

Some of these dances were composed by Susato himself and, as he was moreover a wind player, it is difficult to imagine they were composed for any other purpose than performance by the Antwerp band. As one can see in the title-page, his publishing business was 'at the sign of the crumhorn.'

One finds here some forty compositions, including basse dances, branles, pavanes, *Allegaingien* and 'new' *gaillarden*. Some, of course, are based on earlier models and are immediately recognizable, such as the 'Mille regretz,' based on Josquin, and the 'Il estoit une fillette,' based on Janequin. In cases where Susato has reworked earlier literature, as for example Attaingnant's 'Bergerette Dont vient cela,' the new composition is always much more interesting than the original. A few of these compositions seem truly Flemish in character and seem to be original works based on local sources, as for example the 'Roboecken dans,' named for a village near Antwerp.

Susato's principal competitor was Pierre Phalèse, who in 1571 also published a collection of one hundred and three four-part dances, mostly of the branle type, also probably intended for civic wind bands. Since copyright laws were as yet unknown, Phalèse took much material directly from earlier sources, including fifteen dances from Susato's collection of 1551. In this case we are grateful for this plagiarism, for the dances include many of the original wind band dances of d'Estrée (1564) which thus survive in their only complete form.[61]

Another volume of dances was published by Phalèse in 1573 which is now lost.[62] This publication is known to have consisted of four- and five-part instrumental dances.

In 1583 this firm published yet another dance collection, the *Chorearum Molliorum Collectanea*, containing one hundred and four separate compositions. Again it was in four part-books, described as for all instruments, for 'maistres Musiciens, & autres amateurs de toute sorte d'Harmonie.'

[61] This collection is discussed, and sources given, in Caroline Cunningham, 'Estienne du Tertre, Scavant Musicien, Jean d'Estr'e, Joueur de Hautbois du Roy' (Unpublished dissertation, Bryn Mawr, 1969), 1:218ff.

[62] *Petit tresor des danses et branles à quatre et cinq parties des meilleurs autheurs propres à jouer sur tous les estrumenz*. Fétis says this publication contained music by Antoine Barbe, among others.

8 Civic Wind Bands in France

IN THE FIRST VOLUME OF THIS SERIES, I have discussed the founding of the minstrel guild in Paris, 'La confrerie Saint-Julien,' in 1321. Like all such guilds it was a quasi-religious society for mutual aid which, at the same time, attempted to control performance.

During the sixteenth century there is evidence that this guild held formal 'assemblies' of its members from time to time to discuss the issues before the guild. The records for one of these assemblies, on 8 August 1586, reveal the purpose was to elect a member to the post of governor of the hospital they had founded. On this occasion they had to wait an hour for enough of the members to arrive to begin the meeting.[1]

The guild at this time had approximately one hundred 'masters,' one of whom always served, by election, as the leader, called, 'the king.' Beginning with Jean Bénard, in 1537, the names of these kings are extant.[2] One of these kings, Claude de Bouchaudon, who served from 1575–1590, instituted a system of 'licenses,' which could be sold to new players in town who were not members of the guild. This allowed them to play, while both retaining some control from the guild and at the same time enriching the guild's treasury. One of these licenses, for example, was sold to Yves de Brie, 'player of violin and hand-drum,' in 1585.[3] His license read that he might play in Paris so long as he was without fault and created no scandal. Some licenses were good for life, some limited the areas where one could perform, but in no case was the recipient ever called a 'master.'

Before the beginning of the century this guild had made an attempt to assert control beyond the city of Paris itself by appointing 'lieutenants' in control of performance in other towns. Thus we read of Nicolas Hestier being made lieutenant at Tours, on 26 March 1508.[4] After mid-century more of these records of lieutenants are extant.[5] The king, Claude de Bouchaudon, seems to have made a particular effort to orga-

---

[1] Most of the material on this guild during the sixteenth century has been taken from Francois Lesure, *Musique et musiciens Français du XVIe Siècle* (Genève: Minkoff Reprint, 1976), 115ff.

[2] During the sixteenth century, they were:

    1537 Jean Bénard
    1541 Nicolas Convers
    1555 Charles Chevallier
    1569 Pierre Roussel
    1575 Claude de Bouchaudon
    1590 Claude Nyon, called, 'Lafont'

[3] 'jouer de violon et de tabourin à main'

[4] Paris, National Archive (MS. Q 1215).

[5] Among them,

    1555: Pierre Germain, lieutenant pour le bailliage de Meaux.
    1558: Médard Cugnechon, lieutenant général et spécial pour la ville de Melun.
    1563: Jean Sauvage, lieutenant pour la ville et le bailliage de Beauvais.
    1568: Nicolas Le Vent, procureur général pour le Vermandois.
    1569: Louis Cozette, lieutenant pour la ville et le bailliage de Beauvais.
    1569: Laurent Ouyn, procureur pour la châtellenie de Pontoise, le comté de Chaumont et Magny et la prévôté d'Andrezy.

nize all the villages within two hundred to three hundred kilometers of Paris under lieutenants and many of these names also survive.[6]

There is also more information regarding the apprenticeship requirements for this guild during the sixteenth century. In one respect this guild seems to have been more liberal than most, in that it did not require residence in Paris as a requirement for being an apprentice. The average apprentice was from ten to sixteen years of age and together with his parents or teacher drew up a legal document regarding all the conditions of his service. The duration of this apprenticeship was officially six years, but few seem to have been required to serve so long, and never if one was the son of a 'master.' The apprentice was assigned to a 'master,' who was required to treat the apprentice humanely and to provide for his welfare.

After serving his period of apprenticeship, one had to play a 'chef-d'oeuvre' before the king and one of his lieutenants. This apparently was a sight-reading examination and the difficulty depended on the amount of control the guild wished to exert at the moment with regard to controlling the number of players. For the son of a 'master,' this examination was a mere formality.

If one failed to thus join the guild of 'masters,' there was a lower order of affiliates known as 'fellows' (Compagnons). In reality few persons seem to actually been designated in this capacity, but those who were had to be content with performing only for minor weddings and banquets.

The inventory of one master, Thomas Roullant, in 1534 suggests that these players also owned a fairly large number of the instruments they might be expected to play, in this case two sackbuts, two shawms, four flutes, and two tabourins.[7]

The better players in this guild were also members of the wind band of the King of France. Such was the case with Jean d'Estrée, who is known to have been a member of the guild from 1552 until 1558. He lived in the St. Merri district near the headquarters of the guild and also near the rue de la Harpe where the publisher Attaingnant was located. When not performing with the king's wind band, d'Estrée is known to have often played with a ten-member civic band, which I assume to have been a wind band as two other members were also wind players, the shawmists, Nicolas Mutet and Julien Le Maistre.[8]

[6] Given in Lesure, *Musique et musiciens Français du XVIe Siècle*, 119–120.

[7] Lesure, *Musique et musiciens Français du XVIe Siècle*, 137.

[8] Francois Lesure, 'La Communauté des "joueurs d'instruments" au XVIe siècle,' in *Revue historique de droit Français et étranger* (1953), 79ff.

From 1559 to 1564, d'Estrée also served as editor and arranger for the publisher, Nicolas Du Chemin, a capacity in which he produced four books of *danseries*. Unfortunately none of these works survive in complete original editions, but it can be seen that they contained an extensive repertoire, mostly of the branle types, although basse dances, galliards, and pavanes are also included. Most are in four-parts, with five and six-part works appearing in the final volume.[9] Musically these dances are melody oriented, with simple harmonic part-writing below. This simple structure, together with d'Estrée's close relationship with the civic wind bands in Paris, lead me to believe that these publications were intended for these organizations. Perhaps the fact that many of these dances were reprinted in Flanders, which also had a very strong civic wind band tradition, also points to this possibility. The demand for music of exactly this nature by the civic wind bands is clear, as one can see by a comment of Arbeau (1588).

> Nowadays there is no workman so humble that he does not wish to have shawms and sackbuts at his wedding.[10]

The civic wind players in Paris, in addition to the private weddings, etc., performed in all great civic celebrations. Surely they were among those heard during the great festivities celebrating the release of the two young sons of Francis I from imprisonment by Charles V, in 1530. Tables were erected on the streets, filled with food and drink, and at the city hall (Hôtel de Ville) a great feast was given and all 'honest people' (honnestes gens) were welcome. An eyewitness reported hearing 'trompettes, clerons, bucinnes, tabours et autres instrumentz musicaulx' on this occasion.[11] A very similar description is found in the text of a chanson by Janequin, published in the same year, which is clearly celebrating the same event.[12]

One can also find evidence of civic wind bands in a number of other cities of France during the sixteenth century. In Toulouse one reads that in mid-century all instrumental music for both private and public functions was organized by the civic wind band.[13] This seems to have been the case in Marseilles as well, for the viols only begin to appear after 1546 and the violins only at the end of the sixteenth century.[14]

[9] See Cunningham, *Estienne du Tertre*, and Grove, 6:264.

[10] Arbeau, *Orchésography*, 51.

[11] Victor-Louis Bourrilly, ed., *Le journal d'un bourgeois de Paris sous le règne de François Ier* (Paris: Picard, 1910), 340–342.

[12] *Trente et six chansons* (Paris, 1530).
Chantons, sonnons, trompetes
Tabourins, phifres et clerons
Sy faisons la grant feste.
Plus nous ne craindrons le son de
   la trompete
Puisque les enfans et paix avons.
Chantés, dancés, jeunes filletes
Bourgeoyses et bourgeoys.
Faites sonner voz
   doulces gorgettes
Distant a haulte voix:
'Vive les enfans du noble
   roy Françoys.'

[13] Grove, 19:93, which also gives the names of two of the wind band players at this time, Jacques Pradas and Mathelin Tailhasson.

[14] Grove, 11:705.

According to Arbeau,[15] even the villages had wind music for their celebrations. Speaking of the soprano shawm and bombard, he writes,

[15] Arbeau, *Orchésography*, 50.

> This pair is excellent for making a tremendous noise, such as is required in village fetes or large gatherings, but if they were played with the flute they would drown the sound of it. It combines well with the tabor or with the big drum.

Several accounts from provincial cities survive which describe the civic wind players appearing in welcome ceremonies for aristocratic visitors. In Valenciennes, in 1539, for example, Charles v was welcomed by the usual trumpets and fifes, but also by the civic wind band playing new chansons.

> des jouers de hautbois qu'il fait moult bon ouyr pour leurs chansons nouvelles.[16]

[16] Jean Jacquot, ed., *Les Fêtes de la Renaissance* (Paris: Centre Nationale de la Recherche Scientifique, 1973), 242.

A more complete description of a provincial wind band's instrumentation is found in connection with the arrival of Henry II in Lyons in 1548. Here, Charles Peyronet and Charles Cordeilles, 'meneur d'aulboys,' led a nine-member civic wind band composed of 'dolcians, cornetts and sordun' in performances for this occasion.[17]

[17] Grove, 'Cordeilles, Charles.'

The most extensive of these accounts comes from Cambrai, in 1540, for the welcome of Charles v, accompanied by the Dauphin and the Duke of Orléans. First they were welcomed by the city officials and the twelve civic trumpeters, dressed in black and red.

> The said twelve trumpeters began to play most melodiously, and without interruption, preceding His Majesty on the way to the episcopal palace.

The city streets were illuminated by more than seven thousand torches, triumphal arches, and heraldic trappings. At the rue Saint-Georges, there were children actors, 'who, when the said Majesty passed under the said arch, began to sing in beautiful, sweet and harmonious counterpoint, "O vera unitas".' The civic band was stationed in the market place, the official point of welcome by the citizens.

Besides and along with the splendid resonance of the said trumpets, there were, at the top of the city hall ... a great number of instruments called clarions and oboes making great melody. And a great many little children all crying out loudly in the Italic fashion, 'Imperio! Imperio!' which filled the said market place and all the town with delightful joy and harmony.

At the episcopal palace the local cathedral choir sang 'songs and motets made and composed' for the occasion, followed by a Te Deum inside the cathedral. As the emperor departed the town he was again saluted by the musicians from the top of the city hall.[18]

[18] This description taken from Wangermée, *Flemish Music*, 176–178.

9 *Civic Wind Bands in the German-Speaking Countries*

NÜRNBERG IS A TOWN which seems to have developed its civic wind band somewhat in advance of many German cities. Closely related, one to the other, is the fact that Nürnberg was also an early center for the manufacture of wind instruments, being a famous center for trumpets already in the fifteenth century. In any case, during the sixteenth century Nürnberg was sufficiently well-known for its civic wind band that one can almost follow its development in the iconography of that century. At the beginning of the century (ca. 1500) a miniature of the butchers guild dance pictures a three-man band of two shawms and a slide-trumpet.[1] A pencil drawing from 1519 still shows three men, but now a sackbut has replaced the slide-trumpet.[2] From the following year there is a famous work by Albrecht Dürer, 'Nürnberger Stadtpfeifer,' which pictures now a four-man band of two shawms and two sackbuts (two percussionists are not playing). Finally, a mid-century engraving, 'Ball in the Town Hall,' shows a five-member civic wind band playing a cornett, three shawms, and a sackbut.[3]

I have mentioned in the introduction to this section the fact that this town maintained some ninety instruments for these players by 1575. It is clear from the various instrument purchases during the century that these included all the new renaissance woodwinds. Already in 1503 the town records mention the purchase of eight 'krumme pfeiffen' (crumhorns?) and two shawms.[4] In 1539 the town purchased a full consort of nine crumhorns from the town of Memmingen, which seemed to have specialized in the making of these instruments.

> 50 gulden to Hans Schnitzer, town player, for 9 crumhorns made in Memmingen and left to the town players with their other instruments belonging to the council for them to use according to a decision of the council.[5]

[1] Nürnberg, Stadtbibliothek (MS. Nor. K. 444, fol. 1).

[2] Anonymous, in the *Nürnberger Schembarthandschrift* (D2, fol. 66) in the Nürnberg, Germanisches Nationalmuseum (Hs. 5664)

[3] Anonymous, Nürnberg Stadtbibliothek.

[4] Ekkehart Nickel, *Der Holzblasinstrumentenbau in der Freien Reichsstadt Nürnberg* (München: Musikverlag Katzbichler, 1971), 22, 26.

[5] Ibid., 69, 412ff.

> 50 gulden rl. Hansen Schnitzer statpfeyffer für 9 krumbhörner zu Memmingen gemacht und den statpfeyffern bei iren andern instrumenten aim rath zugehorig auch gelassen nach eins rats gefallen für die zu geprauchen.

The Nürnberg Stadtpfeifers, ca. 1449, playing for a dance by the city's butchers' guild at their annual carnival playing two shawms and a slide trumpet.

The town seems to have maintained consorts of crumhorns until the end of the century, as records for 1575 and 1598 prove. The second of these is an inventory which reveals the family members of their crumhorn consort.

> Item 1 case with crumhorns, 1 bass with 2 keys, 1 bass with 1 key, 1 tenor with 1 key, 2 tenors without keys, 2 altos and 2 sopranos. Total 9. Note. All are there including a small box containing the reeds.[6]

[6] For 1575: Nürnberg, Stadtbibliothek (Rep. A. 2b, Nr. 96). For 1598: Nickel, *Der Holzblasinstrumentenbau in der Freien Reichsstadt Nürnberg*, 339.

> Item 1 Futter mit Krumphörnern, 1 Bass mit 2 Schlossen, 1 Bass mit 1 Schloss, 1 Tenor mit 1 Schloss, 2 Tenor one Schloss, 2 Discant und 2 klaine Discant St. 9. Nota. Seind alle da, samb einem Schechtelein, darinnen die Mundstuckh sein.

Nürnberg, Germany, ca. 1520, a mural attributed to Albrecht Dürer shows the town wind band playing from a balcony.

Records for 1538–1539 mention payments for the construction, by the band members themselves apparently, of a bombard and the outdoor reed-cap instruments, the Rauschpfeifen.

> It has been decided in the council to negotiate with the town musicians to make for the council a large bombard together with the Rauschpfeifen which go with it, such as they have made for Friedrich the Count Palatine, so that they can be used to the general honor of the town.
>
> …
>
> When the town musicians completed the large bombard and Rauschpfeifen which go with it, as ordered on fol. 37 above, with the intention of using them in this year's Carnival, it has been decided that first of all nothing will be paid in respect of the bill until an inventory of all these instruments is answered in the accounts room, and they are also to be instructed to look after these instruments well and not to lend them out too much.[7]

Beginning with 1575 the town records also carry frequent references to the purchases of the proto-type bassoons.[8]

It is obvious from the kinds of instruments purchased, that most towns expected their wind bands to perform both indoor and outdoor functions, as indeed they do today. In Augsburg, for example, which had five civic wind band members in

[7] Nickel, ibid., 58–59.

> Beim Rat ist verlassen, mit den stadtpfeiffern ze handeln eim rath auch ein grossen Bommart sampt dazugehörigen rauschpfeiffen ze machen, wie, si dem pfalzgrafen Friderich zugericht haben, damit man die zu gemeiner stat ehrn geprauchen mög.
> ……
> Als die statpfeiffer den grossen bommart und zugehorige rauschpfeiffen auf den heioben fol. 37 eingeschriben bevelch verfertigt, des vorhabens, diesel ben noch dise fass nacht zu geprauchen, ist verlassen, das mans zuverderst inen dem gemachten anschlag gemes betzalen, volgends aller stuckh hal ben ein vertzaichnus in dj losungstuben antwurten, und inen bevelch thun soll, solche instrumenta wol zu verwaren und nit zu gemein zu machen.

[8] Ibid., 35, 338, 342.

1555 and seven by the end of the century,⁹ one finds an inventory of 1540 which includes a full consort of crumhorns for indoor performance.

> There are also 4 crumhorns, alto, 2 tenors, 2 bass, which Wolff Ganss has. In addition there have also been made 1 alto and 1 tenor in a case covered in leather and locked with key.¹⁰

In the same inventory one finds the outdoor consort of Schreyerpfeifen.

> First of all Schreyerpfeifen: 2 altos, 2 tenors, 1 bass—in the keeping of Mr. Hans Drechsel.¹¹

There is a similar record of a consort of Schreyerpfeifen belonging to the civic wind band in Munich,¹² although we know little else about this band. According to Grove, there were four members at this time who performed not only private and official civic music, but also helped out at court. Apparently they did not form an independent guild until the seventeenth century.¹³

In Leipzig one again finds the purchase of the same instruments: Schreyerpfeifen in 1523 and crumhorns in 1542.¹⁴ Our real interest in the Leipzig civic wind band is with regard to the nature of the sixteenth-century traditions which would

Patriziertanz im Grossen Nürnberger Rathaussaal, an anonymous image showing a wind band of three shawms and two sackbuts playing for a dance in the Nürnberg town hall, ca. 1550

⁹ Salmen, *Musikleben im 16. Jahrhundert*, 16.

¹⁰ Adolf Sandberger, 'Bemerkungen zur Biographie Hans Leo Hasslers und seiner Brüder sowie zur Musikgeschichte der Städte Nürnberg und Augsburg im 16. und zu Anfang des 17. Jahrhunderts,' in *Denkmäler der Tonkunst in Bayern* (Leipzig: Breitkopf & Hartel, 1904), V/1, lvii.

> Mer sein verhannden 4 krwmhörner discant 2 tennor 1 bass Canter die hat wolff gannss. Dar Zwe ist noch gemacht worden 1 Discannt vnd 1 tennor vnd ein fueder mit leder yber zogen vnd verspert mit ainem schlissel.

¹¹ Ibid.

> Zwm ersten schreyetpfeiffen 2 discant 2 tennor 1 bass canter— die het her hannss trexel.

¹² Nickel, *Der Holzblasinstrumentenbau in der Freien Reichsstadt Nürnberg*, 66.

¹³ Grove, 12:781.

¹⁴ Rudolf Wustman, *Musikgeschichte Leipzigs bis zur Mitte des 17. Jahrhunderts* (Leipzig: Siegel, 1926), 36.

The Nürnberg Stadtpfeifers, ca. 1545, *Fastnachtstanz von Metzgern im Jahre 1519* (Carnival Dance of the Butchers in the Year 1519), playing two shawms and a sackbut.

result in the great Abblasen[15] literature of the seventeenth century which is still widely performed today. Traditional scholarship always dates this practice from the reconstruction of the civic hall in 1599 at which time the town council ordered the wind band to perform every morning at ten o'clock, 'in honor of God,' from a newly constructed balcony. But is it possible that the Abblasen tradition could have begun so late in Leipzig? I do not think so.

Consider Dresden, which apparently began its civic wind band at the relatively late date of 1572,[16] prior to which there was but a single musician being paid by the city.[17] Yet, when this civic band was organized in 1572 the contract specified the performance of four-part music from the tower, which is a clear indication that the Abblasen tradition was known during the sixteenth century. Additional duties called for in this contract included the usual guard duties and helping to 'strengthen, and enhance' the Kreuzchor,

> on feast days, Sundays and at weddings and other occasions when polyphony was performed.[18]

[15] 'Abblasen' is used to designate the multi-part music played by tower musicians, as opposed to the ancient tradition of simple musical signals.

[16] Grove, 5:615. According to Smithers, *The Music and History of the Baroque Trumpet*, 123ff., Berlin began its civic music even later, the oldest extant payment being made in 1590 to 'Steffan Pfugenn, Stadtpfeiffer.'

[17] Reinhard Kade. 'Die Leipziger Stadtpfeifer,' in *Monatshefte für Musik-Geschichte* 21, no. 10 (1889), 195.

[18] Grove, 5:615.

Municipal Wind Players, an image from the *Heldt'schen Trachtenbuch*, shows the Nürnberg civic wind band, ca. 1560–80.

Aside from this indication that Abblasen were known by 1572 in Dresden, it should be pointed out that during the earlier years when this city had no civic wind band of its own it sometimes imported the Leipzig civic wind band, as it did, for example, for the Midsummer Fair in 1522. Is it possible that they learned of the Abblasen tradition from the Leipzig band, indicating an earlier tradition in Leipzig?

Evidence of civic multi-part tower music which is very similar to the later seventeenth-century tradition in Leipzig can also be found in Lübeck. Here the civic wind band first performed a chorale at four o'clock in the morning to awaken the farm hands and then another chorale to mark the mid-day pause. They performed again to mark the resumption of work at noon and at nine o'clock to indicate the time to sleep.[19]

In Zürich one also finds a civic contract calling for performances by the civic wind players 'at noon on Fridays, Sundays, holidays, and on "unserer Herren Tag".'[20]

As in the low countries, one sometimes finds references to fine civic wind bands in even the smallest towns in sixteenth-century Germany. Memmingen, for example, had such a reputation for the quality of its wind band that in 1502 the Emperor Maximilian wrote to the town council asking them to send him 'two of your town musicians, Jörg Eyselin and Ulrich Plaser ... who are reputed to be good at playing high and low parts on shawms and trombones.'[21]

During the sixteenth century, some German towns still placed a strong emphasis on the medieval watch duties. This can be seen in a Memmingen town council order in 1518 regarding the necessity for substitutes for watch duty when the band wanted to leave town to enter a contest.

> Jack the town player is to be allowed to go with the other players for ten days to Augsburg, if they wish to win an award with the crumhorns, but in the meantime he must arrange for the watch to be maintained.[22]

Many sixteenth-century contracts for the civic wind players stress the importance of this duty. In a contract for the Stadtpfeifer, Abraham Hut, in Zwickau, in 1569,[23] for example, one reads that he must keep careful watch day and night in the tower and announce each hour by blowing on his 'hörnlein' (whereas in the welcoming of official guests he plays the trumpet). In case of fire, he announces it with a signal-bell and if during the day by a red flag and if at night by hanging out a lantern. As we shall see below, this contract is rather typical in also requiring him to help out in the church with his instrument when polyphonic music is performed.

[19] Wilhelm Stahl, *Musikgeschichte Lübecks* (Kassel: Barenreiter Verlag, 1952), 2:45ff.

[20] Antoine-Elisee Cherbuliez, *Johann Ludwig Steiner: Stadttrompeter von Zurich*, Neujahrsblatt der Allgemeinen Musikgesellschaft in Zurich (Zurich: Hug, 1964), Bd. 148, 18.

[21] Stadtarchiv (MS. 1/1).

> Wir vernemen Wie Ir zwen genannt Jörg Eyselin Vnnd ulrich plaser vnnder Euren Stat pfeiffern habt, die mit den Schalmeyen vnd Pussaunen zu altieren vnnd passieren guot sein sollen. Die wir geen by unns haben vnnd geprachen wolten.

> One of this town's wind players got in trouble with a rival guild by selling drinking glasses on the side. The town council ordered a stop to this infringement (Ratsprotokolle, 22 November 1521).

> The selling of drinking glasses. The shopkeepers guild have complained that Jörg Wier has drinking glasses and other glasses for sale, which he is not allowed to do. A member of the small trader's guild, he has always been a woodworker and claims for this reason always to have had them for sale and therefore requests them to be allowed to remain. It has been decided to send for Jörg Wier and anyone else not a member of the shopkeepers guild who have glasses for sale.

[22] Memmingen, Stadtarchiv (Ratsprotokollbuch 1517–1519).

> Jacken dem plaser will man x tag gen augspurg mit den anndern pfeiffern erlauben ob sie mochten ain geblin gewynnen mit den krumen hornern, doch das er uns mittler zeyt die wacht wol versehe.

[23] This entire document is quoted in its original form in Arno Werner, *Vier Jahrhunderte im Dienste der Kirchenmusik* (Leipzig: Carl Merseburger, 1933), 275ff.

Smithers[24] quotes an interesting example of an actual oath taken by a new civic trumpeter in Wismar, in 1586.

> I swear that I shall be true, obedient and loyal to the honorable council of the town of Wismar, to bear in mind their and the town's best interest, and to avert harm to the best of my ability while on the tower of St. Nicholas where I have been appointed tower watch. I swear to watch carefully day and night, to look after light and fire with all diligence so no harm may come to the town and church from them; in other respects I also swear to behave modestly and peacefully with everyone and to lead an honorable and respectable life, so help me God.

Finally, there is one very unusual sixteenth-century reference to tower watch-musicians performing their surrogate clock duty. Here the poor citizens are not only awakened at three or four o'clock in the morning, but are awakened to the sound of crashing cymbals(!), together with an interesting variety of other instruments.

> (They) are to give the time hourly with cymbals, and also every day in the morning around daybreak, at about three or four o'clock, they are to play on flutes, crumhorns, cornetts or shawms; similarly around midday at eleven o'clock and then again in the evening … at about nine or ten o'clock.[25]

The civic wind band in Delitzsch had a contract in 1580 which required their playing at the very same times as above, but with the additional responsibility of winding the town clock![26]

During the sixteenth century the universities were, as they are in Europe today, very closely connected with local civic government, thus the great university ceremonies were also civic celebrations as well. In Köln the doctoral ceremonies for lawyers included a procession with trumpets and drums.[27] Even more interesting was the celebrations of the Doctors of Theology, who in 1591 not only engaged four wind players, but provided them with wine and three persons to carry their instruments.[28]

An account[29] of the awarding of degrees ceremony at the University of Leipzig, in 1541–1542, permits one to see how elaborate these festivities could be. On the evening before, the

---

[24] Smithers, *The Music and History of the Baroque Trumpet*, 120ff.

[25] H. Moser, 'Zur Mittelalterlichen Musikgeschichte der Stadt Köln,' in *Archiv für Musikwissenschaft* I (1918), 136ff.

> (Sie) sollen alle stunden mit dem Zimbel den uhren nachschlagen, auch alle tag des morgens, wenn der tag bald beginnet heranzubrechen, ungefährlich um drei oder vier uhren, in ihre pfeifen, krumhörner, zincken oder schalmeien blasen, zu mit tag um eilf uhren gleichergestalt und dann des abends … ungefährlich um neun oder zehn uhren abermalen.

[26] Smithers, *The Music and History of the Baroque Trumpet*, 123.

[27] Hermann Keussen, 'Die alte Universität Köln,' *Universität Köln* (Köln, 1929), 43.

[28] Franz Joseph von Bianco, *Die alte Universität Köln und die spätern Gelehrten-Schulen dieser Stadt* (Köln, 1856), 89–90, 100.

> Spielleuten: Item den vier unseren Herren Spielleuten aus Beuelch jederem 1 Goigulten—6 Thlr. 8 Alb.
> Voigt was an obgemeltem Werck zerbrochen: Item fur ein weisse Krug, 80 die Spilleuth hinweggenohmen, far 8 alb.
> Item den Spilleuten die Kost geben, wie den Gasselbotten. NB. haben am vorigen Tag ein weisse Krug sampt dem Wein gefordert und hinweg genohmen, nobis invitis sagten, es wer der Brauch also, sein uber 4 Q. Wein.
> Organist W. Kubertus. Item hat W. Kubertus vor sein Theil nichts haben wollen, sonder vor seine zween Jungen gefordert 1 Reichsthlr. Item noch vor drey Personen, so die Instrumenta musicalia hin und wider getragen, und einem so geblasen, zusammen 18 Alb. thut so W. Kubertus empfangen—1 Thlr. 22 Alb.

civic trumpeters announced the event to the entire city. At the first official ceremony, the *Promotionsakt*, where the vice-chancellor empowers the dean to accept the successful candidates into the *magisterium*, the civic wind band plays a musical interlude followed by participation in a procession with the trumpeters. Later these same wind players, together with singers from St. Thomas Church, performed at a great banquet in honor of the candidates.

A description of the ceremonies of those being promoted to the degree of Doctor of Medicine in Basel, in 1557, mentions a four-man wind band playing in the cathedral before the ceremony and in the procession afterward.[30]

A basic part of all civic wind band's expectations was their participation in welcoming distinguished visitors. An eyewitness to the arrival of visiting princes attending the wedding of Duke Ludwig of Württemberg to Dorothea Ursula, of Baden-Durlach, in Stuttgart in 1575, reported,

> Such a noise of cornets and crumhorns, of bombards, racketts and shawms that one could not even hear oneself speak.[31]

An ink drawing by Johann Twenger shows the Breslau civic wind band (cornett, trombone, trumpet, and dulzian) on a triumphal arch, welcoming Rudolf II on 24 May 1577.[32]

Civic wind bands also were required to perform for all important civic banquets, and a typical civic contract in Zwickau, in 1569, calls upon the four-man civic wind band, the 'zwen Zincken, Posaun vnd Bomhardt' to play fanfares and dance music at all 'Festtage.'[33]

Finally, an anonymous woodcut from 1541 shows a civic trumpeter performing a typical, if more mundane, task of accompanying a civic official making his rounds making accouncements.[34]

Civic wind bands in Germany, as everywhere in Europe, augmented their salary by performing for private weddings. We can gain an insight into this custom, which was often highly organized, in the sixteenth-century civic regulations in Weissenfels.[35] When the civic wind band was requested to perform by the bridegroom, at the church, banquet, or dance,

[29] Georg Erler, *Leipziger Magisterschmäuse* (Leipzig: Giesecke & Devrient, 1905), 150ff. I have taken my account from the version as it appears in Nan Cooke Carpenter, *Music in the Medieval and Renaissance Universities* (Norman: University of Oklahoma Press, 1954), 253.

[30] Heinrich Boos, *Thomas und Felix Platter* (Leipzig, 1878), 309–310.

> ... ich stalt mich in die undere cathedram, D. Issac in die obere und nach dem bleser, so do waren, ufgeblasen, hült D. Issac die oration und proponiert mir die themata.
> ......
> ... doruf die vier bleser anfiengen blosen und zogen in der procession also uss dem sal zu der Cronen. do dass pancquet angestelt war und gieng mit mir der rector D. Wolfgangus Wissenburger, hernoch der alt herr doctor Amerbach und andre academici in zimlicher zal, der pedel vor mir und die bleser, so durch die gassen biss zur herberg bliesin.

[31] Nicodemus Frischlin, quoted in G. Pietzsch, 'Beschreibungen deutscher Fürstenhochzeiten von der Mitte des 15. bis zum Beginn des 17. Jahrhunderts ala musikgeschichtliche Quellen,' in *Anuario Musical*, vol. 15 (1960), 46.

> Von Zincken, krumphoernern ein schreien, Von Bomhart, Racketen, Schalmeien, Dass einer gleich sein eigen wort Bey jme selber nimmer hort.

[32] Nürnberg, Germanisches Nationalmuseum (Sign. HB 235).

[33] Salman, *Musikleben im 16. Jahrhundert*, 74.

[34] Found in Joannes Millaeus, *Praxis criminis*, copy in Nürnberg, Germanisches Nationalmuseum (Sign. R. 3134 m. 4v.).

the band received four Groschen from each guest. If any bridegroom preferred not to have 'music,' but only fife and drums, there was a standard charge of twelve Groschen. The wind band, moreover, was permitted to 'pass the hat,' twice for a morning wedding and once for an evening wedding, but could make no further demands on the guests. For purposes of the security of the players, they could not be asked to remain later than ten o'clock in the evening (nine o'clock in the winter).

The civic wind band had the right to a 'Brautsuppe,' eating and drinking in the home of the bridegroom, but the excesses of some band members led to a loss of this privilege in 1598.

During war time, or during a period of economic decline, the civic wind band played for more modest compensation.

There is a very interesting account of the dance music played by wind bands at these wedding celebrations in the 1532 contract for the civic wind band at Reval (Tallinn).

> Item after the evening meal they should play four popular double dances and then they can play a double dance with recorders or crumhorns, as well a girl's dance and the bride's dance, which adds up to ten dances ... Whoever wishes to hold board for an evening in the hall or houses and wishes to be entertained on recorders and crumhorns with four double dances, one girl's dance (and) one bride's dance, for this the payment is six farthings.[36]

Every resourceful civic wind band no doubt found many individual means of seeking more money from the citizens. I close this discussion with an account[37] of the civic wind band in Delitzach which had started a tradition of performing a 'Neujahrsblasen.' This consisted of the band, with their apprentices, going around the town on New Year's Day, playing in front of the citizens houses for donations. It seems this was quite unpopular with the townspeople and so in 1599 the town council passed a special bonus of one Taler for the civic wind band, if they would not carry out this New Year's performance.

---

35 Arno Werner, *Stadtische und furstliche musikpflege in Weissenfels* (Leipzig: Breitkopf & Hartel, 1911), 36.

36 H. Moser, 'Zur Mittelalterlichen Musikgeschichte der Stadt Köln,' in *Archiv für Musikwissenschaft* I (1918), 139.

> Item nah der auendt maltidt sollen seh spellen IIII dubbelde dentze gelevet idt en szo mogen sze eynen dub belden dantz mith flouten off krum hornern spelen hier tho eynen yunckfrouwen dantz unde den bruth danstz szind tho samende X denze ... Szo we eyne auendts kost holden will ym gylstauen off yn huyszen unde will zick an flouten unde krum hornen genoegen lathen III dubbelde dentzse eyn yunckfrouwen dantz I brudt dantz hir vor sall men en geven VI ferding.

37 Werner, *Vier jahrhunderte im dienste der kirchenmusik*, 231.

Civic Wind Bands in the German-Speaking Countries 195

An engraving by Johann Twenger featuring a wind band performing for the arrival of Emperor Rudolf II at Breslau, Poland, 1577.

10   *Civic Wind Bands in Italy*

Every sixteenth century Italian town of almost any size had two civic wind ensembles. First there was an ensemble of trumpets which were used in particular for ceremonial purposes. When great state visitors would arrive, these civic trumpets would often join with the aristocratic visitor's trumpets, and perhaps with borrowed trumpets from other towns, to form large numbers. One reads, for example, of the welcome given Louis XII of France in Milan in 1499 when not only the six 'trombatori del Comune' played their silver trumpets, but one hundred additional trumpets encircled the king, in front and to the rear.[1] The statutes of Urbine (1559) contain an interesting suggestion that the repertoire of these official trumpeters was not always merely of the fanfare type, for here it specifies 'devout' music.

> … shall be preceded by trumpets … and … with a devout and sonorous sound of trumpeters playing on loud trumpets.[2]

Each town also had a civic wind band, usually called 'musica di piffari,' or 'compagnia di piffari,' or simply 'piffari,' but it is clear that during the sixteenth century some combination of shawms, trombones, and cornetts were intended by this term and not primarily instruments of the flute family.[3]

A curious exception was Torino, which called its civic wind band, 'Banda di tromboni. This band, which performed at all civic functions, wore uniforms of silver and gold, embossed with the duke's arms. It had seven members by 1585, with many members, including the leaders, Giovanni De Ler (1567) and Anselmo Sergiusi (1580), imported from Lucca, which had flourishing music schools.[4]

Most civic wind bands in Italy seem not to have organized themselves into guilds, as was the case in most of Europe, and so had more difficulty in collective bargaining with their town councils.[5] No doubt this accounts for the Italian civic wind bandsmen being paid less than almost any other musicians in their country.[6]

---

[1] Alessandro Vessella, *La Banda*, 80.

[2] Don Smithers, *The Music and History of the Baroque Trumpet*, 77.

[3] Dietrich Kämper, *Studien zur INstrumentalen Ensemblemusik des 16. Jahrhunderts in Italien*, 50.

[4] Vessella, *La Banda*, 130.

[5] Exceptions may have been Florence, see Orazio Bacci, ed., *Vita di Benvenuto Cellini* (Florence: Sansoni, 1901), 12ff.; and Venice, see Francesco Caffi, *Storia della musica sacra* (Venice, 1855), 1:57.

[6] An excellent discussion of this point can be found in Carl Anthon, 'Some Aspects of the Social Status of Italian Musicians during the Sixteenth Century,' *Journal of Renaissance and Baroque Music* (1946), part 2, 222ff.

One of the many large towns which had both kinds of ensembles was Bologna, as we can read in an eyewitness description of both in 1602.

> When they appear in public, these 'Signori' (the town council) are dressed in rich robes of silk, and during the winter they are muffled up with very precious furs as well. They are accompanied by a very respectable household of eight trumpeters, with a drummer or player of the nakers, who with these trumpets play certain Moorish drums. To both the drums and trumpets are attached banners with the arms of liberty; also eight excellent musicians with trombones and cornettos; a herald; a 'spenditore'; nine pages dressed in scarlet cloaks and stockings in the livery of the city—white and red.[7]

This band, called the 'Concerto Palatino,' had a regular instrumentation of four cornets and four trombones and was famous throughout Italy for its concerts.[8]

In Florence the civic wind band traditions seem to have been so deeply rooted that they continued to flourish despite the great political upheavals which began the century.[9] It is said that there was such a close relationship between music and the other arts in Florence, that the father to Benvenuto Cellini began flute lessons for his son at an early age believing that, whatever craft he might wish to follow when he was older, the entry to a craft would be facilitated by his son's having been a musician.[10]

The civic wind band in Florence, 'I pifferi della Signoria,' consisted of three shawms and two sackbuts in 1510, with a sixth player added in about 1520.[11] One must assume that, as was usually the case, these players played all the basic wind instruments of the time, except for the trumpet. We also know that in 1512 Benvenuto Cellini himself was granted provisional membership as a player of the flute due to his unusual ability, even though he was only twelve years of age.[12]

Polk believes that the impression in general history texts that the members of the string instrument family were popular by this time in Florence may be quite in error; indeed, he was unable to find a *single* reference to a string instrument in the civic archives between 1490 and 1532!

In addition to the wind band, Florence also had civic trumpets, who are called 'trombetti,' or 'trombatori' These two terms represent a distinction in the instrument used, as one can see in a description of a civic procession held during the final years of the Republic (1525–1530).[13] First one saw eight 'trom-

[7] Smithers, *The Music and History of the Baroque Trumpet*, 78.

[8] Grove, 3:2; also 19:160, which contains the biography of one of the cornett players in this band during the sixteenth century, Ascanio Trombetti. Accounts of the concerts by the Padua civic wind band at the annual carnival in 1549 speak of performances more in the nature of cabaret or variety shows. (Kämper, *Studien zur Instrumentalen Ensemblemusik des 16. Jahrhunderts in Italien*, 181–182)

[9] This period of upheaval began with the French invasion of 1494 and the subsequent rule of Savanarola. A pro-French, anti-Medici, faction followed and then in 1512 the return of Medici power under the man who would become Pope Leo x. Another anti-Medici faction took power in 1528 and then the return of the Medicis occurred again in 1532, thanks to Charles v.

[10] Vessella, *La Banda*, 92.

[11] The civic wind music in Florence during the fifteenth and sixteenth centuries is extensively discussed in an unpublished paper, 'Civic Patronage and Instrumental Ensembles in Renaissance Florence,' by Keith Polk.

[12] 'Deliberazioni dei Signori e Collegi,' Archivio centrale di Stato in Firenze (Vol. 104, 1511–1512, carte 46).

[13] Vessella, *La Banda*, 92–93.

betti,' with long, ornate, silver trumpets, 'very heavy,' weighing 3 pounds, 3 ounces. Next came six 'trombadori,' with equally ornate trumpets, weighing 6 pounds, 6 ounces. Now an ensemble of two trombetti, two trombadori, a drum player (naccherino),[14] and a cymbal player (ciambanelle di Bronzo) appeared. Finally, in this procession, the civic band appeared, described here as '4 pifferi' and two silver trombones (tromboni d'argento).

Finally, I might add that there was a kind of children's band in Florence, consisting of children of the civic orphanage. This band seems to have been a wind band, or at least an account of 1586 speaks of 'cornetto, traversa, viola (or) trombone.'[15] This ensemble was popular with the Florentine nobility and under its leader, Franciosio, gave concerts in Pistoia, Ferrara, and Lucca.

Another town which maintained a relatively large civic wind band during the sixteenth century was Lucca. This band had eleven members by 1517[16] and at least ten throughout the century.[17] Among the members of this band were the Dorati family, chiefly Nicolao Dorati (d. 1593), who was hired as a trombonist in 1543 and became the leader of the band in 1557. His brother, Bartolomeo, was also a trombonist in the band from 1546 until his death in 1603. The two sons of Nicolao also were members during the latter part of the century.[18]

This civic wind band was named the 'Musica di Palazzo' and we have a very interesting municipal decree of 1557 which provides an excellent picture of their organization and duties.

[14] One civic drummer during the sixteenth century who seems to have been much appreciated was Gulielmus Gallus, of Ferrara. There is an extant record of a special gift to him by Alfonso I (Modena, Archivio di Stato, Musica e Musicisti, Busta 2).

p(raedic)ti Ill.(ustrissi)mi n(ost)ri familiaris & Tamborinus civis ferrariensis.

[15] Reese, *Music in the Renaissance*, 546.

[16] Salmen, *Musikleben im 16. Jahrhundert*, 16.

[17] Anthon, 'Some Aspects of the Social Status of Italian Musicians during the Sixteenth Century,' 225.

[18] Grove, 5:574.

> Nicolao Dorati is to be the director and head of said musicians, and they must obey him in performing whatever music in whatever manner he may choose. When playing at the city hall, before and after the dinner of the *Signoria*, Messer Bernardino da Padova is to play the first soprano, and Vincenzo di Pasquino Bastini the second soprano; but when playing in the hall or the chambers of the *Signoria*, each one is to play or sing the part assigned to him by said Messer Nicolao, their director. However, outside of the city hall, in church, on the public square, at weddings, feasts, serenades, or other events, where they will number at least six, Messer Giulio is to play the first soprano, Messer Bernardino, his father, the second, and Messer Vincenzo the third, that is, contralto. And if by chance, which God forbid, there should arise among them a quarrel, ill-will, or other trouble, Messer Nicolao is to intervene and restore peace, and if anyone should refuse to listen to reason, he is to be reported to the *Signoria* in office at the time, so that steps can be taken accordingly. And since beautiful music and perfect harmony are the result of constant practice, there should be assigned to them for this purpose a room …

equipped with tables and benches in which they are to meet for practice twice a week for two hours, namely, Wednesdays and Saturdays. From the first of February to the last of September they shall meet in the morning, two hours before dinner, and from the first of October to the last of January, in the afternoon, two hours before supper. In order to enforce these rules, the *maestro di casa* shall take the attendance, and those who are absent, shall be fined one *carlino* for each time, except in case of illness or other legitimate excuse.[19]

[19] Anthon, 'Some Aspects of the Social Status of Italian Musicians during the Sixteenth Century,' 225.

This general pattern seems to have been followed in many of the smaller towns in Italy. Udine had five civic wind band members in 1560 and seven by 1575, consisting of 'piffari' and trombones who played outdoor concerts, processions, for civic guests, and in the church.[20] Perugia during the sixteenth century had six civic trombetti and a wind band of four 'pifferi' and a trombone.[21]

[20] Kämper, *Studien zur Instrumentalen Ensemblemusik des 16. Jahrhunderts in Italien*, 179.

[21] Vessella, *La Banda*, 45.

Parma's wind band was called the 'compagnia di piffari,'[22] which at the beginning of the century consisted of four 'pifferi,' in addition to four civic trombettieri. In 1526 the town council decided to increase the wind band to five players, with the understanding they were not to travel without the permission of the town and the breaking of any rules would result in the suspension of their pay.[23] Their pay, which came in part from the town and in part from the 'Camera Apostolica,' was raised in 1527 and the town also provided new uniforms for every major civic festival. The highest paid players were two trombetti, called 'trombetti foresi,' for it was their responsibility to go outside the walls of the town to recruit new players.

[22] Nestore Pelicelli, 'Musicisti in Parma,' in *Note d' Archivio*, vol. 9 (Rome: Edizioni 'Psalterium', 1932), 42ff.

[23] Vessella, *La Banda*, 89.

The civic wind band in Palermo is called in a document of the sixteenth century, 'musici bifari salariati della citta.' Two extant accounts describe their appearances: in 1574, for the arrival of Monsenior Monreale, who came in four galleys, where they are called 'pifferi, trombeti e timpani'; and in 1593 when they joined the procession celebrating the arrival of the relics of Saint Ninfa.[24]

[24] Ibid, 128.

Because of the unique government of Venice, it was the Doge's wind band which usually appeared as the official representative at both civic and church festivities. The processions which were so typical of all renaissance cities were, of course, water processions in Venice. The doge's boat would always contain the six-member wind band. This band also gave an hour-long concert each day in the Piazza St. Mark.[25]

[25] Eleanor Selfridge-Field, *Venetian Instrumental Music from Gabrieli to Vivaldi* (New York: Praeger, 1975), 14ff.

Venice also had at least six independent piffari bands which were associated with the religious fraternities of the city and which will be discussed below. Perhaps it was the activity of these bands which contributed to a civic ordinance of 1548 requiring 'street musicians and public bands' to obtain a license from the *Messetaria*, an official civic department which superintended a variety of minutiae.[26]

Our greatest interest is reserved for a civic wind band which seems to have been created at the end of the sixteenth century, conducted by, and perhaps founded by, Girolamo Dalla Casa. The name of the band is seen in his title, 'Capo de Concerti delli stromenti di fiato della Illustriss. Signoria di Venetia,' or, 'Leader of the Venetian Civic Wind Band.'[27]

While virtually nothing is known of the function of this civic wind band, an extraordinary portion of their actual repertoire is extant in the two volumes of Dalla Casa's *Il Vero Modo di Diminvir* (1584). Dalla Casa was one of the greatest performers of the cornett during the sixteenth century and these volumes represent his solo literature which was accompanied by the wind band. They consist of the solo part fully written out, with identification of the madrigal or motet over which the solo line is to be played. It is, then, the most extensive body of early literature for a solo wind instrument and wind band accompaniment.

Verona had a famous civic institution, the Accademia Filharmonica, which sponsored concerts. An inventory[28] of its instrument collection in 1569 lists five sets of viols, a lira, a rebechino, seven lutes, two harpsichords, a regal, and the following wind instruments:

A chest of 22 recorders (with crooks for the three lowest) and two incomplete chests
A case of 5 flutes (with the bass made in two pieces), another set of 5, and two incomplete sets
2 tabor-pipes; 2 tamburi
5 crumhorns (pivete)
3 fifes (fiffari da campo)
3 trombones, with their crooks and tuning bits (pezzi)
5 tenor cornetts
4 silver-mounted ordinary cornetts
8 mute cornetts
3 dragon-belled cornetts (con testa di bissa)
1 fagoto with reeds (canelli)

[26] Carew Hazlitt, *The Venetian Republic* (London: A&C Black, 1915), 2:1015.

[27] Original Italian found in Kämper, *Studien zur Instrumentalen Ensemblemusik des 16. Jahrhunderts in Italien*, 204.

[28] Quoted in Anthony Baines, *Woodwind Instruments and Their History* (New York: Norton, 1962), 239.

PART 3
Church Wind Bands

Church Wind Bands

I BELIEVE THAT STUDENTS OF MY GENERATION were given a rather incomplete picture of sixteenth-century church music, the professors and textbooks following the concentration of nineteenth-century scholarship on the great Roman Church music of Josquin, Palestrina, etc., left at least one student with the impression that this was an 'a cappella' era. Nothing could be further from the truth. In the English-speaking world, our perspective has been blinded in particular by the fact that the crucial third volume of Praetorius' *Syntagma Musicum* has never been published in an English translation.

Nothing demonstrates the significance of this misunderstanding of sixteenth-century church practices more than the view given my generation of the great wind masterworks of Gabrieli and his school. This body of music, while acknowledged as important, was presented as something of an isolated phenomenon, as something which somehow just appears at one place and one time. As a result of this unexplainable and isolated appearance, it was taken as somewhat 'odd,' in the greater context of sixteenth-century church music, rather than as the logical climax of something which was going on throughout the century.

We can see today that there were much wider traditions of church music during the sixteenth century. That portion which I document in the following pages—the use of wind bands—is clearly evident in the contracts and payments to civic wind bands throughout Europe; in the personal wind ensembles maintained by the church princes themselves, first and foremost being the wind bands of the popes, which I have documented above; and in the known protests of some clerics against the use of instruments in the church, together with the replies which these provoked from musicians.[1]

The rich iconography of the sixteenth century stands as an additional testimony to this wider tradition. First, there are icons which clearly picture these wind bands participating in the actual service. The most striking example is the often reproduced engraving by Adrian Collaert, 'Mass, with several

[1] For the latter category, see Denis Arnold, 'Brass Instruments in the Italian Church Music of the Sixteenth and Early Seventeenth Centuries,' *Brass Quarterly* (1957), 81.

choirs' (1595), in which one sees not one but two separate wind bands, consisting of cornetts nd trombones, performing with the choirs.[2] Another widely reproduced icon which shows a wind band perforing during the service is the woodcut appearing in Hermann Finck's *Musica Practica* (1556).[3]

[2] After a drawing by Johannes Stradanus in the Cabinet des Estampes, Paris, National Library; a copy of the Collaert engraving can be found in the West Berlin Staatliches Institut für Musikforschung.

[3] A copy can be found in the Brussels, Bibliothèque Royale (Fonds Fetis, Nr. 5322).

Musical Celebration of a Mass (1595), by Adriaen Collaert (1560–1618)

A woodcut from Hermann Finck's *Musica Practica* (1556)

CHURCH WIND BANDS 207

In addition to these examples, which show the wind band performing for the Mass itself, there are many icons which demonstrate the participation of wind bands in other kinds of church formalities. Foremost among these are, of course, weddings, and a typical example is a painting on wood called *Wedding of the Holy Ursula* (ca. 1520) which pictures a wind band of four shawms and a trombone.[4]

[4] Anonymous, Lisbon, Museu Nacional de Arte Antiga (Inv.-Nr. 597).

Wedding of the Holy Ursula, ca. 1520, picturing a wind band of four shawms and a trombone (see detail above)

As the coronations of the secular princes always included wind bands, so the church princes wanted for their ceremonies no less regal splendor. An altar painting by Christophorus Moya (1580) depicts the ordination of a bishop and includes a wind band which appears to be three shawms and a slide-trumpet.[5]

[5] Tarragona, Museo Provincial.

Detail from an altar painting, *La consagración de San Agustín*, by Christophorus Moya, 1580

Sixteenth-century icons portraying the stories of the bible sometimes interpolate the modern (sixteenth century) wind band into the picture. A series of drawings illustrating the Old Testament, *Historiarum Veteris Testamenti*, by Hans Holbein, done in Basel, ca. 1525, are an excellent example. In illustration Nr. 56, one sees the Arc of the Covenant surrounded by a wind band consisting of two (and possibly three) slide-trumpets, a trombone, an unidentifiable wind instrument, a pipe and tabor player, together with the more biblical harpist. Similarly, the *Encomium Musices* (Antwerp, ca. 1595), by Philippus Gallaeus,[6] provides music by a wind band of cornetts, shawm, and pipe and tabor, for the crossing of the Red Sea.

[6] A facsimile edition was published in Cambridge in 1943.

A drawings from *Historiarum Veteris Testamenti*, by Hans Holbein, ca. 1525, showing the Arc of the Covenant surrounded by a wind band.

Because the sixteenth century was still fond of allegorical lessons, many such icons include the wind band. One of the more frequently reproduced examples is the 'Gebyn aller Menschen,' from the *Dance of Death* series of woodcuts by Hans Holbein (Basel, 1525). Here one sees a wind band of skeleton figures playing a slide-trumpet, two straight trumpets, a shawm, two woodwinds (possibly crumhorns), timpani, and a hurdy-gurdy. There are several icons which portray wind bands of 'angels,' an extraordinary example being the anonymous Czech painting, 'Coronation of the Virgin and Child' (1520).[7] Here three separate wind consorts are seen: on the left, three cornetts and a trombone; in the center, a trio of recorders; and on the right a consort of four crumhorns. Another example, from the same year, is the Litoméřice Song Book, which includes a consort of angels playing shawms.[8]

Finally, one must mention the new pipes being included in sixteenth-century organ construction, for they are clearly an imitation of the contemporary wind band sounds. A very interesting example is found in a contract for a new organ in the cathedral in Antwerp, dated 1509, which includes the specification,

7 Národní Galerie, Prague.

8 A reproduction can be found in Barra Boydell, *The Crumhorn and Other Renaissance Windcap Instruments* (Buren: Knuf, 1982) ,283.

two types of flutes and hollow pipes as well as tabor pipes, hunting horns, flutes, trumpets, shawms, cornetts, *ruyspypen* (Rauschpfeife?), and tambors and yet other strange sounds which have not been heard in organs.[9]

The 'ruyspypen' appears again in Arnold Schlick's *Spiegel der Orgelmacher und Organisten* in 1511. In describing new registers, he mentions,

> certain new registers or pipes ... such as *russpfeiffen*, crumhorns and trumpets which are now made.
>
> ...
>
> I can point to *rausspfeifen* and trumpet stops existing and in use in an instrument for nine years.[10]

It is my hope that these iconographic examples will suggest, and the following pages will document, the rather evident conclusion one must reach: there is more to the story of sixteenth-century church music than the masterpieces of a cappella music!

[9] Jean Auguste Stellfeld, *Bronnen tot de geschiedenis der Antwerpsche clavecimbel- en orgelbouwers in de XVIe en XVIIe eeuwen* (Antwerpen: Drukkerij Resseler, 1942), 45.

> ... twee maniren van fluten ende hoelpypen noch sweegelen walthoernen scheelpipen trompetten schalmeyen sincken ruyspypen ende tamborynen ende noch meer andere seltseme stemmen die noyt in orgelen gehoirt geweest.

[10] Quoted in ibid., 19.

> ... Etlicher neüwer register oder pfeiffen ... als rüss pfeiffen, oder kromphörner und Trommeten so man nun macht ...
>
> ...
>
> Ich kan zeigen rausspfeiffen und trompten bey neun jaren in eim werck gestenden und gebrucht ...

A woodcut from the *Dance of Death* series by Hans Holbein (Basel, 1525) showing a wind band of skeleton figures playing a slide-trumpet, two straight trumpets, a shawm, two woodwinds (possibly crumhorns), timpani, and a hurdy-gurdy.

11 *Church Wind Bands in the Low Countries*

EXTANT DOCUMENTATION from the sixteenth century suggests that in the Low Countries, as in Germany, performance in the church may have been a regular duty of the civic wind band; Polk believes that such performances were common by 1550.[1]

A typical contract from early in the century is found in Mechelen (1505), where the civic band was required to 'play on cornets and other instruments during the solemn masses celebrated by order of the magistrates.'[2] In Mechelen this tradition seems to have continued for in a civic document of 1550–1551 one again reads of payments to members of the civic band for performing during the Mass, as well as in church processions.[3]

A new series of regulations for the civic band in Mons in 1588 is not quite so specific but also seems to imply regular performance in the Mass, as the players are directed to 'assist with the Mass.'[4]

For Antwerp, one finds a document regarding the purchase of two 'trompers' (trombones or slide-trumpets) by the city to be used by Susato,

> in the processions and also in the church with the singers (during the mass).[5]

---

[1] Polk, 'Ensemble Instrumental Music in Flanders,' 24.

[2] Wangermée, *Flemish Music*, 180.

[3] Mechelen *Stads Rekeningen*, 1550–1551, fol. 229.
> Item den stadtspelieden ... voer dat zy gespeelt hebben inde processie mitgaders noch ... dryen van inde misse gespeelt te hebben.

[4] Vander Straeten, *La Musique aux Pays-Bas*, 2:32.
> Premiers, que tous joueurs de ladicte ville, debveront estre de ladicte connestablie et payer pour leur entrée chacun la somme de cincq gros, pour employer à faire célébrer la messe chacun mois, pour pryer Dieu et madamme sainte Cécile, pour les âmes des trepassez d'icelle connestablie, à laquele messe debveront adsister tous joueurs et ceulx de ladicte connestablie, sauf légitisme excuse, à peine d'encheyr en cincq solz tournois chacun.

[5] Antwerp *Stads Rekeningen*, 1541–1542, fol. 88.
> Inde omegangen ende Inder kerken metten sangers op hooge dagen te spelen.

There is also a reference to the actual literature used by the Antwerp wind band in the church in a 'lovely large songbook,' created by Anthony Barbe, chapel master of the Cathedral of Our Lady in 1550. The music was to be used at High Masses, 'to be sung out of by the choir, and to be played out of by the city musicians.'[6]

A similar volume of motets to be used by a civic wind band in the church was commissioned in 1484 of Casin de Brauwer, Master of the Children at St. Donaes, by the town council of Bruges.[7] Following this, the civic wind band apparently did not appear in the church for a few years at the turn of the century for one finds that the choir master, Obrecht, no less, received an order from the city demanding correction. In 1509 the accounts again note the presence of the 'chapel master, singers, organist and wind players.'[8]

In Audenarde an extant civic regulation, dated 5 September 1514, calls for the civic wind band (scalmeyers) to participate in the Mass in the church of Sainte-Walburge.[9] In another document, of 1539, one reads of a member of the wind band being sent to Antwerp to purchase a 'beautiful case of crumhorns' to be used in the annual procession of the sacrament.[10] I might add that while there are accounts of harps and lutes in these processions, the violin does not appear in the church records before 1691![11]

---

[6] Leon de Burbure, 'Notes historiques de Antwerp' (Unpublished volumes of notes in the Antwerp City Archive), 1:103.

… gegeven Mr. Athoni Barbe, zangmeester ter maken van eenen schoonen grooten zanckboeken die hij … doen schrijven voor de stadt, omme hoochdaeche in de choor daer uyt te zingene, ende de stadtspeellieden deser stadt daer uyt te spelene …

[7] Vander Straeten, *La Musique aux Pays-Bas*, 4:99.

Betaelt heer Casin de Brauwer, priester ende cantor van den Kinderen van Sint-Salvators, voor zyn salaris van den moyte by hem gliehadt van ghestelt ende ghemaect te hebben, ten divers chen stonden, zekere motetten, omme die by den menestreulen van deser stede ghespeelt te werdene, uut gracien.

[8] Bruges, *Stads Rekeningen*, 1508–1509, fol. 66v.

De Cantre, zanghere, oorghelare ende blasere 't sint donanes … ter causen van den … alle tlof ende salve sint donaes.

[9] Vander Straeten, La Musique aux Pays-Bas., 4:143.

[10] Ibid., 145. .

Betaelt Arent Van Curtenbosch, van dat hy, by ordonnantie van scepenen deser stede, ontrent Sacramentsdach laetsleden, tot behouve deser stede, gecocht heeft t'Antwerpen, eenen schoonen cokere cromhoorens, die der selver stede toebehoort, tsamen de somme van lxxx lib. par.

[11] Ibid., 152.

Finally, there is perhaps an example of a regular church wind player found in a document from Ieper, dated 1592, regarding a 'bass flute,' helping out in the choir.[12]

The court chapels in the Low Countries seem to have had permanent wind players, rather than resorting to borrowing the local civic wind bands. A list of personnel of the royal chapel in Brussels for 1576 lists three priests, nine singers, two cornett players, one trombonist, an organist, and an organ tuner.[13]

Similarily, the court of Margaret of Austria, the Regent of the Low Countries, also maintained wind players for use in the service.

> Paid to Hans Nagel and Jehan van Vincle, instrumentalists ... for ... having served continually ... in singing and playing daily in discant the divine hours and services.[14]

[12] Vander Straeten, *La Musique aux Pays-Bas*, 2:265.

> Prima augusti 1592.—Domini concluserunt instrumentum seu fistulam pro basso esse, expensis fabrice.
> ......
> Ex venditione instrumenti ad formandum bas sum.

[13] Vander Straeten, *La Musique aux Pays-Bas*, 3:319ff.

> A Théodor Rixstel, sonneur de trombon ...
> A Stévin Denooter, sonneur de cornet ...
> A Michel Francs, sonneur de cornet ...

[14] Vander Straeten, *La Musique aux Pays-Bas*, 7:269.

> ... et Hans Naghele et Jehan Van Vincle, joueurs d'instruments d'icellui sr., la somma de huit cens livres ... pour, par ordonnance d'iceulx srs et de madite dame de Savoye, avoir servy continuellement devers mondit sr, en sadite chapelle, en chant ant et jouant journellement en discant les heures et service divin.

> For additional information regarding these two players, see above, pages 89–90, fn. 12, 15.

12 Church Wind Bands in France

A WELL-KNOWN EXAMPLE OF FRENCH WIND PLAYERS participating in a Mass is the one which occurred on 23 June 1520, during the historic meeting between Francis I and Henry VIII. Cardinal Wolsey, richly clad with even his sandals set with jewels, was the celebrant, even though he had not personally conducted a Mass in years.[1] But then, this was a very special occasion,

> being present ... xxi bishops, in pontificall, iii cardinals and i legate under a cloth of estate, at which mass there were iii kings, iii queens, with divers and many noble estate.[2]

It appears that the English and French royal chapels alternated in singing the movements of a Mass written by a composer named Perino. One account indicates some movements were accompanied by organ and others by sackbuts and fifes (certainly shawms is meant).[3] Another account indicates the entire Mass was accompanied by organ, sackbuts and cornetts.[4] One listener was moved to declare, 'it was heavenlie hearing.'[5]

There is at least one indication that under Francis I the court wind band participated in the Mass while in Paris as well. One of Wolsey's correspondents heard High Mass in the chapel of Francis I and mentioned that it was accompanied by 'hautbois (shawms) and sackbutts.'[6]

Speaking of Wolsey, his counterpart in Paris was John, Cardinal of Lorraine (1498–1550), a close companion of Francis I, and a very wealthy church prince as he held eight bishoprics, four archbishoprics and several of the wealthier abbeys, including Cluny. A contemporary noted that to attend a Church council, he merely had to commune with himself! And like the similarly princely Wolsey, this Cardinal also maintained his own personal wind players.[7]

---

[1] According to the Venetian ambassador to London, quoted in Joycelyne Russell, *The Field of Cloth of Gold*, 173–174.

[2] Ibid.

[3] Ibid., 174.
[4] Ibid., 175.
[5] Ibid., 174.

[6] Stevens, *Music & Poetry in the Early Tudor Court*, 313.

[7] Daniel Heartz, *Pierre Attaingnant: Royal Printer of Music*, 83, where a poem (Chantilly, Musée Condé, MS 530) by one of the Cardinal's shawm players, Florent Copin, is also quoted in part—apologizing for his inadequacy to the task of sufficiently gratifying his master.

> Car pour assez, o des princes le prime
> Joyeulx te rendre oyant beaulx vers en rithme
> Un sainct-Gelais, poete tant supreme
> Omere grec, Marot ny maro mesme
> Ne suffiroient a te donner plaisir.

John, Cardinal of Lorraine (1498–1550), sixteenth century

A court document from late in the reign of Francis I gives the personnel of the *schola cantorum*, founded in 1543, as 'two undermasters, six children, two cornett players, twenty-six singers, twelve clerics, and two grammar teachers for the children.'[8]

[8] Guillaume Du Peyrat, *L'histoire ecclésiastique de la Cour* (Paris, 1645), 479.

It is probable that the wind players who performed with the court chapel also traveled with the king. An account, taken from Bayonne during the great tour of 1564–1566 by Charles IX and Catherine de' Medici, mentions a Te Deum sung by the king's chapel singers and accompanied by 'excellent cornetts.'[9]

[9] *Recueil des choses notables, qui ont esté faites a Bayonne …* (Paris, 1566), 7.

An account recording the arrival of Elizabeth of Austria at Notre Dame Cathedral mentions she was greeted by 'great numbers of trumpets, clarions, and cornetts.'[10]

[10] Simon Bouquet, *Bref et sommaire recueil de ce qui a este faict …* (Paris, 1571).

Finally, there is an indication that in some of the provincial cities the town wind bands also assisted in the church music. In Toulouse, during the sixteenth century, the civic band supplied 'oboes, trumpets and drums for ceremonial motets and masses in the principal churches.'[11]

[11] Grove, 19:93.

13 *Church Wind Bands in Spain*

According to Salmen,[1] during the sixteenth century it was a normal occurrance for 'ministriles' to participate in the performance of polyphonic music in the great Spanish cathedrals. By this date, as I have noted above, 'minstrel' almost always means the players of wind instruments. So here too, one reads in a description of the instrumental music of the Granada Cathedral,

> Instruments were used at first only to accompnay certain processions (when portative organs were also used), but from 1563 six instrumentalists were employed for the daily services; they played flutes, trumpets, trombones and bassoons.[2]

In Seville in particular one finds accounts of the use of wind band in the cathedral, under the leadership of Francisco Guerrero (1528–1599), a musician second only to Victoria in importance as a composer of Spanish church music and himself a cornett player. According to Salmen, the instruments he used were shawms, sackbuts, and bassoons.[3] Robert Stevenson gives a somewhat broader range of consorts of instruments used in the cathedral.

> Throughout his long tenure at Seville Cathedral, instruments such as families of shawms, cornetts, flutes and bassoons were constantly used to add divisions, embellishing and alternating with his vocal lines.[4]

In another place, Stevenson quotes an actual cathedral document, dated 11 July 1586, which specifies,

> At greater feasts there shall always be a verse played on recorders. At Salves, one of the three verses that are played shall be on shawms, one on cornetts and the other on recorders; because always hearing the same instrument annoys the listener.[5]

Stevenson also comments that the music of Guerrero, much more than the music of either Morales or Victoria, was copied and recopied for use in the cathedrals of the New World.[6] This

[1] Salmen, *Musikleben im 16. Jahrhundert*, 182.

[2] Grove, 7:627.

[3] Salmen, *Musikleben im 16. Jahrhundert*, 182.

[4] Robert Stevenson, 'Francisco Guerrero,' Grove, 7:789.

[5] Robert Stevenson, *Spanish Cathedral Music in the Golden Age* (Berkeley: University of California Press, 1961), 152–167.

[6] Grove, 7:789.

Spanish composer Francisco Guerrero, by Francisco Pacheco, 1599

perhaps helps explain the fact that one finds evidence that the New World churches also made extensive use of wind bands in their services. Regarding Mexico, for example, one finds in Geronimo de Mendieta's *Historia Eclesiastica Indiana* (ca. 1571–1596) the interesting observation that,

> nowhere in all of Christendom are there so many recorders, shawms, sackbuts, orlas, trumpets and drums as in the Kingdom of New Spain.[7]

Further south, in Guatemala, there is a document recording the purchase of a case of recorders for the main cathedral already in 1549.[8] I might mention that Indiana University

[7] Quoted in J.A. Guzmán-Bravo, 'Mexico, Home of the First Musical Instrument Workshops in America' *Early Music* 6, no. 3 (1978): 355.

> en todos los reinos de la Cristiandad no hay tanta copia de flautas, chirimías, sacabuches, orlas, trompeta y atables como solo en este Reino de La Nueva España.

[8] Robert Stevenson, 'European Music in 16th Century Guatemala,' *The Musical Quarterly* 50, no. 3 (1964): 341–352.

owns several volumes of manuscripts, dating from sixteenth-century Guatemala, which contain polyphonic instrumental compositions.⁹

Even in South America, one reads that when Fernandez Hidalgo was in charge of the cathedral music in La Plata (now Sucre, Bolivia), he,

> lured a number of other musicians from Cuzco and maintained a rich establishment which included players of cornetts, sackbuts, flutes and shawms as well as singers.¹⁰

Finally, a few notes about Portugal are appropriate here, especially regarding an important individual player, Andre de Escobar (fl. 1560–1580). This man held the title of 'Master of the Shawms' at both the Evora Cathedral and the University of Coimbra.¹¹ He also was the author of a method book for the shawm, the *Arte musica para tanger o instrumento da charamelinha*, which unfortunately does not survive.¹²

There was also a wind band in residence in the cathedral in Lisbon. We know, for example, that in 1592 the musicians of this cathedral consisted of twenty-four adult and twenty-two boy singers, two bassoons, a cornettist and two organists.¹³

[9] See the sixth volume in this series.

[10] Grove, 6:475.

[11] According to a document dated February 4, 1579, in the city archives.

[12] Grove, 6:243.

[13] Grove, 11:24.

14 Church Wind Bands in England

REFERENCES TO THE USE OF WIND BANDS in English churches, especially in the performance of *Te Deums* are fairly frequent in the literature of the sixteenth century. One author believes this tradition was already strong before that period.

> I have tried to show elsewhere that the *alta capella* (wind band) was probably used early on for the ceremonial performance of 'Te Deum' with bells. The first likely use of it is in 1306, in the service which ended the Prince of Wales' vigil before he was knighted: Matthew of Westminster remarks that the noise of trumpets and shawms, and the raising of voices was so loud that the 'shout of praise' (iubilatio) with which the choir entered could not be heard.[1]

[1] Richard Rastall, 'Some English Consort-Groupings of the Late Middle Ages,' *Music & Letters* 55, no. 2 (1974): 194.

One reads of Henry VIII and Cardinal Wolsey attending Mass at St. Pauls, in 1525, after which 'the quere sang Te Deum, and the mynstrelles plaied on every side.'[2] This reference and a similar one in 1527, mentioning the 'King's trumpetts and shalmes' again in St. Pauls,[3] follow a familiar pattern of the importation of royal or civic wind bands into the church for special occasions.

[2] Hall, *Hall's Chronicle*, 693.

[3] William Dugdale, *The History of Saint Paul's Cathedral* (London, 1818), 433.

Canterbury Cathedral, on the other hand, seems to have been an early example of a cathedral which maintained its own small wind band from an early date. As early as 1532, a cathedral statute calls for the employment of '2 sackbutteers and 2 cornetteers.'[4] A similar document of 1549 speaks of 'two sackbutters and two cornetters,' who were to 'support the melody on feast days and their vigils.'[5] A visiting Italian heard this wind band in 1589 and was very impressed.

[4] Woodfill, *Musicians in English Society*, 149.

[5] Stevens, *Music & Poetry*, 313.

> ... seeing him (the Archbishop) upon the next Sabaoth day after in the Cathedrall Church of Canterburie, attended upon by his Gentlemen, And servants ... also by the Deane, Prebendaries, and Preachers in their Surpleses, and scarlet Hoods, and heard the solemne Musicke with the voices, and Organs, Cornets, and Sagbutts, hee was overtaken with admiration, and tolde an English Gentleman of very good qualitie, 'That they were led in great blindnesse at Rome, by our owne Nation, who made the people there believe, that there was not in England, either Archbishop, or. Bishop, or Cathedrall, or any Church or Ecclesiasticall government; but that all was pulled downe to the ground, and that the

people heard their Ministers in the Woods, and Fields, amongst Trees, and bruite beasts; But, for his owne part, he protested, that (unlesse it were in the Popes Chappell) he had never saw a more solemne sight, nor heard a more heavenly sound.'[6]

[6] George Paule. *The Life of the most reverend and religious prelate John Whitgift Lord Archbishop of Canterbury* (London, 1612), 79.

Another eyewitness from the period of Elizabeth I makes a similar comparison with the pomp of the Roman Church.

> ... the alter was furnished with rich plate, with two gilt candlesticks, with lighted candles, and a massy crucifix in the midst; and that the service was sung not only with organs, but with the artificial music of cornets, sacbuts, etc., on solemn festivals ... That, in short, the service performed in the Queen's Chapel, and in sundry cathedrals, was so splendid and showy, that foreigners could not distinguish it from the Roman, except that it was performed in English.[7]

[7] Quoted in Duncan, *The Story of Minstrelsy*, 177.

Such descriptions of the use of cornetts and sackbuts continue throughout the reign of Elizabeth. An eyewitness, writing of her visit to Oxford in 1566, notes, 'and afterwards ... she entered into the church, and there abode while the quyer sang and played with cornets, a *Te Deum*.'[8] Another observer of the same service wrote, 'in the middle of which service was an anthem called *Te Deum*, sung to cornets.'[9] Both visits by the queen to Worcester Cathedral in 1575 included cornetts and sackbuts, the Sunday Service being, 'a great and solemn noise of singing of service in the quire both by note and also playing with cornetts and sackbuts.'[10]

[8] Mr. Neale, Reader of Hebrew at Oxford, quoted in Nichols, ed., *The Progresses and Public Processions of Queen Elizabeth*, vol. 1.

[9] 'Mr. Gutch, from Wood's Mss.,' quoted in ibid., vol. 3.

[10] Woodfill, *Musicians in English Society*, 149.

During a visit to the queen by Frederick, Duke of Württemberg, in 1592, one finds an account of the use of winds in the more private surroundings of the queen's palace at Windsor, one of his secretaries writing,

> This Castle stands upon a knoll; in the outer or first court there is a very beautiful and immensely large church, with a flat even roof, covered with lead, as is common with all churches in this kingdom. In this church his Highness listened for more than an hour to the beautiful music, the usual ceremonies, and the English sermon. The music, especially the organ, was exquisitely played; for at times you could hear the sound of cornets, flutes, then fifes (shawms?) and other instruments ... After the music, which lasted a long time, had ended.[11]

[11] Jacob Rathgeb, *A True and Faithful Narrative...* (Tübingen, 1602), quoted in William Brenchley Rye, ed., *England as Seen by Foreigners* (New York: Bloom, 1967), 15–16.

A similar gathering of the court at Whitehall in 1597 included, 'a short service, the clergy all being in their rich copes, with princely music of voices, organs, cornetts, and sackbuts, with other ceremonies and music.'[12]

While these accounts describe the music surrounding royalty, as the reader has seen above at least some cathedrals maintained wind players on a more regular basis. A further indication that this practice was more common in England can be seen in the writings of Roger North (1695–1728), who, in speaking of this earlier period, comments, 'wind musick was frequently used in churches, instead of voices, or else to enforce the chorus.'[13]

In many of the smaller towns it was the civic wind band, the waits, who must have provided the wind music when it was needed by the church. I have mentioned above the participation of these bands in the church Miracle plays. One interesting example, in 1512, called for a dance to follow the play, the musicians being called upon to 'do their diligence' and afterwards to 'geve us a daunce.'[14]

One also reads of the civic waits participating in the great church processions, an eyewitness to one in 1554 noting,

> On the sixth of May there was a goodly Evensong at Guildhall College ... with singing and playing as good as ever you heard ... And after the Mass was done, every clerk went their procession two and two together, each having on a surplice and a rich cope and a garland. Then fourscore standards, streamers and banners; each one that bore them had also an alb or surplice. Then came the waits playing.[15]

On reads of the civic wind band assisting with the actual church service in St. James Church, in Bristol, in 1583;[16] in Norwich for the Christmas Service in 1575; and in Chester in 1591.[17]

A final interesting reference seems to have required the town wind band, as the resident musical authorities, to serve as adjudicators of the new town carillon, the wind band of Cornhill being required in 1589 to go to St. Michael's Church to 'take note of a new church bell.'[18] In this case the town band seems to have failed to satisfy the churchwardens for another group of musicians was called in 'to take further note.'

[12] Harrison, ed., *The Elizabethan Journals*, 184.

[13] John Wilson, ed., *Roger North on Music* (London: Novello, 1959), 341.

[14] Edward W. Naylor, *Shakespeare and Music* (New York: Da Capo Press, 1965), 163.

[15] Hugh Baillie, 'A London Gild of Musicians, 1460–1530,' *Proceedings of the Royal Musical Association* 83 (1957), 22.

[16] Langwill, *Waits, Wind Band, Horn*, 174.

[17] Woodfill, *Musicians in English Society*, 150.

[18] Unsigned article included in Crewdson, *The Worshipful Company of Musicians*, 167.

15 *Church Wind Bands in the German-Speaking Countries*

DURING THE SIXTEENTH CENTURY in the German-speaking lands, one can see an extraordinary development in the use of wind bands in the church. In the first part of the century one can still see many examples of the aristocratic wind bands continuing the traditions of the fifteenth century, yet by the end of the century one finds the post-Luther, Protestant, multi-choral works for voices and winds which one usually associates with the early German Baroque.

The use of the aristocratic wind band in the private chapels of the noble continues as a strong tradition in sixteenth-century Germany and Austria, following the example set by the Emperor, Maximilian I, who had many 'trumetten, pfeiffen (shawms) und orgeln' in his private church music, 'des kunigs cantarei.' During the Reichstag meeting he attended in Trier, in 1512, one heard *only* trombones, cornetts, and trumpets with the church music.[1] His son, Philip the Fair, followed his example, as is suggested by an eyewitness who describes hearing a Mass in Philip's chapel, during which the trombones joined in playing the 'Deo gratias' and the 'Ite messa est.'[2]

The interest these nobles had in their chapel music can be seen in the last will and testament of the Elector Ottheinrich of Heidelberg. In this document he expressed his hope that his chapel musicians would be maintained, his famous 'Organisten, pusauner, ... zincKhenbleser vnd Trumetter.'[3]

An example of such a private chapel later in the century is that of the Elector Moritz of Saxony, who hired six cornett and sackbut players in 1549 for his church music. One of those hired was the composer Antonio Scandello (1517–1580), who was also a cornettist of such fame that cornett students came from great distances to study with him.[4]

The most familiar examples of these aristocratic wind bands performing in the church are found in the descriptions of the weddings of the nobles, an excellent example being the often cited wedding in Torgau, in 1500, of John the Steadfast (later, Elector of Saxony). During the wedding ceremony an eyewitness recounts a Te Deum, sung by a court singer with

[1] Wolfgang Suppan, *Lexikon des Blasmusikwesens* (Freiburg: Schulz, 1976), 23.

[2] Michel Brenet, 'Notes sur l'introduction des instruments dans les élglises de France,' in *Riemann-Festschrift* (Leipzig: Max Messes Verlag, 1909), 281.

    A Innsbruck, Philippe se recontra avec le Roi des Romains, dont la chapelle comprenait des 'sacqueboutes' qui pendant la messe 'comenchèrent le grade (graduell) et jouèrent le *Deo gratias* et *Ite missa est*, et les Chantres de Mgr chantèrent l'offertoire.'

[3] Quoted in Suppan, *Lexikon des Blasmusikwesens*, 24.

[4] Grove, 16:547.

organ and 'my lord's trumpets, trombones, shawms, and other instruments of which the German princes have so many.' On the following Tuesday, a mass was sung in the castle chapel, under the direction of Adam von Fulda, accompanied by organ, three trombones, zink, and four crumhorns. It was, says an eyewitness, 'almost joyous to hear.'[5]

The wedding of Casimir von Brandenburg in Augsburg, in 1518, featured wedding music of great solemnity, performed by singers, organists, trombones and cornetts.[6]

An eyewitness account of the wedding of Duke Ludwig of the Württemberg court in Stuttgart, in 1575, describes the wedding music as an eight-part work for singers and trombones which was 'so lovely and noble that the heart was refreshed.' Later, in a descriptive poem, the same observer makes a reference to one of the performances by the duke's wind band.

> Zinks and five shawms,
> Held with flying fingers,
> Faster than an eye blink,
> They played the best pieces.[7]

---

[5] Gustave Reese, *Music in the Renaissance* (New York: Norton, 1959), 655; and Wilhelm Ehmann, *Tibilustrium* (Kassel: Barenreiter-Verlag, 1950), 38.

> So balde aber diss beschehen, sein vorordnet die fürstlichen singer zu einem Zeichen merer frölichkeit ze singen das gotlich lob te deum laudamus mit sambt der orgall, vber welche auch meiner gnedigste vnd gnedige Hern Drampter, Posawner, pfeiffer vnd andere Instrumentisten vor alle andere deutsche Fürsten viel haben …
> ……
> … haben die genannten synger meiner gnedigsten vnd gnedigen Hern zwue messen gesungen mit Hulf der orgall, dreyer posaun vnd eins zincken. dasgleichen vier Cromhorner zum positief fast lustig zu hören.

[6] Ehmann, *Tibilustrium*, 150.

> … mit grosser Solennität vnnd Zirheit vnnd sunnderlichen durch key. Mst. Cantores, Organisten, Passawner vnnd Zinnkenplasser Triumphlich gehalten worden ist.

[7] Nicodemus Fiischlin, quoted in Josef Sittard, *Geschichte der Musik und des Theaters am Württembergischen hofe* (Stuttgart, 1890), 1:18–19.

> Verdembte Zinken, und funft Pfeiffen,
> Mit gschwinden Fingern konten greiffen,
> Geschwinder dan ein Augenblick,
> So ghrad pfiffen die besten Stück.

Another connection between the Württemberg court and the Church seems to lie in the use of the Rector of Bempflingen who, apparently served as an agent for purchasing crumhorns, bombards, curtals and other instruments for the court. See, G. Bossert, 'Die Hofkantorei unter Herzog Christof,' in *Württembergische Vierteljahreshefte für Landesgeschichte* (1898), Neue Folge, VII, 153.

There are also extant accounts of the royal trumpet choirs performing in the church during the sixteenth century, a practice which, as the reader will see below, is discussed at length by Praetorius. A contemporary account says one frequently heard the trumpet choir in the church on great festival days when the Te Deum was sung.[8] Meyer documents such a practice in the Mecklenburg court early in the century.[9]

An excellent account of how these trumpet choirs actually functioned in church music is given in a description of the ordination service of Bishop Amsdorf in Naumberg, in 1542. The principal musical performance, a work given as 'Nun bitten wir den heiligen Geist,' consisted of the first verse heard in the organ, the second by a five-part choir, and the third by the five-part trumpet choir.[10]

As prevalent as the appearance of aristocratic wind bands and trumpet choirs must have been during the sixteenth centuries, the greater number of surviving accounts of wind bands in the church are descriptions not of these ensembles but rather of the participation of civic wind bands. Of these accounts, most are descriptions of music in the Protestant services for it was there that the new multi-part music in the Italian style was first championed. Nevertheless, one does find descriptions of civic wind bands appearing in the Catholic Mass as well.

The Zwickau civic wind band was paid in 1559–1560 to perform the Mass and in the same city in 1565 a visiting wind band was paid for performing in the church.[11]

One account from St. Anne's Church in Dresden, in 1578, also gives us the actual repertoire performed. On this occasion the student choir of St. Anne, together with the Dresden civic wind band, performed a six-part motet, 'Jubilato Deo,' by Clemens non Papa and a six-part motet, 'Te Deum Patrem,' by Orlando di Lasso.[12]

There are also a few sixteenth-century accounts of wind music in the Catholic convents and monasteries. Kellner writes that one often heard the local civic wind band perform during the important festivals at Kremsmunster in Austria.[13] Melk had a salaried cornettist at the end of the century,[14] while the convent at Hall (now Solbad Hall, near Innsbruck) had a full wind band of cornett and trombone players for which it was famous at the time.[15]

---

[8] Flemming, quoted in Ehmann, *Tibilustrium*, 41.

Die musikalischen Trompeter [those who could read music?] sind bey Hofe die angenehmsten, sie müssen zur Tafel blasen, in der Capelle mit aufwarten, wenn bey Solemitäten das Te Deum laudamus angestimmt wird.

[9] Clemens Meyer, *Geschichte der Mecklenburg-Schweriner Hofkapelle* (Schwerin: L. Davids, 1913), 5.

[10] Ehmann, *Tibilustrium*, 149.

[11] Arno Werner, *Vier jahrhunderte im dienste der kirchenmusik* (Leipzig: Carl Merseburger), 204.

... in der Kirchen in die Masse geblasen ...
......
die in der Kirchen in die Kantorei geblasen.

[12] Ehmann, *Tibilustrium*, 149.

[13] Altmann Kellner, *Musikgeschichte des Stiftes Kremsmünster* (Kassel: Barenreiter Verlag, 1956), 149ff.

[14] Grove, 12:107.

[15] Groves, 10:157.

Traditional accounts of the early Protestant Church sometimes make the assertion that the early church leaders were opposed to the use of instrumental music in the services and celebrations of the church.[16] Numerous accounts of the use of civic wind bands in their services during the sixteenth century, particularly in polyphony, suggest that this idea was short-lived at best. Even as early as 1539 one finds Martin Luther himself praising a church procession which included trombones, harps, timpani, cymbals, and bells.[17]

The most complete account of the use of a civic wind band in the Protestant church during the sixteenth century is found relative to an Easter celebration in Halle. On Palm Sunday there was a procession with trumpets and fifes[18] and on Easter morning, during the service, a band of shawms performed, twice, a 'beautiful motet.'[19] On Ascension Day trumpeters played for a procession which carried a picture of the Saviour and the shawm band played an artistic piece from the roof.[20]

The Linz (Austria) civic wind band played in the Lutheran Landhauskirche after 1550.[21] Towns which had no civic wind bands would import them, so the Wurzen band appeared in Finsterwalde in 1581 and the Altenburg band in Oschatz in 1598.[22] Two such accounts are more valuable as they hint at the musical function of the civic wind band. In Berne, in 1572, they were used to help accompany the congregational singing[23] and in Zwickau, in 1558, the band was ordered to play with the organ (in die Orgel pfiffen), an expression which Ehmann takes to mean playing a chorale over an organ cantus firmus.[24]

Additional clues to the role of the civic wind band in the Protestant Service can perhaps be found in the surviving music itself. Ehmann mentions a three-part chorale composed in 1540 by Johann Kugelmann (in this case, a court wind player) and the 'Instrumental Songs' of Martin Agricola, Kantor at Magdeburg. The latter three-part works are unspecified but Ehmann believes that they were for winds, as this was the prevailing practice.[25] One should also mention the *26 Fugen* (1542) composed by Johann Walther (1496–1570), Luther's musical advisor, composed 'especially for cornetts.'[26]

It was, however, for the performance of polyphony that civic wind bands were most used in the Protestant Service. Jakob Gallus, who was one of the first German composers to

[16] Werner, *Vier jahrhunderte im dienste der kirchenmusik*, 203.

[17] Curt Sachs, *Musik und Oper am kurbrandenburgischen Hof* (Berlin, 1910), 25.

Haben auch jre Churfürstliche G. nich genug an einem Circuitu oder· Processio/ das jr vmbher gehet/ klingt vnd singet/ So gehet sieben mal mit herumb/ Wie Josua mit den Kindern von Jsrael vmb Hiericho giengen machten ein Feldgeschrey/ vnd bliesen mit Posaunen. Vnd hat euer Herr der Marggraue ja lust darzu/ mogen jre Churfürstliche Gnad vorher springen vnnd tantzen/ mit Harpffen/ Paucken/ Zimbeln vnnd Schellen/ Wie Dauid vor der Lade des HERREN that/ da die inn de Stadt Jerusalem gebracht ward/bin damit sehr wol zufrieden.

[18] Ibid, 26.

Simul cum tubicinibus et fistulatoribus in supremitate arcis vel secundum exigenciam in ecclesia.

[19] Ibid.

Deinde ligant crucem cum stola, Et tibicines fistulabunt bis optimam mutetam.

[20] Ibid.

Et mox tibicines super testudinem personabunt canticum aliquod artificial iter compositum.

[21] Grove, 11:12.

[22] Werner, *Vier jahrhunderte im dienste der kirchenmusik*, 219.

[23] Grove, 2:621.

[24] Ehmann, *Tibilustrium*, 156.

[25] Ibid, 133.

[26] This manuscript, now in DDR:LEu (MS. Cod. Mus. 50, 'Thomaskirche'), and available in a modern edition in *Johann Walter Samtliche Werke* (Kassel: Barenreiter, 1973), 4:77–120, contains seventeen fugues in three-parts and nine in two-parts.

write multi-part church music, wrote in his *Opus Musicum* (1587)[27] that where there were small numbers of singers the winds *must* help out.

It is evident that the use of winds with multi-part music in the protestant church increased greatly during the latter part of the sixteenth century. A report by a trumpeter in the service of the protestant Bishop of Halle a.d. Saale says that winds were used all the time for this kind of church music.[28]

This increase in the performance of multi-part music is clear from the numerous examples of new contracts specifically requiring the civic wind band's participation. A new order from the Zwickau civic council in 1569 tells the civic wind band they must serve in the church with their instruments whenever multi-part music is performed.[29] An almost identical regulation is found in Delitzsch in 1580 in the contract for new civic band members.[30]

In this same year (1580) the civic wind band in Munich began playing in the cathedral[31] and a payment was made in Weissenfels for the performance of the civic wind band in church.[32] An interesting document relative to the wind band playing in the Easter Service in Weissenfels the following year reveals that the payment included a measure of wine![33] Still another payment was made in 1582 to the civic wind band for playing the Christmas Service.[34]

When the Dresden civic wind band was reorganized in 1772, the four members were called upon to 'strengthen and enhance the Kreuzchor with their playing on feast days, Sundays and at weddings and other occasions when polyphony was performed.'[35] A civic council ordinance of 1571 in Ulm speaks of the civic wind band playing on cornetts and trombones in the Münster Cathedral (in die Cantorey blasen).[36] A similar ordinance is found in Torgau in 1596.[37]

Further examples could be given, but the point must be clear by now that during the second half of the sixteenth century the civic wind bands in Germany were actively engaged to help perform multi-part music in the protestant churches. But how exactly did they function with the choir in performing this music? The answer to this question is found in a fascinating discussion by Praetorius in the third volume of his *Syntagma Musicum*.[38]

[27] In Part Three, 'Instructio ad musicos.'

> Aber da es whol schwerlich eine einigermassen angesehene Gemeinde gibt, bei der nicht Bläser angestellt wären, ... falls wegen der geringen Anzahl von Sängern Orgel und Instrumente zu Hilfe kommen müssen, so sehe ich nicht ein, warum meine Stücke unausführbar sein sollen.

[28] Ehmann, *Tibilustrium*, 149.

> wan man in unser kyrchen feygeriret allezeit so ehr vorhanden.

[29] Quoted in Ehmann, *Tibilustrium*, 149.

> ... mit seinen Dienern, inn der Kirchen, so offt man figural singett ... mit den Instrumenten den Chor stercken helffen.

[30] Ibid.

> ... auf die hohen Feste und sonst der Kantorei zur Zier neben den Gesellen mit Blasen und Pfeiffen in dem Figuralgesange sich brauchen lassen.

[31] Salmen, *Musikleben im 16. Jahrhundert*, 18; also Grove, 12:781. Wind music in the Bavarian court chapel in Munich dates from at least 1557, as one can see in a document regarding the purchase of a 'false bombard' for the choir. See Sandberger, *Beitrage zur Geschichte der bayerischen Hofkapelle unter Orlando di Lasso*, 3:5.

> den 8 Martij Bezallt für die Canntorej Vmb Ain falschen Pomhartt 3 gld. 3 h.

[32] Arno Werner, *Städtische und fürstliche Musikpflege in Weissenfels* (Leipzig: Breitkopf & Hartel, 1911), 37.

[33] Ibid.

> 4 gr. ahn ein stüblein Wein, dass die Stadtpfeifer die Heilige Ostern Inn der Kirchen geblasen.

[34] Ibid.

[35] Grove, 5:615.

For the reader who may not be familiar with this volume, I must begin with a note regarding why it is chronologically appropriate to discuss this work here. Although this volume was published in 1619, scholars today consider it important as an insight into the late Renaissance, rather than the early Baroque.[39] This judgement seems to be confirmed by such comments by Praetorius as, 'For *many years* it has been this author's fervent wish that someone (else) would undertake to write about these matters.' Indeed, one passage clearly suggests that Praetorius did not yet see the new Baroque style on the horizon.

> In the third and fourth volumes, I have included the most important facts a conductor and practical musician will need to know, especially at this time when music has reached such a high level that any further advance would seem inconceivable.[40]

The portion of the third volume which appears to me to hold the key to discovery of the function of the civic wind bands, when they were brought into the church service, is an extensive and surprising discussion relative to the impromptu forming of *additional* instrumental choirs from pre-existant multi-part church music. I might add that Praetorius says many times that while he and other German musicians are observing the principles below, the original idea came from Italy and specifically from the generation including Gabrieli.[41] Praetorius begins this discussion of the extraction of material to form new and additional choirs of voices and instruments under his definition of 'capella.'

> In my opinion the Italians originally used it (the term *capella*) only to designate an additional separate choir, extracted from several different choirs with various kinds of instruments and voices, as are employed in the larger Imperial, Austrian, and other Catholic musical establishments. This choir is called *chorus pro capella*, because the whole vocal choir or the whole *capella* performs this as a group, placed entirely apart from the other choirs and chiming in like the full *Werk* on an organ. This produces a glorious richness and splendor in such music ... In every *concerto* [a term Praetorius uses for any large scale musical, 'concerted' composition] one, two, or three such *capallae* can be extracted and set up in different parts of the church, each of them consisting only of four persons, or more if available.[42]

36 Salmen, *Musikleben im 16. Jahrhundert*, 18.

37 Ehmann, *Tibilustrium*, 149.

38 Unfortunately this, the most important of the three volumes, has never been published in an English translation. A fine translation has been done by Dr. Hans Lampl (California State University, Long Beach), to whom I am indebted for making a copy for me to read. All following references are to his translation.

39 No one believes Praetorius when he writes here, 'On the spur of the moment I did this, at Nürnberg, on April 30th, 1619.'

40 Praetorius, *Syntagma Musicum*, trans. Hans Lampl, vol. 3, 3.

41 Ibid., 127, 129, 199, 325, etc.

42 Ibid., 148.

As startling as this may seem to the modern reader, the implication is that a multi-choral vocal or instrumental composition by a composer such as Gabrieli is to be considered only a kind of 'basic source material' from which one may construct larger, spatial configurations. I might add that this extraordinary principle is also mentioned by other composers at this time, an example being the discussion found in the preface of Giovanni Fergusio's 'Gloria in altissimis.'[43]

The basic principles which Praetorius sets forth for the creation of the 'new' choirs or ensembles are rather simple. First, the use of unisons, that is, the performance of material in the new ensemble which is drawn directly from a pre-existent ensemble, 'can be used throughout without hesitation in high, low, and middle parts by voices as well as instruments.'[44] Second, one may create music in the new ensemble which is either an octave higher or lower than the pre-existent music, provided that one part is sung and the other part played on an instrument.[45]

Praetorius particularly recommends the addition of lower octave doubling of the bass line, going so far as to say that in multi-choral music the bass lines can be three octaves apart![46] The justification for this idea is based in part on the tradition of organ coupling.

> Accordingly [the use of octave doublings] may be done in all voices, and it does not offend the ears when the part of the singer in an ensemble is played an octave higher or lower on cornetts, *Geigen*, recorders, trombones, or bassoons. For some melody instruments, especially recorders ... are to be played one or two octaves higher than written. This compares with the practice of combining many different stops on an organ in unisons, octaves, super-octaves, and sub-octaves and (as some call them) contrabasses. Provided enough players are available, quite a splendid sound is produced in tuttis, if one assigns to a bass—at the regular pitch—a common or a bass trombone, a Chorist-bassoon, or pommer; in addition a double bass trombone, double bassoon, or large double pommer, and double bass, which all sound an octave lower, like the sub-basses on organs. This is particularly common in contemporary Italian *concerti* and can be sufficiently justified.[47]

The only real caution which Praetorius adds to this seemingly rather free concept has to do only with the placement of these new ensembles in the church building. When one begins to add new ensembles and as a result has three or four

---

43 See Grove, 6:471.

44 Ibid., 123.

45 Ibid., 124.

46 Ibid., 126.

47 Ibid., 125. Praetorius, speaking of such Italian practice, makes an interesting reference to what may be lost works by Gabrieli.

> In some manuscript copies of *Concerti* by Giovanni Gabrieli I have seen a variety of such *capallae*. They cannot, however, be found among those published last year. (Ibid., 149)

His reference to the 'works published last year' can only be the final book of *Sacre symphoniae* and the *Motets*, both published in 1615—the final works published by this composer.

ensembles spread out in the building, one must be careful that the congregation hears, either through doubling or placement, the true bass line.[48]

The choice of which instruments to use seems to Praetorius only a question of range. He engages in a lengthy discussion of the clefs appropriate to the more common instruments, and in particular (given the sixteenth-century's preference for *consorts*) the clefs which must be used to transcribe a vocal work for an ensemble of like instruments.

For the cornett choir, Praetorius recommends only four parts, due to the limitation he heard in the instrument in both the higher and lower registers.[49]

For the flute choir, Praetorius demonstrates how one can transcribe specific works by Gabarieli, Herulo, and Hassler for eight-parts, using three parts for flutes and the remaining parts for bassoons, soft pommers, or trombones. For flutes, he recommends in particular the Dorian, Hypodorian, and Hypoaeolian (transposed down a tone) modes.[50]

Because of the numerous sizes of recorders known to Praetorius, he gives the 'Omnes gentes' of Gabrieli as an example of a sixteen-part work which can be played by recorders alone! The use of the recorder consort he finds particularly effective if one uses only the lower five sizes, for the smaller instruments he finds 'make too much noise.'[51] On the other hand, in larger rooms, such as a church building, he finds the larger instruments cannot be heard well.

Given the preference of the sixteenth-century ear for lower instruments in general, it is no surprise that Praetorius devotes a lengthy discussion to the various possibilities of combining trombones, bassoons or dulcians, and pommers or bombards.[52] The bassoon players he finds are improving and if they have a good reed can play rather high with good intonation. Because the bassoons, and also the large bass pommers, cannot play fast notes well, he suggests that motets, concerti, sonatas, and canzonas for these instruments may be transposed to a suitable range. For the larger instruments, he recommends the Hypodorian and Hypoionian modes as the most suitable.

The crumhorn consort requires great care, due to the natural limitation of this instrument which could not overblow the octave. The shawm consort was also found limited by Praetorius, in particular because he found the smaller,

[48] Ibid., 120, 123, 150.

[49] Ibid., 203ff.

[50] Ibid., 204ff.

[51] Ibid., 205ff.

[52] Ibid., 208ff.

higher members difficult to play in tune. Better, he says, to leave the 'squeaky discant shawm alone' and use only the larger instruments.[53]

[53] Ibid., 218ff.

Regarding the use of string instruments in the church, which Praetorius calls *capella fidicina*, his remarks suggest that as a consort these instruments were not commonly known.

> But it is up to anyone's pleasure to use this *capella*, or leave it out. For, as mentioned above, I have only added it (to this discussion) because of the approbation of certain listeners and would not otherwise have deemed it very important. If one would thus want to compose and arrange such a *capella fidicinia* … one would attract those listeners in Germany who still do not know what to make of (this) new style.[54]

[54] Ibid., 154.

Praetorius sums up this discussion by giving examples of his own compositions for the church which demonstrate this rich instrumental practice, including compositions with up to thirty-four parts in nine choirs![55]

[55] Ibid., 274ff.

This is not to suggest that one heard at all times a large *tutti* sound. Indeed, Praetorius suggests that for variety one may use a different consort for each verse, a practice he found common in secular music.[56] Also, one may place the various vocal and instrumental choirs on opposite sides of the church, which adds to variety from the listener's perspective and helps guard against the possibility of the instrumental forces overpowering the voices.[57]

[56] Ibid., 237.

[57] Ibid., 241, 272.

Another interesting source of variety in church music, which Praetorius found possible, was the insertion of instrumental compositions between the movements of the mass, magnificats, or motets, in the manner of the *intermedii* found in the theater.[58]

[58] Ibid., 145.

In more general terms, Praetorius suggests that in the performance of church music a more moderate concept of both tempo and dynamics are appropriate, as compared to secular music.[59] In particular his comments on dynamics seem to suggest that in his experience he had heard some rather dire results from the natural competition among performers.

[59] Ibid., 145–146.

> No one must cover up and out shout the other with his instrument or voice, though this happens very frequently, causing much splendid music to be spoiled and ruined. When one thus tries to outdo the other,

> the instrumentalists, particularly cornett players with their blaring but also singers through their screaming, rise in pitch so much that the organist playing along is forced to stop entirely.[60]

[60] Ibid., 194.

Although the introduction of consorts must have greatly improved ensemble intonation in the sixteenth century, one can see in Praetorius' remarks that musicians, then as now, were constantly checking their pitch. Praetorius could not understand why the responsible instrumentalist could not do this unpleasant task at home before he came to play!

> But it creates great confusion and din if the instrumentalists tune their bassoons, trombones, and cornetts during the organist's prelude and carry on loudly and noisily so that it hurts one's ears and gives one the jitters. For it sounds so dreadful and makes such a commotion that one wonders what kind of mayhem is being committed. Therefore everyone should carefully tune the cornett or trombone in his lodging before presenting himself at the church or elsewhere for a performance, and he should work up a good embouchure with his mouthpiece in order that he may delight the ears and hearts of the listeners rather than offend them with such cacophony.[61]

[61] Ibid., 198.

At the conclusion of this long discussion of the possibilities of instrumental music in the church service, Praetorius attempts to categorize such music into several general styles. The first of these, which he calls *Polyhymniae Tubiciniae* and *Tympanistriae*, are those works during which the noble trumpet choirs could participate. The trumpets were clearly optional, however, for if 'one cannot, will not, or must not use the trumpeters and timpanists, these compositions can nevertheless be performed quite well in town churches without trumpeters.'[62] Praetorius cautions that if one does use the trumpets, care must be taken that their 'powerful sound and reverberation' not 'drown out the entire music.' He suggests placing them not in the main church but elsewhere, such as a nave (an einen sondern Ort, nahe bey der Kirchen).

[62] Ibid., 222ff.

One must conclude from Praetorius' discussion that it was his experience that most of these trumpeters did not yet read music. He cautions the composer to write only simple parts, for 'it is up to any well-trained musician to improve upon them,' that is, improvise in the style of their noble art. Even more interesting is the possibility he holds out that a composer could compose a church work in such a way that the trumpet choir could superimpose their (quasi-secret) memorized repertoire pieces, which Praetorius identifies as 'Sonadas, of various kinds, those played at banquets, before and after dances, the *Intrada*, and the *final*.' This was apparently possible due to the simple and predictable harmonic structures of the natural trumpet. But, even if these pieces should co-ordinate harmonically, how, in performance in the church, does one control a group of trumpeters who do not read music and are not accustomed to having to follow a conductor? The answer, says Praetorius, is to follow them!

> One thing should be remembered here: since the trumpeters are in the habit of hurrying (particularly because the trumpets require a good deal of breath, which cannot be sustained very well at a slow pace), one should accelerate the beat when the trumpeters enter, otherwise they always finish their *sonatas* too soon. Later the beat may be lengthened, until the trumpeters start in again.

16 *Church Wind Bands in Italy*

I HAVE GIVEN EXAMPLES ABOVE[1] of the private wind bands maintained by the sixteenth-century popes. In addition, many of the lesser church princes maintained musical establishments and some were apparently extensive.[2] Given this example it is only natural to find instrumental music in the church as well.

As in other countries, one finds the personal wind bands of the nobility accompanying the great family celebrations of weddings and baptisms in church ceremonies. In some cases such ensembles participated in the normal services of the church as well. One reads that the trumpet choir of Duke Guidobaldi I of Urbino accompanied the hymns, ca. 1507, frequently making 'loud noises'[3] and again in 1556 there were five trumpets serving in the capella of the Urbino church.

The most convenient source of wind players for use in important church services and celebrations were, of course, the civic wind bands, the 'piffari.' In some cases this duty was actually part of the civic players contract with the town council, as one can see in a typical contract from Bergamo.

> (The players were instructed) to serve on festivals in the choir with their instruments, and in the morning and evening; and further to play without extra pay either in part or altogether at all feasts, solemnities and other public occasions on request.[4]

A similar contract can be found for the ten members of the civic wind band in Lucca[5] and accounts of civic wind bands performing for regular church festivals can be found in Florence and Bologna.[6]

One town which seems to have had both an active civic wind band and a tradition of winds in the actual church service was Udine; it was this civic band which first employed the Dalla Casa brothers of the famous wind music in St. Mark's in Venice. A document, dated 1556, from the cathedral in Udine reads,

---

[1] See pages 119–126.

[2] Otto Kade, 'Zwei archivalische Schriftstücke aus dem 16. Jahrhundert,' in *Monatshefte für Musikgeschichte*, vol. 4 (1872), 47ff., quotes a letter of Count Philip of Hessen describing a banquet given by the Cardinal Madruzzo of Trent during which the music,

> was quite wonderful and such as never had been heard anywhere … there were about fifty singers there … and up to eighty players of all types of instruments.

[3] Don Smithers, *The Music and History of the Baroque Trumpet*, 77.

[4] Denis Arnold, 'Brass Instruments in the Italian Church Music of the Sixteenth and Early Seventeenth Centuries,' *Brass Quarterly* (1957), 84.

[5] Ibid.

[6] Grove, 6:647; 19:160.

> To the shawm and crumhorn (?) players in the service of the city, five in number, serving in the choir of the aforementioned church of Udine …[7]

Another source of wind bands for appearances in the church were the unique Italian religious fraternities, called academies, companies, or sometimes, as in Venice, 'Scuola.' These lay organizations existed in part to help support the church and they contributed to the celebration of all church festivals as well as the funerals of their members.

The regulations of the 'Compagnia della Serenissima Madonna della Steccata' of Parma required its musicians to sing and play at all the greater festivals, including the feasts of the Circumcision, Epiphany, Ascension, Corpus Christi, St. Peter, St. John the Baptist, the various feasts of the Blessed Virgin Mary, Christmas and the ten days following it, Holy Week and Easter, with all their Vigils.[8] We must assume these musicians were for the most part wind players and singers, as the pay records of this organization do not mention a single string player before 1621![9]

The 'Scuole' of Venice are the best known of these religious fraternities today. One reads of the Scuola di Sant' Orsola hiring trumpets and piffari to perform at the Rialto bridge and in the Piazza di San Marco on the eve of Saint Ursula's day.[10]

An English visitor described a musical performance in the luxurious building of the Scuola di San Rocco, in 1608, which was 'so, good, so delectable, so rare, so admirable, so superexcellent,'

> that it did even ravish and stupifie all those strangers that never heard the like. But how others were affected with it I know not; for mine owne part I can say this, that I was for the time even rapt up with Saint Paul into the third heaven. Sometimes there sung sixteene or twenty men together, having their master or moderator to keepe them in order; and when they sung, the instrumentall musitians played also. Sometimes sixteene played together upon their instruments, ten Sagbuts, foure Cornets, and two Violdegambaes of an extraordinary greatness; sometimes tenne, sixe Sagbuts and foure Cornets.[11]

This same Scuola di Rocco, by the way, issued a very interesting document to its wind players, in 1550, which read, 'Those players was cannot play canzoni in procession shall be

---

[7] G. Vale, 'La Capella Musicale del Duomo di Udine dal Secolo XIII al XIX,' in *Note d' Archivio*, vol. 7 (1930), 106.

> Tibicinibus et aduncorum cornuum inflatoribus, numero cinque, pubblico stipendio huius civitatis servientibus in choro praedictae Ecclesiae Utinensis …

[8] Arnold, 'Brass Instruments in the Italian Church Music of the Sixteenth and Early Seventeenth Centuries,' 87.

[9] Ibid., 88. Only ca. 1650 do the strings 'take over.'

[10] Leland Earl Bartholomew, *Alessandro Rauerij's Collection of Canzoni per Sonare, Venice, 1608* (Fort Hays: Kansas State College, 1965), 36.

[11] Ibid., 36–37.

deprived of their employment.' To American band directors of the twentieth century this has a familiar ring, 'If you are not in the marching band, you can not be in the concert band!'[12]

Some larger cathedrals employed their own instrumentalists to perform regularly with the choir. The cathedral in Padua, when it reconstituted its cappella in 1594, after a period of decline, employed in addition to the singers, two trombones, a cornettist and a violonist, with an additional two trombones 'on call' for special occasions.[13] One of these trombonists, Bartolomeo Faveretto, was employed at the same time in the chapel of St. Antonio in Padua.[14]

Another cathedral which seems to have employed its own wind band was in Treviso. The 'maestro di cappella,' Pietr' Antonio Spalenza, once took his choir and wind band of trumpets, trombones, and cornets to a nearby convent for Augustinian nuns for a performance and was reprimanded as the organ was the only instrument allowed in closed convents.[15]

The best known example of a cathedral which employed winds is, of course, St. Mark's in Venice. The first permanent instrumental music in St. Mark's dates from the employment of a group of musicians in 1568, which included the famous cornettist, Girolamo Dalla Cassa (ca. 1543–1601) together with his brothers Zuanne and Nicolò. The music director, Zarlino, specified that the group was to play concerts from the organ lofts, but they probably also accompanied the singers.[16] A pay record from the cathedral, dated 21 April 1568, mentions four mute cornetts, two alto cornetts, and a *fifero* (shawm?).[17]

Reports of concerts by as many as twelve players continue during the tenure of Dalla Cassa. As Reese points out, these musicians seem to have been mostly players of cornett and trombone.

> Gabrieli shows a decided preference for cornets and trombones, a choice no doubt influenced by the fact that these instruments were used at St. Mark's, having been commonly included in performance there after Zarlino became *maestro di cappella* in 1565.[18]

[12] Dietrich Kämper, *Studien zur Instrumentalen Ensemblemusik des 16. Jahrhunderts in Italien* (Koln, 1970), 197.

> Che li sonadori non possano in Procession sonar Canzoni, e sonandole siano privi dell'impiego.

[13] Arnold, 'Brass Instruments in the Italian Church Music of the Sixteenth and Early Seventeenth Centuries,' 86.

[14] Grove, 6:440.

[15] Grove, 17:814–815.

[16] Eleanor Selfridge-Feld, *Venetian Instrumental Music from Gabrieli to Vivaldi* (New York: Praeger, 1975), 13–16.

[17] Denis Arnold, 'Con Ogni Sorte di Strumenti: Some Practical Suggestions,' *Brass Quarterly* 2 (1959): 104.

[18] Reese, *Music in the Renaissance*, 551.

A composite list of players on salary at St. Mark's during the lifetime of Gabrieli, for example, would show five different cornett players, nine different trombonists (one of whom also played the bassoon), one large string instrument and two players of the prototype violins.[19]

Dalla Casa was succeeded as *maestro di concerti* (ensemble conductor) by another cornettist, Giovanni Bassano (d. 1617). During the tenure of Bassano the permanent players consisted of two cornets and two trombones, with extra players hired for special events at the rate of a half-ducat per service.[20] It was only under the tenure of the next ensemble director, the violinist, Francesco Bonifante (b. 1576), that string instruments began to equal in number the winds.

The best description of the function of these wind bands in the actual church service is found in the extensive discussion by Praetorius in the third volume of his *Syntagma Musicum*. As I have indicated above, in reference to his discussion, while Praetorius was writing of performance practice in Germany, he indicated many times that this tradition originated in Italy.

Instrumental Forms in the Italian Church Service

The earliest multi-part music played by wind bands was the direct transcription and the paraphrasing of vocal polyphony, much of it sacred in origin. Just as the original wind dance literature grew out of this tradition, so also, in Italy, an entirely new imitative form begins to develop in the sixteenth century.

The first prototypes of what would become the canzona begin to appear near mid-century and are called *ricercare, fantasie*, and *capriccio*.[21] These early prototypes do not seem particularly identifiable, but rather all are synonyms for the same style: three- and sometimes four-voice works which begin in imitation, but fail either to continue the imitation or to present clear formal designs. Willaert, Rore, Bassano and Julius de Modena are all represented by such compositions.

[19] Selfridge-Feld, *Venetian Instrumental Music from Gabrieli to Vivaldi*, 297ff.

[20] Dalla Casa's original salary, in 1568, was seventy-five ducats for the year.

[21] Traditional scholarship dates these works as beginning ca. 1550 and the canzona beginning ca. 1570, however I have pointed out above, with reference to the Scuola di San Roco, that the canzona was clearly known in Venice already in 1550.

This activity led to the body of literature called *canzoni*, extant examples of which date from ca. 1570. For about a fifty-year period hundreds of canzoni were composed and published; those well-known examples by Gabrieli being only the 'tip of the iceberg.'

One group of canzoni composers centered in Milan; Paolo Cima, Costa, Pellegrini, Rognioni, Soderino, and others, composed thoroughly original works which tend toward polyphony throughout.[22] In Bologna, two important composers, Adriano Banchieri and Aurelio Bonelli,[23] contributed canzoni which are more progressive and begin to feature the sectional repetition associated with Baroque music.

The center for canzoni publication, and perhaps composition as well, was Venice. In the first generation of canzoni composers here, including Andrea Gabrieli, Guami, and Merulo, one still finds the borrowing of earlier vocal materials. The second generation includes a broad range of talented composers, among them Cifra, Massaino, Quagliati, Troilo, Viadana, Bona, Radino, Spongia, Stivori, and of course, Giovanni Gabrieli. A third generation of Venetian canzoni composers followed and I will discuss them in a later volume.

Where were all these canzoni performed? The evidence is that they were intended to be used during the Mass[24] and are perhaps best thought of as a kind of sacred 'interlude' music, in substitution for the organ. This is consistent with the remarks by Praetorius in his *Syntagma Musicum*, vol. 3, and also a catalog[25] kept by the organist, Carlo Milanuzzi, of Venezia, who listed such items as,

> Canzon a 5 detta la Zorzi per l'Epistola
> Concerto a 5 per l'Offertorio
> Canzon a 5 detta la Riatelli per Ii Post Communio

Near the end of the century another instrumental form appears in contrast to the popular canzona, the *sonata*. The definition of this new form as given by Praetorius seems to correspond with the extant music.

[22] The most valuable study of this form and its composers is by Egon Kenton, *Life and Works of Giovanni Gabrieli* (American Institute of Musicology, 1967), 469ff.

[23] Bonelli also composed a Toccata, 'Athalanta,' for the Bologna civic wind band.

[24] Grove, 9:369. 'The *Canzona per sonar* was a composition of some length ... generally played during Mass.'

[25] Quoted in Arnold, 'Brass Instruments in the Italian Church Music of the Sixteenth and Early Seventeenth Centuries,' 89.

> In my opinion the distinction between sonata and canzona lies in this: the sonatas are made to be grave and imposing in the manner of the motet, whereas the canzonas have many black notes running briskly, gayly, and rapidly through them.[26]

[26] Praetorius, *Syntagma Musicum*, 48.

The Wind Ensemble Music of Giovanni Gabrieli

> Ye Immortal God! What a man was that!

So the great German Baroque composer, Heinrich Schütz, described his teacher, Giovanni Gabrieli.[27] Except for an occasional hint, such as the fact that in 1586 he received a bonus equal to a year's pay, there is little biographical information to prepare us for such a judgment by Schütz. It is, of course, the man's music which in our view sets Gabrieli apart from most of his contemporaries. How *is* his music so different?

To consider only his canzona contributions, he was the first to write for more than eight parts, the first to assign parts for specific instruments, and the first to treat the canzona as a polychoral (cori spezzati) composition. No one else's canzoni were so varied in their alternation of polyphonic and homophonic textures and binary and ternary metric structures. Harmonically, one sees his bass lines beginning to move in fifths, pointing to later concepts of modulation, and his use of unprepared and unresolved dissonances and faster harmonic rhythms gave his music a great deal more harmonic color[28] than that found in the older Roman polyphonic style of his contemporaries.

Many of his numerous canzoni are designated for specific instruments, usually combinations of cornetts and trombones, and are thus unusual in a period when the publisher preferred to suggest, 'Con Ogni Sorte di Stromenti.'[29] In doing this the publishers may have been hoping to encourage sales, but, it is equally true to say they were only reflecting the common practice; music directors then did not share our concern for instrumentation. Reese points to a performance of Annibale Padovano's eight-part *Battagha*, which was published specifi-

[27] Heinrich Schütz, in the dedication of his *Sacrae Symphoniae* to the Elector of Saxony.

[28] One must remember that Venice itself, lying on the border of East and West, was a colorful city. This confluence of cultures produced St. Mark's, a Roman church looking more like a richly golden Mosque, and the passionate colors of Titian.

[29] 'To be played on all/any sorts of instruments,' or *per sonare* (to be played) in distinction with *per cantare* (to be sung).

cally for wind band (strumenti da fiato), by eight trombones, eight *viole da arco*, eight *grandi flauti*, one *strumento da penna*, one lute, and voices![30]

The church wind music of Gabrieli, which one should properly call *concerti da chiesa*, are important for their own inherent musical worth and as the climax of a thousand-year march of the wind instrument toward acceptance in the church service. But the influence of this music does not end here, these *concerti da chiesa*, together with their accompanying *concerti da camera*, are also a beginning. They are the first link in a chain that will result in the *Harmoniemusik* of the Classic Period. This is a discussion proper to the Baroque and so I beg the reader's patience to await a further volume.

[30] Reese, *Music in the Renaissance*, 550.

Notes on Performance Practice

Notes on Performance Practice

I should like to present here a few thoughts, which have not otherwise found a place in this volume, on performance practice of the sixteenth century. In particular I should like to include a few more general suggestions by Praetorius, in the belief that his third volume of his *Syntagma Musicum* has not been generally available to the English reader.

Regarding the performer's approach to the notation, Praetorius first cautions against merely playing the composition 'the way the composer wrote it.' This, he says, is a frequently heard flaw.

> The discrimination of the performer does not go far enough to explore and grasp the artfulness of the written composition.[1]

[1] Praetorius, *Syntagma Musicum*, trans., Lampl, 3:121.

In a discussion of tempo, Praetorius states that the general practice was to use the common time signature when a slower tempo was needed and the allabreve signature when a faster tempo was desired, that is, it was a characteristic of speed, and not necessarily an indication to conduct in two or in four. He goes on to say that the Italian composers were just beginning (1619) to replace this system with Italian words, such as '*adagio, presto*, etc.,' but that recent Italians, Gabrieli in particular, were not consistent. In summary he suggests that the conductor should decide for himself where the beat is to be slow or fast and cautions that if the conductor conducts too fast he risks,

> making the spectators laugh and offend the listener with incessant hand and arm movements and give the crowd an opportunity for raillery and mockery.[2]

[2] Ibid., 99.

Another interesting discussion deals with how to end a composition in performance. Most musicians today understand that a *ritard* as we understand it is not in the style, but Praetorius mentions a practice which seems to be entirely lost in our performance of sixteenth-century music today. It is not very commendable or pleasant, he writes, when singers, organists, and other instrumentalists from habit hasten directly,

> from the penultimate note of a composition into the last note without any hesitation. Therefore I believe I should here admonish those who have hitherto not observed this as it is done at princely courts and by other well constituted musical organizations, to linger somewhat on the penultimate note, whatever its time value—whether they have held it for four, five, or six *tactus*—and only then proceed to the last note.[3]

Praetorius places considerable importance on the listener hearing the bass line, cautioning that in multi-choral works the 'true' bass line be doubled as needed so that it stands apart from the various bass lines of the several choirs and ensembles.[4] He reminds the conductor to be careful that the placement of the various choirs and ensembles in the building, relative to the listener, not upset this relationship.

Related to this is a somewhat surprising reference to what some today call the 'pyramid' principle, the necessity of strengthening the lower voices in wind band music. In this regard he suggests that in cadences the lowest voice, and not the upper voices, be heard last.

> As a piece is brought to its close, all the remaining voices should stop simultaneously at the sign of the conductor or choirmaster. The tenors should not prolong their tone ... after the bass has stopped. But if the bass continues to sound a little longer, perhaps for another two or four *tactus*, it lends charm and beauty to the music, which no one can deny.[5]

As the dance music forms so large a part of the surviving wind band repertoire of the sixteenth century, I should like to include here a few more stylistic hints found in Praetorius[6] for the reader to have in addition to the well-known suggestions found in Arbeau's *Orchesographie*.

> *Pavane* ... mainly designed for grave dancing ... it has to be executed with characteristic, slow, and graceful steps and Spanish gravity.
> *Galliard* ... has to be executed with straightness and a good disposition, more than other dances ...
> *Branle* ... not as violent as in the galliards and courantes, but quite gentle, from the knees only and without skips.

---

[3] Ibid., 105.

[4] Ibid., 120–122, 126.

[5] Ibid., 105. This preference for the lower partials is, of course, demonstrated throughout the sixteenth century in the preference for the new lower family members of consorts.

[6] Ibid., 51–54.

Courantes … executed with certain measured up and down skips, as if one were running while dancing.

Allemande … not as quick and nimble as the galliard, but somewhat heavier and slower.

In his discussion of notation, Praetorius touches on the most important characteristic of sixteenth-century instrumental interpretation, the question of articulation. There are two very important questions here, the first of which deals with their system of syllabication on wind instruments.

Syllabication is the use of specific linguistic components to produce the modern equivalent of notated articulations. The modern brass player's double-tonguing pattern, 'tu–ku–tu,' is a very distantly related example.

If our knowledge of the sixteenth-century use of syllabication is very incomplete, its significance is very apparent. It was one of the keys, for example, for executing the extraordinary virtuoso passages for cornett by Dalla Casa or the similar passages in the canzoni of Gabrieli. The sixteenth-century player was well aware of the importance of this basic skill as one can see in a poem by Agricola (1528).

> If a wind player you'd like to be,
> Learn well your 'diridiride,'
> Which belong to the notes small,
> Lest you look a fool before all.[7]

7 Translation by the present writer.
> Wiltu das dein pfeiffen besteh
> Lern wol das diridiride,
> Dans gehort zu den Noten klein
> Drum las dir nicht ein Spot sein.

On one level, syllabication was simply a technique for making something happen, through controlling the force and speed of the air column. Only in this regard is the modern 'tu–ku–tu' the equivalent.[8] Dalla Casa, in his *Il vero modo di diminuir* (1584), recommends for the fastest passages on the cornett the 'lingua riversa,' a range of patterns from the softest palate tonguing, 'le–re–te–re,' to the dental, 'te–re–te–re.' The latter, he wrote, though gay and more harsh, is easier to hold back in sixteenth-note passages. But at even at this more technical level, there is a great deal which has been lost to us. What, for example, does Mersenne mean, during the early seventeenth century, when he calls 'te–te–re–te' a *coup de levre* (blow of the lip)?

8 Dalla Casa called the sound of this pattern, 'crude and terrifying.'

Much more important is the fact that syllabication was used not merely as a technical device, but also for musical purposes, as the equivalent of the modern notation of articulations. Here, unfortunately, we have only the slightest surviving clues. A good example of how this use of syllabication worked is a pattern carried over into the nineteenth century by the English flute teacher, Drouet. He taught the use of the word, 'territory,' to produce the equivalent of two slurred and two tongued notes, but with a much more subtle final two tongued notes than the usual 'ta' would produce. It seems apparent that the sixteenth-century player had a whole range of degrees of attack, produced by syllabication, whereas the modern player has relatively few.[9]

Another important question has to do with the longer, legato slurs of modern notation, which are missing entirely from printed sources of the sixteenth century (very few manuscripts are extant). An early treatise on bass viol playing, the Spaniard Diego Ortiz's *Trattado* (1553) has given some modern readers the impression that most string playing was single stroke, and by extension, that wind players must have tongued everything. But when I consider the overall style of renaissance music, I find this difficult to believe. Surely those fine players were too sophisticated to be content with so unaesthetic an approach.

The use of syllabication helped, as in the case of 'territory' which gives a quasi-slurred effect. A very important clue is found in Praetorius, when he mentions a 'new' slur symbol.

> I agree with Lippius, Hassler, and others, that all complex ligatures should be eliminated except the one indicating (two) whole-notes, and that their place should be taken by the sign ' ... I believe that at the present time, when faster notes are used, the slurred notes can just as conveniently be indicated by the sign .[10]

He first of all indicates here that faster notes were not single tongued. More important is a suggestion that I believe has been overlooked by modern writers on sixteenth-century instrumental techniques. He seems to suggest here that the

[9] Suggested treatises for further study of this question include the *Opera institulata Fontegara* (Venice, 1535), by the flutist, Sylvestro Ganassi; the *Selva di varii passaggi secondo l'uso moderno per cantare e suonare con ogni sorte de stromenti* (Milan, 1620), by Francesco Rognoni Taeggio; in addition to the Dalla Casa work cited and the Arbeau, *Orchésographie*. The trumpet may have been slow to adopt this idea, for Bendinelli claims, ca. 1585, that he was the first to apply them to the instrument. The system continued somewhat into the eighteenth century in the oboe tutor by Freillon-Poncein (1700) and the famous Quantz flute book (1752).

[10] Praetorius, *Syntagma Musicum*, 3:56.

ligatures were not merely for the convenience of the scribes, but may have been a specific means of indicating legato, or slurred notes. This is a very significant clue and deserves further scholarly attention.

Notes on the Instruments

Notes on the Instruments

During the central portion of this volume I have tried to avoid such things as technical information about instruments so as not to block the flow of the narrative. On the other hand this information is not without importance and the following is included for those readers who may want to recall some of the basic characteristics and developments of the sixteenth-century instruments.

As I pointed out above, in the introduction to 'Court Wind Bands,' toward the beginning of the sixteenth century there seems to have been remarkable advances in the craft of wood-turning. This, coming at a time when musical preferences were changing as well, led to an almost total replacement of the woodwind instruments of the fifteenth century.

Taken together, the result is first the distinctive new concept of consorts, or ensembles and bands consisting of different sizes of the same instrument, which seems to have been applied to virtually every known wind instrument.[1] This gave a more aesthetic homogeneity and also helped an ensemble avoid pitch problems, assuming the consort was made by the same maker. The second characteristic of these sixteenth-century ensembles was the new lower family members, which also improved the sound by giving a darker texture to the entire ensemble.

The Shawm

The rapid and far-flung work in improving the rough sounding medieval shawm has left us with a large number of sixteenth-century names for this instrument. 'Shawm' comes from the Latin *calamus*, for reed, as does the French *chalemie*, the Spanish *chirimia*, and the German *Schalmey*. *Chalumeau*, which also comes from this root, and which later we associate with the clarinet, also means a double-reed during the sixteenth century—the chanter of the bagpipe. The Latin *bombus* (to drone or buzz) is the root for the larger instruments of the shawm family, the *bombard*, or in German *Pumhart*. The French word, hautbois (high wood), begins to be found just before

[1] Praetorius in *Syntagma Musicum*, trans., Harold Blumenfeld (New York: Da Capo Press, 1980), 2:43, cites a curious attempt at creating a self-contained consort of bagpipes.

> An inventor ... gave this matter much thought and fashioned an entire set of five of these bagpipes controlled with bellows, such that a piece for four or five voices could be played by them. But I do not find the sound of such a combination very pleasing.

the dawn of the sixteenth century, but the instrument is still a shawm. Finally, the Italian *piffaro* is used to mean shawm,[2] although in English it has frequently been mistranslated as the etymologically more literal, 'pipe,' and thus fife or flute.

The most prominent characteristic of the new sixteenth-century shawm was the pirouette, the funnel-shaped reed-shield against which the player pressed his lips. This was developed because of the most important new playing characteristic, the fact that the player was now controlling the reed with his lips, an enormous step forward in terms of tone control.

[2] Praetorius, *Syntagma Musicum*, 37, gives shawm as the only definition of *piffaro*, but adds that the Latin *gingrina* was sometimes used, 'because it sounds just like the cackling of a goose—from gingrire, to cackle.'

The Bassoon Prototypes

The sixteenth-century advances in wood-turning led to the important idea, or perhaps capability, of boring *two* parallel tubes through the same piece of wood. This made possible an instrument capable of playing in the lower range without resorting to the huge, unwieldy instruments of the bass shawm types. These various early bassoon prototypes were bored with two conical tubes (the shawm was the model), each cone bored in a different direction.

These experiments were carried out in many countries at about the same time during the sixteenth century, accounting for the great variety of names for the bassoon's first generation. Many of the early terms and references are Italian, suggesting perhaps the first work may have been done there. The German *Dulzian*, the English *dulcian*, and the Italian *dolzane* come from the Latin root *dulcis* (sweet), as Praetorius suggests.

> In their lower range and in tone, dulcians are similar to the basset bombard, though still quieter and softer; and perhaps it is from this loveliness of sound that they are called dulcians.[3]

[3] Ibid., 38.

Perhaps this was also an expression of satisfaction for this new instrument as compared to the bombard, which was named for a cannon!

Curtal, and its variants, however, also had meant a cannon—but then, it was only a 'small' cannon. 'Bassoon' (Spanish, *bajon*) comes from the Latin *bassus*, which means, of course, 'bass.' But how does one explain 'fagotto?' In Italian it means a bundle of sticks, which the bassoon is today but was not yet during the sixteenth century. Probably the name was taken from an experimental organ-variant called *phagotum*, made by an Italian cleric, Afranio. His instrument has nothing whatever to do with the bassoon, neither did his instrument ever make the slightest place for itself, yet through someone's error the *name* he gave it will probably be known forever!

Among the new bass instruments developed along these lines, but which have not quite survived are the sordun and the wonderful rackett. In the case of the rackett, the wood-turner's masterpiece, there are not two, but nine parallel tubes bored into a single piece of wood. Hence a confusion of the senses; the eye sees a tiny instrument, but the ear hears the low tones of a great one. The largest rackett can play lower than the contrabassoon, yet is scarcely a foot high!

The Crumhorn

Perhaps no other instrument is so associated today with the sixteenth century as the crumhorn. It represented a new family of double reed instruments, differing in the cap which covered the reed. This was an instrument anyone could produce a tone on and, taken together with its limited range (it could not over-blow the octave), was therefore very popular with those members of the aristocracy who were eager to be musicians.

The outdoor variants, the Rauschpfeife and the Schreierpfeife, probably sounded very similar to a modern bagpipe.

The Flutes

In using the term 'flute,' sixteenth-century literature does not always clearly distinguish between the recorder and the transverse instrument. Both now appeared in families, the flute in at least three sizes and the recorder, according to Praetorius,[4] in no fewer than eight!

[4] Ibid., 34.

> the small flute—two octaves higher than the cornett
> the discant flute—a fourth lower than the small flute
> the discant flute—a fifth lower than the small flute
> the alto flute—an octave lower than the small flute
> the tenor flute—a fifth lower than the alto flute
> the basset flute—another fifth lower

the bass flute—a fifth lower than the basset flute
the large flute—an octave lower than the basset

Both kinds of flutes are so well known today that no discussion is necessary, except perhaps to point out that Praetorius[5] warns that both instruments sounded an octave higher than written during the sixteenth century.

[5] Praetorius, *Syntagma Musicum*, (original version), 2:21.

The Cornett

This is another instrument one associates with the sixteenth and seventeenth centuries in particular. It could be a virtuoso instrument, as one can see in the extraordinary collection by Dalla Casa composed for his Venetian State Wind Band, but its popularity must have been due to its beautiful tone quality. During the early years of the seventeenth century, Mersenne wrote,

> It seems like the brilliance of a shaft of sunlight appearing in the shadow or darkness, when one hears it among the voices in cathedrals or in chapels.[6]

[6] Quoted in Gerald Ravenscourt Hayes, 'Instruments and Instrumental Notation,' *New Oxford History of Music* (London, 1968), 4:761.

Roger North, during the early years of the eighteenth century, said, intending a complement, 'one might mistake it for a choice eunuch.'[7]

This instrument came in three forms, all made in different sizes. The straight and curved kinds had detachable mouthpieces, the mute cornett did not. The curved cornett was easier to hold, but the design probably was created to help the problem arising in finger stretches in the straight form. Because of this problem, straight cornetts were never made larger than the alto instrument. The modern English maker, Christopher Monk, however, notices a further distinction. He writes, 'the bend does to some extent act as a baffle and obscures some of the incidental breath and tongue sounds.'[8]

The mute cornett (*stiller Zink* in German) had a built-in mouthpiece of a narrow bore, but with a wide backbore. It seems therefore to have been a softer instrument, ideal for blending in ensembles.[9]

[7] John Wilson, ed., *Roger North on Music* (London: Novello, 1959), 40.

[8] Letter to Howard Mayer Brown, quoted in 'Sixteenth-Century Instrumentation,' in *Musicological Studies & Documents* (1973), 63–64.

[9] Praetorius, in *Syntagma Musicum*, trans., Blumenfeld, 2:36, observes, 'These instruments are quite soft and quiet in tone and lovely to listen to.'

Unlike the modern brass player, early iconography clearly demonstrates that the cornett player played with the mouthpiece on the *side* of his lips. This reflects the assumption held today that the cornett player used much more sophisticated embouchure changes than today to control tone and pitch. Mersenne also wrote that this style of playing allowed greater ease in soft playing and allowed the player to use less breath, and thus play for longer periods. He maintains that he knew one Frenchman who could play a hundred measures in one breath.[10]

But, there is too much we do not know about the cornett, particularly in the areas of articulation and embouchure. The instrument survived in some church towers of Germany until the nineteenth century but then died shortly before the revival of modern interest. Thus a gap of perhaps only a single generation in the first-hand passing down of its traditions has forever cut us off from the secrets, and the very sound, of this historic instrument.

[10] Marin Mersenne, *Harmonie Universelle* [Paris, 1635], trans., Roger Chapman (Hague, 1957), 346.

The Sackbut

During the sixteenth century the trombone was also found in a number of sizes, including two bass trombones.[11] Already during the sixteenth century there were virtuoso players of the trombone. Praetorius mentions in particular one Erhardus Borussus, of Dresden, 'who is said to be living in Poland at present.'

> He mastered this instrument to such a high degree that he could play almost as high as a cornett (he goes on to say a total of nearly four octaves) ... and was able to execute rapid coloraturas and jumps on his instrument just as is done on the viola bastarda and cornett.[12]

[11] Praetorius, *Syntagma Musicum*, 32.
One is exactly twice as long as the ordinary trombone without crooks ... the other kind is not quite twice as long as the common trombone, but its depth is brought about by its rather wider tubes and by the use of crooks. Octave trombones of this kind were already in use many years ago at various chapels.

[12] Ibid., 31, another he mentions with great range abilities was 'the famed master, Phileno, of Munich.'

The Trumpet

The sixteenth century seems to have been the transition period in the history of the trumpet for it is here that the older clarion types finally begin to disappear. Such great strides in the craft of metal working occurred at the dawn of this century that many of the trumpets of this time are works of art in their own right. The European center remained Nürnberg, whose craftsmen traded and traveled in numerous countries.

Virdung, in *Musica getutscht* (1511) mentions three kinds of trumpets. The tower trumpet he identifies with the old S-trumpet, the last stage of the busine development. The other two, *Clareta* and *Felttrummet* have a different look entirely, the oblong form of the modern instrument. In 1519, the English historian, William Horman, made a similar distinction, 'A trumpette is streyght; but a clarion is wounde: in and out with an hope (hoop).'[13]

We know little more about the new instrument's use, for it was a carefully guarded possession of the sophisticated royal trumpet choirs—their repertoire and playing techniques were a guild secret. We do know they played in parts, but where literature survives, such as the three hundred and thirty-two sonatas of Bendinelli, only the one part is given above which the remaining parts were improvised. One famous example of documentation of what this multi-part trumpet literature may have sounded like is found in the famous 'Toccata' by Monteverdi (1607).

[13] Quoted in Don Smithers, *The Music and History of the Baroque Trumpet*, 79, fn.

Bibliography

Bibliography

Aber, Adolf. *Die Pflege der Musik unter den Wettinern und Wettinischen Ernestinern.* Leipzig: Siegel, 1921.

———. *Die Pflege der Musik unter den Wettinern und wettinischen Ernestinern, von den Anfängen bis zur Auflösung der Weimarer Hofkapelle, 1662.* Bückeburg: C.F.W. Siegal, 1921.

Aerde, Raymond Joseph Justin Van. *Ménestrels communaux ... à Malines, de 1312 à 1790.* Mechelen, 1911.

Alenda y Mira, Jenaro. *Relaciones de solemnidades y fiestas públicas de España.* Madrid: Sucesores de Rivadeneyra, 1903.

Altenburg, Detlef. *Untersuchungen zur Geschichte der Trompete im Zeitalter der Clarinblaskunst.* Regensburg: G. Bosse, 1973.

Ammerbach, Elias. *Orgel oder Instrument Tabulaturbuch.* Leipzig, 1571.

Ample Discours de l'Arrivee de la Royne Catholique soeur du Roy à sainct Jehan de Lus: de son entrée à Bayonne ... Paris, 1565.

d'Ancona, Allessandro, ed. "Giornale del viaggio di Michele de Montaigne in Italia nel 1580 e 1581." In *L'italia alla fine de secolo XVI.* Città di Castello: Lapi, 1889.

Anglès, Higino. "Die Instrumentalmusik bis zum 16. Jahrhundert in Spanien." In *Natalicia Musicologica.* Hafniae: Hansen, 1962.

———. *La musica en la Corte de Carlos V.* Barcelona: Consejo superior de investigaciones cientificas, 1944.

Anglo, Sydney. *The Great Tournament Roll of Westminster.* Oxford: Clarendon, 1968.

Anthon, Carl. "Some Aspects of the Social Status of Italian Musicians during the Sixteenth Century." *Journal of Renaissance and Baroque Music* part 2 (1946).

Arbeau, Thoinot. *Orchésography.* Translated by Mary Stewart Evans. New York: Kamin Dance Publishers, 1948.

Armstrong, Edward. *The Emperor Charles V.* London: MacMillan, 1910.

Arnold, Denis. "Brass Instruments in the Italian Church Music of the Sixteenth and Seventeenth Centuries." *Brass Quarterly* (1957).

———. "Con ogni sorte di strumenti: Some Practical Suggestions." *Brass Quarterly* 2 (1959).

Auton, Jean. *Chroniques de Louis XII.* Vol. 2. Paris, 1889.

Bacci, Orazio, ed. *Vita di Benvenuto Cellini.* Florence: Sansoni, 1901.

Baillie, Hugh. "A London Gild of Musicians, 1460–1530." *Proceedings of the Royal Musical Association* 83 (1957): 15.

Baines, Anthony. "Crumhorn." *Grove's Dictionary of Music and Musicians.* London: Macmillan, 1954.

———. *European and American Musical Instruments.* London: Batsford, 1966.

———. "Two Cassel Inventories." *The Galpin Society Journal* 4 (1951): 30.

———. *Woodwind Instruments and Their History*. New York: Norton, 1962.

Bartholomew, Leland Earl. *Alessandro Rauerij's collection of Canzoni per Sonare, Venice, 1608*. Fort Hays: Kansas State College, 1965.

Bertolotti, Antonino. "Speserie segrete e pubbliche di papa Paolo III." In *Atti e Memorie delle RR. Deputazioni di Storia Patria, per le provincie dell'Emilia*. Nuova serie III, ia, 1878.

Bianco, Franz. *Die alte Universität Köln und die spätern Gelehrten-Schulen dieser Stadt*. Köln, 1856.

Boetticher, Wolfgang. *Aus Orlando di Lassos Wirkungskreis*. Kassel: Bärenreiter, 1963.

Boos, Heinrich. *Thomas und Felix Platter*. Leipzig, 1878.

Bossert, G. *Württembergisches Vierteljahrheft für Landegeschichte*, 1912.

Bottrigari, Hercole. *Il Desiderio or Concerning the Playing Together of Various Musical Instruments*. American Institute of Musicology, 1962.

Bouquet, Simon. *Bref et sommaire recueil de ce qui a esté faict, et de l'ordre tenüe à la joyeuse et triumphante Entrée de tres-puissant, tres-magnanime et tres-chrestien Prince Charles IX de ce nom Roy de France, en sa bonne ville et cite de Paris …* Paris, 1572.

Bourrilly, Victor-Louis, ed. *Le journal d'un bourgeois de Paris sous le règne de François 1er 1515-1536*. Paris: Picard, 1910.

Boydell, Barra. *The Crumhorn and other Renaissance Windcap Instruments*. Buren: Knuf, 1982.

Brantôme. "Vie du connétable de Bourbon", n.d.

Brenet, Michel. "Notes sur l'introduction des Instruments dans les Églises de France." In *Riemann-Festschrift*. Leipzig: Max Messes Verlag, 1909.

Bridenbaugh, Carl. *Vexed and Troubled Englishmen, 1590–1642*. New York: Oxford University Press, 1968.

Bridge, Joseph. "Town Waits and Their Tunes." *Proceedings of the Musical Association* 54 (1928): 63–92.

Bridgman, Nanie. "Charles-Quint et la Musique Espagnole." *Revue De Musicologie* 43, no. 119 (1959): 44.

———. "Fêtes Italiennes de plein air au Quattrocento." In *Hans Albrecht in Memoriam*, edited by Wilfried Brennecke and Hans Haase. Kassel: Bärenreiter, 1962.

Brown, Howard. *Sixteenth-Century Instrumentation: The Music for the Florentine Intermedii*. Dallas: American Institute of Musicology, 1973.

Burton, Elizabeth. *The Pageant of Elizabethan England*. New York: Scribner, 1959.

Caffi, Francesco. *Storia della musica sacra nella già cappella ducale di San Marco in Venezia dal 1318 al 1797*. Venice, 1855.

Carpenter, Nan Cooke. *Music in the Medieval and Renaissance Universities*. Norman: University of Oklahoma Press, 1958.

Castellani, Marcello. "A 1593 Veronese Inventory." *The Galpin Society Journal* 26 (May 1, 1973): 15–24.

Cavendish, George. *The Life and Death of Cardinal Wolsey*. Edited by Richard Sylvester. London: Oxford University Press, 1959.

Ceccherelli, Alessandro. *Descrizione di tutte le feste e maschera te fatte in Firenze per il carnouale, questo anno 1567*. Florence, 1567.

Cellini, Benvenuto. "La Vita." In *Opere*. Milano, 1968.
Chamberlin, E.R. *Marguerite of Navarre*. New York: Dial Press, 1974.
Chambers, David. *The Imperial Age of Venice, 1380–1580*. New York: Harcourt Brace Jovanovich, 1971.
Chambers, E.K. *The Elizabethan Stage*. Oxford: Clarendon, 1923.
Chapman, Hester. *The Last Tudor King: A Study of Edward VI, October 12th, 1537–July 6th, 1553*. New York: Macmillan, 1959.
Cherbuliez, Antoine-Elisée. 'Johann Ludwig Steiner: Stadttrompeter von Zürich.' In *Neujahrsblatt der Allgemeinen Musikgesellschaft in Zürich*. Zürich: Hug, 1964.
Chybinski, Adolf. "Polnische Musik und Musikkultur des 16. Jahrhunderts in ihren Beziehungen zu Deutschland." *Sammelbände der Internationalen Musikgesellschaft* 13 (1912).
Cosma, Viorel. "La Culture Musicale Roumaine a l'Epoque de la Renaissance." *Musica Antiqua-Acta Scientifica* (1969).
Crewdson, Henry Alastair Ferguson. *The Worshipful Company of Musicians*. London: Knight, 1971.
Cunningham, Caroline. "Estienne du Tertre, 'Scavant Musicien,' Jean d'Estrée, 'Joueur de Hautbois du Roy,' and the Mid-Sixteenth Century Franco-Flemish Chanson and Ensemble Dance". Diss., 1969.
Cuyler, Louise. *The Emperor Maximilian I and Music*. London: Oxford University Press, 1973.
Dart, Thurston. "Origines et Sources de la Musique de Chambre en Angleterre (1550–1530)." Edited by Jean Jacquot. *La Musique Instrumentale de la Renaissance* (1955).
———. *The Interpretation of Music*. New York: Harper & Row, 1963.
Devillers, Léopold. *Essai sur l'histoire de la musique à Mons*. Mons, 1868.
Dilich, Wilhelm. *Historische Beschreibung der Fürstlichen Kindtauff Fräulein Elisabethen zu Hessen*. Cassel, 1598.
Dugdale, William. *The History of Saint Paul's Cathedral*. London, 1818.
Duncan, Edmondstoune. *The Story of Minstrelsy*. Detroit: Singing Tree Press, 1968.
Dunlop, Ian. *Palaces and Progresses of Elizabeth I*. London: Cape, 1962.
Durant, Will. *The Reformation: A History of European Civilization from Wyclif to Calvin, 1300–1564*. New York: Simon and Schuster, 1957.
Van Dyke, Paul. *Catherine de Médicis*. New York: Scribner, 1922.
Ehmann, Wilhelm. *Tibilustrium*. Kassel: Bärenreiter-Verlag, 1950.
Eitner, Robert. "Briefe von Jorg Neuschel in Nürnberg, nebst einigen anderen." In *Monatshefte für Musikgeschichte*. Vol. 11. Leipzig, 1877.
Elsner, Emilie. *Untersuchung der instrumentalen Besetzungspraxis der weltlichen Musik im 16. Jahrhundert in Italien*. Berlin, 1935.
Erickson, Carolly. *Bloody Mary*. Garden City, NY: Doubleday, 1978.
Erler, Georg. *Leipziger Magisterschmäuse im 16., 17. und 18. Jahrhundert*. Leipzig: Giesecke & Devrient, 1905.
Fabyan, Robert, A.H. Thomas, and I.D. Thornley. *The Great Chronicle of London*. London: Printed by G.W. Jones at the sign of the Dolphin, 1938.

Federhofer, Hellmut. *Musikpflege und Musiker am Grazer Habsburgerhof.* Mainz: Schott, 1967.

Federmann, Maria. *Musik und Musikpflege zur Zeit Herzog Albrechts.* Kassel: Bärenreiter-Verlag, 1932.

Fenlon, Iain. *Music and Patronage in Sixteenth-Century Mantua.* Cambridge: Cambridge University Press, 1980.

Fitzgibbon, H. Macaulay. "Instruments and Their Music in the Elizabethan Drama." *Musical Quarterly* 17, no. 3 (1931): 319.

Fox, Lilla. *Instruments of Processional Music.* London: Lutterworth, 1967.

Friis, Niels. *Det kongelige Kapel.* Copenhagen: Haase, 1948.

Fronsperger, Leonhart. *Fünff Bücher von Kriegsregiment.* Frankfurt, 1555.

Fyvie, John. *The Story of the Borgias.* New York: Putnam, 1913.

Galle, Philippe. *Encomium musices.* Cambridge: Heffer, 1943.

Ganassi, Silvestro. *Opera intitulata Fontegara.* Venice, 1535.

Garzoni, Tomaso. *Allgemeiner Schauplatz aller Künst, Professionen und Handwercken.* Franckfurt am Mäyn, 1659.

Gesner, Conrad. *Pandectarum.* Zurich, 1548.

Giambullari, Pierfrancesco. *Apparato et feste nelle nozze del Illustrissimo Signor duca di Firenze, et della Duchessa sua consorte, con le sue Stanze, Madriali, Comedia et Intermedii, in quelle recitati.* Florence, 1539.

Gilliodts-Van Severen, Louis. "Les Ménestrels de Bruges." In *Essais d'Archéologie Brugeoise.* Bruges: Plancke, 1912.

Giustinian, Sebastian. *Four Years at the Court of Henry VIII.* London, 1854.

Glahn, Henrik. *Music from the Time of Christian III: Selected Compostions from the Part Books of the Royal Chapel (1541).* Denmark: Edn Egtved, 1978.

Graham, Victor E., and W. McAllister Johnson. *The Royal Tour of France by Charles IX and Catherine de' Medici: Festivals and Entries, 1564–6.* Toronto: University of Toronto Press, 1979.

Gregorovius, Ferdinand. *Lucretia Borgia.* Translated by John Leslie Garner. New York: Appleton, 1904.

Grose, Francis. *Military Antiquities: Respecting a History of the English Army from the Conquest to the Present Time.* London, 1801.

Grove, George. *The New Grove Dictionary of Music and Musicians.* Edited by Stanley Sadie. London: Macmillan, 1980.

Guizot, François Pierre Guillaume. *The History of France.* London, 1872.

Gutierrez de la Vega, Luis. *De re militari.* London, 1582.

Guzmán-Bravo, José-Antonio. "Mexico, Home of the First Musical Instrument Workshops in America." *Early Music* 6, no. 3 (1978): 350.

Hackett, Francis. *Francis the First.* New York: The Literary Guild, n.d.

Hall, Edward. *Hall's Chronicle.* London, 1809.

———. *The Triumphant Reigne of King Henry VIII.* Vol. 1. London, 1542.

Harrison, Frank, and Joan Rimmer. *European Musical Instruments.* London: Studio Vista, 1964.

Harrison, George B. *The Elizabethan Journals*. New York: Doubleday, 1928.
Hartnoll, Phyllis, ed. *Shakespeare in Music*. London: Macmillan, 1964.
Hayes, Gerald Ravenscourt. "Instruments and Instrumental Notation." *New Oxford History of Music*. London, 1968.
———. *King's Music: An Anthology*. London: Oxford University Press, 1979.
Hazlitt, William Carew. *The Venetian Republic*. London: A. & C. Black, 1915.
Heartz, Daniel. *Pierre Attaingnant: Royal Printer of Music*. Berkeley: University of California Press, 1969.
Henderson, Daniel. *The Crimson Queen*. New York: Duffield and Green, 1933.
Hentzner, Paul. "Travels in England." In *England as Seen by Foreigners in the Days of Elizabeth and James the First*, edited by William Brenchley Rye. London, 1865.
Herre, Volkmar, and W. Schrammek. *Museum Musicum: Historische Musikinstrumente*. Leipzig: Musikinstrumenten-Museum der Karl-Marx-Univ., 1976.
Hibbert, Christopher. *The House of Medici*. New York: Morrow, 1975.
Houwaert, Jan Baptist. *Sommare Beschrijvinghe van den triumphelijcke Incomst van den door luchtigen Aertshoge Matthias binnen die Princelijcke Stadt van Brussele*. Antwerp, 1579.
Illustrium Hollandiae et Westfrisiae Ordinum alma Academia Leidensis, 1614.
Jackson, Catherine Hannah Charlotte. *The Court of France*. Boston: Grolier Society, 1900.
———. *The Last of the Valois: And Accession of Henry of Navarre*. Paris: Grolier Society, 1900.
Jacquot, Jean, ed. *La Musique Instrumentale de la Renaissance*. Paris: Centre Nationale de la Recherche Scientifique, 1955.
———. *Les Fêtes de la Renaissance*. Paris: Centre National de la Recherche Scientifique, 1973.
Jahn, Fritz. "Die Nürnberger Trompeten- und Posaunenmacher im 16. Jahrhundert." *Archiv für Musikwissenschaft* 7, no. 1 (1925): 23.
Janssen, Johannes. *History of the German People at the Close of the Middle Ages*. New York: AMS Press, 1966.
Jeffery, Brian. "Antony Holborne." *Musica Disciplina* 22 (1968): 129–205.
Jouan, Abel. *Recueil et Discours du Voyage du Roy Charles IX*. Paris, 1566.
Kade, Otto. "Zwei archivalische Schriftstücke aus dem 16. Jahrundert." In *Monatshefte für Musikgeschichte*. Vol. 4, 1872.
Kade, Reinhard. "Antonius Scandellus 1517–1580. Ein Beitrag zur Geschichte der Dresdener Hofkantorei." *Sammelbände der Internationalen Musikgesellschaft* 15 (1914).
———. "Die Leipziger Stadtpfeifer." *Monatshefte für Musikgeschichte* 21, no. 10 (1889).
Kämper, Dietrich. *Studien zur Instrumentalen Ensemblemusik des 16. Jahrhunderts in Italien*. Köln, 1970.
Kastner, Georges. *Manuel Général de Musique Militaire à l'usage des Armées Françaises*. Paris, 1848.
Kazdin, Andrew. "Notes for 'The Glorious Sound of Brass'". Columbia Recording, MS 6941, n.d.
Kellner, Altmann. *Musikgeschichte des Stiftes Kremsmünster*. Kassel: Bärenreiter Verlag, 1956.
Kenton, Egon. *Life and Works of Giovanni Gabrieli*. [n.p.]: American Institute of Musicology, 1967.

Keussen, Hermann. "Die alte Universitat Köln." In *Universitat Köln*. Köln, 1929.
Kinkeldey, Otto. *Orgel und Klavier in der Musik des 16. Jahrhunderts*. Leipzig: Breitkopf and Härtel, 1910.
Kist, F.C., and J. van Flensburg. "De Geschiedenis der Musijk te Utrecht van het Jaar 1400 tot op onzer tijd." In *Caecilia-Algemeen Musikaal Tijdschrift van Nederland*, 1848.
Köchel, Ludwig. *Die Kaiserliche Hof-Musikkapelle in Wien von 1543–1867*. Hildesheim: G. Olms, 1976.
Lacroix, Paul. *Military and Religious Life in the Middle Ages and the Renaissance*. Frederick Ungar, 1964.
LaFontaine, Henry Cart De. *The King's Musick*. London, 1909.
Landucci, Luca. *A Florentine Diary from 1450 to 1516*. Translated by Alice de Rosen Jervis. London: Dent, 1927.
Langwill, Lyndesay Graham. *Waits, Wind Band, Horn*. London: Hinrichsen, 1952.
Laurengie, Lionel de la. "Les Debuts de la Musique de Chambre en France." *Revue de Musicologie* 15, no. 49 (February 1, 1934): 25–34.
Lawrence, W.J. "Music in the Elizabethan Theatre." *Musical Quarterly* 6, no. 2 (1920): 192.
Lesure, François. "La Communauté des joueurs d'instruments au XVIe siècle." *Revue Historique de droit francais et étranger* (1953).
———. *Musique et Musiciens Français du XVIe Siècle*. Genève: Minkoff Reprint, 1976.
Llorens, J. "Estudio de los instrumentos musicales que aparecen descritos en la relación de dos festives celebrados el año 1529 en la corte de Ferrara." In *Anuario-Musical*, 25:22–24, n.d.
Machiavelli, Niccolò. *The Art of War*. Translated by Peter Whitehorne [ca.1560]. New York: AMS Press, 1967.
Mahoney, Irene. *Royal Cousin: The Life of Henri IV of France*. Garden City, NY: Doubleday, 1970.
Manifold, John. "Theatre Music in the Sixteenth and Seventeenth Centuries." *Music & Letters* 29, no. 4 (1948): 366.
Mariéjol, Jean-H. *A Daughter of the Medicis: The Romantic Story of Margaret of Valois*. New York: Harper, 1929.
Marzetti, Pietro. "Memorie di Pesaro", n.d. MS., Bibl. Oliveriana, Psearo.
Matthieu, Pierre. *Histoire de France sous les règnes de François I, Henry II, François II, Charles IX, Henry III, Henry IV, Louis XIII*. Paris, 1631.
Mayer, Dorothy Moulton Piper. *The Great Regent: Louise of Savoy, 1476–1531*. New York: Funk & Wagnalls, 1966.
McGuigan, Dorothy Gies. *The Habsburgs*. Garden City, NY: Doubleday, 1966.
Mee, Charles L. *Daily Life in Renaissance Italy*. New York: American Heritage, 1975.
Mellini, Domenico. *Descrizione dell'Apparato Della Comedia Et Intermedii D'essa, Recitata in Firenze il giorno di S. Stefano l'anno 1565 ...* Florence, 1565.
Mersenne, Marin. *Harmonie Universalle*. Translated by Roger Chapman. Paris, 1635.
Messisburgo, Christoforo. *Banchetti, Compositioni di vivande et apparecchio generale*. Ferrara, 1549.
Meyer, Clemens. *Geschichte der Mecklenburg-Schweriner Hofkapelle*. Schwerin: L. Davids, 1913.

Minor, Andrew, and Mitchell Bonner. *A Renaissance Entertainment: Festivities for the Marriage of Cosimo I, Duke of Florence, in 1539*. Columbia: University of Missouri Press, 1968.

Morley, Thomas. *The First Book of Consort Lessons*. Edited by Sydney Beck. New York: Peters, 1959.

Moser, H. "Zur Mittelalterlichen Musikgeshichte der Stadt Köln." *Archiv für Musikwissenschaft* 1 (1918).

Motley, John Lothrop. *History of the United Netherlands*. New York, 1861.

Motley, John Lothrop. *The Rise of the Dutch Republic*. New York, 1864.

Munrow, David. *Instruments of the Middle Ages and Renaissance*. London: Oxford University Press, 1976.

Murray, John Joseph. *Antwerp in the Age of Plantin and Brueghel*. Norman: University of Oklahoma Press, 1970.

Navières, Charles de. *La Renommée ... sus les receptions à Sedan, Mariage à Mesiere, couronnement à Saindenis, et entrees à Paris du Roy & de la Royne*. Paris, 1571.

Naylor, Edward W. *Shakespeare and Music*. New York: Da Capo Press, 1965.

Nichols, John, ed. *Literary Remains of King Edward the Sixth*. London, 1857.

Nichols, John, ed. *The Progresses and Public Processions of Queen Elizabeth*. London, 1788.

Nickel, Ekkehart. *Der Holzblasinstrumentenbau in der Freien Reichsstadt Nürnberg*. München: Musikverlag Katzbichler, 1971.

North, Roger. *Roger North on Music*. Edited by John Wilson. London: Novello, 1959.

Olaus, Magnus. *Historia de gentibus septentrionalibus*. Rome, 1555.

Orliac, Jehanne. *The Moon Mistress*. Translated by F. McCurdie Atkinson. Philadelphia: J.B. Lippincott, 1930.

Panóff, Peter. *Militärmusik in Geschichte und Gegenwart*. Berlin: K. Siegismund, 1944.

Paule, George. *The Life of the Most Reverend and Religious Prelate John Whitgift, Lord Archbishop of Canterbury*. London, 1612.

Pearson, Hesketh. *Henry of Navarre: The King Who Dared*. New York: Harper & Row, 1963.

Pelicelli, Nestore. "Musicisti in Parma." In *Note d' Archivo*. Vol. 9. Rome: Edizioni "Psalterium," 1932.

Percival, Rachel, and Allen Percival. *The Court of Elizabeth the First*. London: Stainer and Bell, 1976.

Du Peyrat, Guillaume. *L'histoire ecclesiastique de la Cour*. Paris, 1645.

Pietzsch, G. "Die Beschreibungen deutscher Fürstenhochzeiten von der Mitte des 15. bis zum Beginn des 17. Jahrhunderts als musikgeschichtliche Quellen." In *Anuario Musical*. Vol. 15, 1960.

Pillement, Georges. *Paris en Fête*. Paris: B. Grasset, 1972.

Polk, Keith. *Civic Patronage and Instrumental Ensembles in Renaissance Florence*. Tutzing: H. Schneider, 1986.

———. *Ensemble Instrumental Music in Flanders, 1450–1550*. unpublished, n.d.

Praetorius, Michael. *The Syntagma Musicum*. Translated by Hans Lampl. Vol. 3. University of Southern California, 1957.

———. *The Syntagma Musicum*. Translated by Harold Blumenfeld. Vol. 2. 3rd ed. New York: Da Capo Press, 1980.
Prescott, H.F.M. *Spanish Tudor: The Life of Bloody Mary*. New York: Constable, 1940.
Prunières, Henry. "La Musique de la Chambre et de l'Écurie sous le Règne de François Ier." *L'Annee Musicale* (1911): 215–250.
Rastall, Richard. "Some English Consort-Groupings of the Late Middle Ages." *Music & Letters* 55, no. 2 (1974): 179.
Recueil des Choses Notables, qui ont esté faites à Bayonne … Paris, 1566.
Reese, Gustave. *Music in the Renaissance*. New York: Norton, 1959.
Reichert, Georg. *Erasmus Widmann, 1572–1634: Leben, Wirken und Werke eines Württembergisch-Fränkischen Musikers*. Stuttgart: Kohlhammer, 1951.
Rhodes, Émile. *Les trompettes du roi*. Paris: Picard, 1909.
Robinson, James Harvey. *Readings in European History*. Boston: Ginn, 1906.
Rodocanachi, Emmanuel. *Le Château Saint-Ange*. Paris: Hachette & cie, 1909.
Rossi, Bastiano. *Descrizione dell'apparato, e degl'intermedi …* Florence, 1589.
Ruhnke, Martin. *Beiträge zu einer Geschichte der Deutschen Hofmusikkollegien im 16. Jahrhundert*. Berlin: Merseburger, 1963.
Russell, Joycelyne Gledhill. *The Field of Cloth of Gold*. New York: Barnes & Noble, 1969.
Rye, William Brenchley, ed. *England as Seen by Foreigners in the Days of Elizabeth & James the First*. New York: Bloom, 1967.
Sachs, Curt. *Musik und Oper am kurbrandenburgischen Hofe*. Berlin: J. Bard, 1910.
———. *Our Musical Heritage*. New Jersey: Prentice-Hall, 1948.
Salmen, Walter. *Musikleben im 16. Jahrhundert*. Leipzig: Deutscher Verlag für Musik VEB, 1976.
———. "Russchische Musik und Musiker in Deutschland vor 1700." *Die Musikforschung* 26 (1973).
Sandberger, Adolf. *Beiträge zur Geschichte der bayerischen Hofkapelle unter Orlando di Lasso*. Leipzig, 1894.
———. "Bemerkungen zur Biographie Hans Leo Hasslers und seiner Brüder, sowie zur Musikgeschichte der Städt Nürnberg und Augsburg im 16. und zu Anfang des 17. Jahrhunderts." In *Denkmäler der Tonkunst in Bayern*. Leipzig: Breitkopf & Härtel, 1904.
Schaal, Richard. "Die Musikinstrumenten-Sammlung von Raimund Fugger." *Archiv für Musikwissenschaft* 21, no. 4 (1964): 212.
Schlosser, Julius. *Die Sammlung alter Musikinstrumente*. Wien, 1920.
Schünemann, Georg. "Sonaten und Feldstücke der Hoftrompeter." In *Zeitschrift für Musikwissenschaft*. Vol. 17. Leipzig, 1935.
Sedgwick, Henry Dwight. *The House of Guise*. New York: Bobbs-Merrill, 1938.
Seely, Grace Hart. *Diane the Huntress: The Life and Times of Diane de Poitiers*. New York: D. Appleton-Century, 1936.
Selfridge-Field, Eleanor. *Venetian Instrumental Music from Gabrieli to Vivaldi*. New York: Praeger, 1975.

Senn, Walter. *Musik und Theater am Hof zu Innsbruck*. Innsbruck: Österreichische Verlagsanstalt, 1954.

Seward, Desmond. *The First Bourbon: Henri IV, King of France and Navarre*. Boston: Gambit, 1971.

Shearman, Dr. John. "Leo X and the Sistine Chapel". London: BBC Radio 3, August 20, 1971.

Sichel, Edith. *Women and Men of the French Renaissance*. Port Washington, NY: Kennikat Press, 1970.

Sittard, Josef. *Zur Geschichte der Musik und des Theaters am Württembergischen Hofe*. Stuttgart, 1890.

Smithers, Don. *The Music and History of the Baroque Trumpet Before 1721*. London: Dent, 1973.

Stahl, Wilhelm. *Musikgeschichte Lübecks*. Kassel: Bärenreiter Verlag, 1952.

Stellfeld, Jean Auguste. *Bronnen tot de Geschiedenis der Antwerpsche Clavecimbel- en Orgelbouwers in de XVIe en XVIIe Eeuwen*. Antwerpen: Drukkerij Resseler, 1942.

Stevens, John. *Music & Poetry in the Early Tudor Court*. London: Methuen, 1961.

Stevenson, Robert. "European Music in 16th-Century Guatemala." *Musical Quarterly* 50, no. 3 (1964): 341.

———. *Spanish Cathedral Music in the Golden Age*. Berkeley: University of California Press, 1961.

Stoltzer, Thomas. "Erzürne dich nicht." In *Das Chorwerk*, edited by Otto Gombosi. Vol. 6. Wolfenbüttel: Möseler Verlag, 1930.

Subirá, José. *Historia de la Música*. Barcelona: Salvat, 1947.

Suppan, Wolfgang. *Lexikon des Blasmusikwesens*. Freiburg: Schulz, 1973.

Taeggio, Francesco Rognoni. *Selva di varii passaggi secondo l'uso moderno per cantare e suonare con ogni sorte de stromenti*. Milano, 1620.

Tassoreau, Ollivier. *La Description de l'Entrée du Treschrestien Roy Charles IX du nom, en sa Ville de Tours*. Tours, 1565.

Thornbury, George Walter. *Shakspere's England: Sketches of Our Social History in the Reign of Elizabeth*. London, 1856.

Trente et six chansons musicales a quatre parties. Paris: Attaingnant, 1530.

Trojano, Massimo. *Discorsi Delli Triomfi, Giostre, Apparati, é delle cose piu notabile*. Munich: Appresso Adamo Montano, 1568.

Tyard, Pontus de. *Solitaire second*, 1555.

Vale, G. "La Capella Musicale del Duomo di Udine dal Secolo XIII al XIX." In *Note d' Archivo*. Vol. 7, 1930.

Vander Straeten, Edmond. *La Musique aux Pays-Bas avant le XIXe Siècle*. Bruxelles, 1885.

———. *La Musique aux Pays-Bas avant le XIXe Siècle*. New York: Dover, 1969.

Vente, Maarten Albert. *Bouwstenen voor een geschiedenis der toonkunst in de Nederlanden*. Utrecht: Vereniging voor nederlandse muziekgeschiedenis, 1965.

Vessella, Alessandro. *La Banda*. Milano: Istituto editoriale nazionale, 1935.

Vioux, Marcelle. *Henry of Navarre*. Translated by J. Lewis May. New York: Dutton, 1937.

Wagner, Johann. *Kurtze doch gegründte beschreibung*. Munich, 1568.

Wallner, Bertha. "Ein Instrumentenverzeichnis aus dem 16. Jahrhundert." *Festschrift zum 50. Geburtstag Adolf Sandbergers* (1918).

———. *Musikalische Denkmäler der Steinätzkunst*. Munich: J.J. Lentnersche Hofbuchhandlung, 1912.

Walter, Johann. *Johann Walter Sämtliche Werke*. Kassel: Bärenreiter, 1953.

Wangermée, Robert. *Flemish Music and Society in the Fifteenth and Sixteenth Centuries*. New York: Praeger, 1968.

Warwick, Alan Ross. *A Noise of Music*. London: Queen Anne Press, 1968.

von Wedel, Lupold. "Journey Through England." In *Elizabethan People*. London, 1972.

Welch, Christopher. "Literature Relating to the Recorder." *Proceedings of the Musical Association* 24 (January 1, 1897): 145–224.

Werner, Arno. *Städtische und fürstliche Musikpflege in Weissenfels*. Leipzig: Breitkopf & Härtel, 1911.

———. *Vier Jahrhunderte im Dienste der Kirchenmusik*. Leipzig: Carl Merseburger, 1933.

Woodfill, Walter L. *Musicians in English Society from Elizabeth to Charles I*. Princeton: Princeton University Press, 1953.

Wustmann, Rudolf. *Musikgeschichte Leipzigs bis zur Mitte des 17. Jahrhunderts*. Leipzig: Siegel, 1926.

Zarlino, Gioseffo. *Le institutioni harmoniche*, 1558.

Index

Index of Names

A

Agricola, Martin, 1486–1556, German composer at Magdeburg, 232
Albert v, duke at Munich, 97ff
Albert, Duke of Prussia, 16th century, 113, 107ff
Albertus Alasco, Palatine of Poland, visits Eliz I in 1583, 44
Alexander vi, Pope, 117
Aloize, Giovanni, famous trombonist at Mantua, 132
Ambra, Francesco, d', playwright, 16th century, 130
Amsdorf, Bishop of Naumberg, description of church music in 1542, 231
Arbeau, Thoinot, writer on dancing, 1588, 46, 80, 181ff, 252
Arundel, Earl of, 46
Attaingnant, Pierre, 1494–1552, Paris publisher, 67ff, 180
August, Elector of Saxony, 16th century, 113
Augustanus, Jacobus Ellendus, merchant, collector of instruments, 144
Augustin de Verona, cornettist, 16th century, 90

B

Banchieri, canzona composer in Venice, 16th century, 245
Barbe, Anthony, choral master in Antwerp, 1550, 214
Barclay, Alexander, author of *Ship of Fools* [1508], 148
Bassano, Giovanni, d. 1617, cornettist and conductor at St. Mark's, Venice, 244
Bénard, Jean, 'king' of minstrels n Paris in 1537, 179
Bendinelli, composer of 332 trumpet sonatas in 16th century, 264
Bevilacqua, Count Mario of Verona, 134
Blanke, John, black trumpeter, court of Henry viii, 18
Bogria, Rodrigo, 1431–1503, Pope Alexander vi, 117
Boleyn, Anne, wife of Henry viii, 26ff
Bonelli, Aurelio, canzona composer in Venice, 16th century, 245
Bonifante, Francesco, b. 1576, head of music St. Marks, first introduced strings, 244
Borgia, Lucrezia, 1480–1519, daughter to Pope Alexander vi, 118ff
Borussus, Erhardus of Dresden, famous 16th century trombonist, 263
Bottrigari, Hercole, 1531–1612, scholar of Italian court life, 126
Bouchaudon, Clude de, 'king' of minstrels in Paris, 1575–1590, 179

Brasser, Jan de, member of the Antwerp town band, 166
Brauwer, Casin de, commissioned band music for church in Antwerp, 214

C

Cardinal Wolsey, court of Henry viii, 22, 23
Casimir von Brandenburg, wedding music in 1518, 230
Catherine de Medici, 16th century, 73ff
Cellini, Benvenuto, 1500–1571, goldsmith, diarist, 112, 198
Champernowe, Sir Richard, associated with Holborne, 16th century, 59
Charles ix of France, reigning 1560–1574, 73ff, 84, 217
Charles v, 1500–1558, Emperor, Holy Roman Empire, 24ff, 63, 88ff, 123, 181ff
Chemin, Nicolas du, publisher of Danseries, 16th century, 71, 181
Christian I of Saxony, 1560–1591, 114, 115 [instrument collection]
Christian III of Denmark, 16th century, 110
Cifra, canzona composer in Venice, 16th century, 245
Clemens, Jacobus [Clemens non Papa], composer, 121, 231
Clement vii, Pope, 1478–1534, 121ff
Cleves, Anne, wife of Henry viii, 27
Collaert, Adrian, artist in Italy, 16th century, 205
Coniac, Pieter de, Dutch instrument maker, 16th century, 165
Cosimo I, Duke of Florence, 1519–1574, 127ff
Curtenbosch, Arent van, member of the Oudenaarde town band, 16th century, 168

D

Dalla Casa, Girolamo, 1530–1601, leader Doge's wind band, Venice, 201ff, 241, 243, 253ff, 262
Dalla Casa, Nicoló, 243
Dalla Casa, Zuanne, 243
De Ler, Giovanni, leader of Torino town band in 1567, 197
Doge of Venice, his wind band, 16th century, 134
Dorati, Bartolomeo, member of 16th century Lucca town band, 199
Dorati, Nicolao, 16th century trombonist and leader of the Lucca town band, 199
Drake, Sir Francis, 1540–1596, English admiral, 154

Drayton, Michael, 1563–1631, English poet, 38
Dudley, Lord Robert, 1531–1588, Earl of Leicester, 161ff
Duke of Württemberg, 235, description of his band's performance, 230ff
Dürer, Albrecht, 1471–1528, German artist, 170, 185

E

Earl of Hertford, visit by Elizabeth I, 53
Earl of Worcester, court of Elizabeth I, 42
Edward VI, King of England, 16th century, 32 [list of wind players for coronation], 29ff
Elizabeth I, 1533–1603, description of church music, 36ff, 50 [visit to Norwich], 157, 226ff
Elizabeth, wife of Philip II of Spain, 16th century, 73, 75ff
Erasmus, Desiderius, 1466–1536, scholar, 119
Ercole d'Este, 16th century, 125ff
Escobar, Andre de, 'Master of Shawms' in Portugal 1560–1580, 223
Estrée, Jean, de, 16th century composer of Danseies, 71

F

Faveretto, Bartolomeo, trombonist employed in church in Padua, 16th century, 243
Ferdinand I, Emperor, 102
Ferdinand II of Insbruck, reigned 1564–1595, [instrument collection], 101ff
Ferdinand, Duke of Bavaria, 16th century, 130
Fergusio, Giovanni, discussion of 16th century German multi-choral music, 235
Finck, Hermann, German artist, 206
Francesco da Milano, lutanist, 16th century, 10
Francesco de' Medici, 16th century, 130ff
Francesco, Giovannni, famous trombonist of Siena, 135
Franciosio, ?, leader of a children's band in Florence in 1586, 199
Franҫis I, King of France, 16th century, 23
Francis II of France, 16th century, 73
Francis, Duke of Brabant, visits Antwerp in 1581, 170
François I of France, 1494–1547, 62ff, 64 [list of players in the shawm and sackbut ensemble], 124, 181, 217ff
Frederick, Duke of Württemberg, 226
Friedrich, Duke of Bavaria, 133
Fronsperger, Lienhart, author of a 1555 manual for the field trumpeter, 111
Fugger, Raimund of Augsburg, merchant, supporter of music, 16th century, 144
Fulda, Adam von, on conducting in Torgau, 16th century, 230

G

Gabrieli, Andrea, canzona composer in Venice, 16th century, 133, 245

Gabrieli, Giovanni, 1554–1612, composer, 134, 235ff, 245ff, 253
Gallus, Jakob, composer of German church music requiring winds, 232
Ganassi, Sylvestro, member of the Doge of Venice wind band, 16th century, 134
Gervaise, Claude, 16th century composer of Danseries, 70
Gonzaga, Viccenzo, coronaton in 1587, 133
Guami, canzona composer in Venice, 16th century, 245
Guerrero, Spanish composer, music copied for use in New World, 221
Guidobaldi I, Duke of Urbino, trumpet choir in church, 241
Gwin, Matthew, professor of music at Oxford in 1582, 39

H

Hans Neuschel, 16th century instrument maker in Nürnberg, 120
Hassler, 236
Henry II of France, reigning 1547–1559, 72
Henry III, King of France, 16th century, 80ff
Henry IV of France, 83ff
Henry VII, King of England, 1457–1509, 8
Henry VIII, King of England, 1491–1547, 6, 9, 15ff [court wind players names], 23 [foreign wind players in his court], 28ff [names of players for funeral], 66ff, 148
Herulo, ?, 16th century Italian composer, 236
Hestier, Nicolas, in charge of civic music in Tours, 1508, 179
Hewet, Robert, leader of York town band in 1567, 152
Heyde, Jörgen, trumpeter for Albert of Prussia, 16th century, 110
Holbein, Hans, German artist, 16th century, 208ff
Holborne, Antony, d. 1606, 58
Horman, William, 16th century English historian, on trumpet vs clarion, 264
Hut, Abraham, Stadtpfeifer in Zwickau in 1569, his contract, 191

I

Isabella d'Este and Mantua, 133ff

J

Janequin, Clément, 1485–1558, French composer, 12, 177
Jehan Van Vincle, performer in court of Charles V, 90
Joachim II of Brandenburg, 16th century, 107
Johann David Wunderer, German historian, 16th century, 11
Johann von Sachsen, German duke, 16th century, 6
Johann, Duke of Mecklenburg, 16th century, 113
John the Steadfast, later Elector of Saxony, 16th century, 229

John, Cardinal of Lorraine, Paris, 1498–1550, 217
Jörg Eyselin, wind player at Memmingen in 1501, 191
Josquin des Prez, 16th century Italian composer, 61, 177
Juana of Spain, 16th century, 87
Julius II, Pope, 1443–1513, 119

K

Karl I, of Graz, 100
Karl II, Archduke in Graz, 16th century, 101
Kenilworth Castle, visit by Elizabeth I, 47ff
Kinckom, Anthony van, member of the Mechelen town band, 16th century, 168
King of Spain, 1510, 18
Kugelmann, Johann, composer, 16th century, 110
Kugelmann, Paul, composer, 16th century, 110

L

Landi, Antonio, playwright, 16th century, 129
Lassus, Orlando da, composer in court at Munich, 16th century, 97, 231
Leicester, Earl of, 45
Leo X, Pope, 1475–1521, 92, 119ff
Leunis, Jan, copyist or composer for the Bruges town band, 16th century, 167
Lorenzo de' Medici, 16th century, not the 'il magnifico', 127
Lorenzo de' Medici, 120
Louis XII, 1498–1515, 61ff, 197
Lübeck, Hendrich, trumpeter and scribe, 16th century, 110
Ludwig III of Duke of Württemburg, reigning 1568-1593, 110, 193
Luther, Martin, 92, 229, 232

M

Machiavelli, Italian politician, writer, 1469–1527, 11
Maes, Paul, member of the Oudenaarde town band, 16th century, 169
Margaret of Austria, 1480–1530, Regent of the Low Countries, 165, 167
Margaret of Austria, 215
Mary Tudor, Queen of England, 16th century, 33ff, 35 [list of wind player names in her court]
Mary, Queen of Scots, 16th century, 21, 73
Massaino, canzona composer in Venice, 16th century, 245
Matthias, Archduke, visits Brussels in 1578, 172
Maximilian I, Emperor of the Holy Roman Empire, 16th century, 18, 87, 191, 229
Maximilian II, Emperor, reigning 1564–1576, 103
Melville, Sir James, courtier, hears Elizabeth I play keyboard, 36

Mendieta, Geronimo de, author of study on music in New World church, 222
Mersenne, 1588–1648, French encyclopedist, 253, 262ff
Merulo, canzona composer in Venice, 16th century, 245
Metzsch, Woff, trumpeter of Albert of Prussia, 16th century, 110
Michelangelo, 1475–1564, 121
Modena, Julius de, 16th century composer of multi-choral works, 244
Moritz of Saxony, Elector, 106 [instrument collection], 229
Moritz, Duke of Dresden, reigning 1541–1553, 113
Moritz, Landgraf of Hesse-Cassel, 16th century, 105ff
Morley, Thomas, 1557–1602, English composer, 151
Moya, Christophorus, 1580 artist, 208

N

Nagel, Hans, 16th century trombonist and spy, 166, 167, 215
Naghele, Hans, performer in court of Charles V, 90
Navieres, Charles de (16th century court poet in Paris), 78
North, Roger, 1651–1734, English biographer, 227, 262
Northbrooke, John Rev., 16th century, 163

O

Obrecht, Jacob, 1457–1505, composer, choir master in Antwerp, 1509, 214
Ottheinrich of Heidelbert, Elector, 16th century, 229

P

Padovano, Annibale, composer of Battagha, for winds, 16th century, 246
Pagani, Matteo, painter of Doge's Procession ca. 1520 in Venice, 134
Paul III, Pope, 1468–1549, 123ff
Peacock, Stephen, Lord Mayor, London, 26
Pelkam, Segar van, leader of the London Waits, 16th century, 152
Pembroke, Earl of, 46
Phalése, Pierre, publisher, 16th century, 177
Philip I of Spain, 1504–1506, Duke of Burgundy, 87ff
Philip II of Spain, 16th century, 34, 73, 94ff [including his instrumental collection]
Philip the Fair, son to Maximilian I, 229
Philip van Wilder, musician, court of Henry VIII, 23
Philipps von Hessen, 16th century, 104
Pontus de Tyard, French poet, 16th century, 10
Praetorius, Michael, German conductor, 1571–1621, important author on performance practice, 5, 205, 233ff, 244, 245, 251ff

Q

Quagliati, canzona composer in Venice, 16th century, 245

R

Radino, canzona composer in Venice, 16th century, 245
Rore, 16th century composer of multi-choral works, 244
Rossetto, Stefano, composer, 131
Rudolf II, Emperor, 103

S

Scandello, Antonio, 1517–1580, famous cornettist, 229
Schlick, Arnold, 1511, author on organ building, 210
Schütz, Heinrich, 1585–1672, German composer, 246
Senfl, Ludwig, composer in Munich, 16th century, 97
Sergiusi, Anselmo, leader of Torino town band in 1580, 197
Shakespeare, English playwright, 16th century, 4, 55ff
Sidney, Sir Philip, 1554–1586, 3, 45 [funeral]
Sofie von Mecklenburg, German, 16th century bride, 6
Sophocles, ancient Greek playwright, 133
Spalenza, Pietr' Antonio, maestro di cappela in Treviso, 243
Spongia, canzona composer in Venice, 16th century, 245
Stivori, canzona composer in Venice, 16th century, 245
Stoltzer, Thomas, court composer in Hungary 16th century, 109
Striggio, Allesandro, composer, 131ff
Susato, Tielman, 1510–1570, composer, composer and leader of Antwerp town band, 166, 213, 175ff

T

Thomsen, Magnus, trumpeter and scribe, 16th century, 110
Troilo, canzona composer in Venice, 16th century, 245
Troisano, Massimo, singer, diarist in court at Munich, 16th century, 98ff
Twenger, Johann, artist in Germany, 1577, 193

U

Ulrich Paser, wind player at Memmingen in 1501, 191

V

Van Vincle, Jehan, wind player in church services for Margaret of Austria, 215
Van Winckle, Cornelis, member of the Ghent town band, 165
Vessella, Alessandro, 19th century author of *La Banda*, 123, 132
Viadana, canzona composer in Venice, 16th century, 254
Virdung, composer of a treatise discussing instruments in 1511, 264
Vivola, Alphonso dalla, composer, court of Ercole d'Este, 16th century, 125

W

Walther, Johann, composer of original German church music for winds, 232
Willaert, 16th century composer of multi-choral works, 244
William V of Munich, 16th century, 98ff
Wolsey, English Cardinal, 1473–1530, 217, 225

Z

Zarlino, Geoseffo, Italian theorist, 16th century, 13

About the Author

Dr. David Whitwell is a graduate ('with distinction') of the University of Michigan and the Catholic University of America, Washington DC (PhD, Musicology, Distinguished Alumni Award, 2000) and has studied conducting with Eugene Ormandy and at the Akademie fur Musik, Vienna. Prior to coming to Northridge, Dr. Whitwell participated in concerts throughout the United States and Asia as Associate First Horn in the USAF Band and Orchestra in Washington DC, and in recitals throughout South America in cooperation with the United States State Department.

At the California State University, Northridge, which is in Los Angeles, Dr. Whitwell developed the CSUN Wind Ensemble into an ensemble of international reputation, with international tours to Europe in 1981 and 1989 and to Japan in 1984. The CSUN Wind Ensemble has made professional studio recordings for BBC (London), the Koln Westdeutscher Rundfunk (Germany), NOS National Radio (The Netherlands), Zurich Radio (Switzerland), the Television Broadcasting System (Japan) as well as for the United States State Department for broadcast on its 'Voice of America' program. The CSUN Wind Ensemble's recording with the Mirecourt Trio in 1982 was named the 'Record of the Year' by The Village Voice. Composers who have guest conducted Whitwell's ensembles include Aaron Copland, Ernest Krenek, Alan Hovhaness, Morton Gould, Karel Husa, Frank Erickson and Vaclav Nelhybel.

Dr. Whitwell has been a guest professor in 100 different universities and conservatories throughout the United States and in 23 foreign countries (most recently in China, in an elite school housed in the Forbidden City). Guest conducting experiences have included the Philadelphia Orchestra, Seattle Symphony Orchestra, the Czech Radio Orchestras of Brno and Bratislava, The National Youth Orchestra of Israel, as well as resident wind ensembles in Russia, Israel, Austria, Switzerland, Germany, England, Wales, The Netherlands, Portugal, Peru, Korea, Japan, Taiwan, Canada and the United States.

He is a past president of the College Band Directors National Association, a member of the Prasidium of the International Society for the Promotion of Band Music, and was a member of the founding board of directors of the World Association for Symphonic Bands and Ensembles (WASBE). In 1964 he was made an honorary life member of Kappa Kappa Psi, a national professional music fraternity. In September, 2001, he was a delegate to the UNESCO Conference on Global Music in Tokyo. He has been knighted by sovereign organizations in France, Portugal and Scotland and has been awarded the gold medal of Kerkrade, The Netherlands, and the silver medal of Wangen, Germany, the highest honor given wind conductors in the United States, the medal of the Academy of Wind and Percussion Arts (National Band Association) and the highest honor given wind conductors in Austria, the gold medal of the Austrian Band Association. He is a member of the Hall of Fame of the California Music Educators Association.

Dr. Whitwell's publications include more than 127 articles on wind literature including publications in Music and Letters (London), the London Musical Times, the Mozart-Jahrbuch (Salzburg), and 39 books, among which is his 13-volume *History and Literature of the Wind Band and Wind Ensemble* and an 8-volume series on *Aesthetics in Music*. In addition to numerous modern editions of early wind band music his original compositions include 5 symphonies.

David Whitwell was named as one of six men who have determined the course of American bands during the second half of the 20th century, in the definitive history, *The Twentieth Century American Wind Band* (Meredith Music).

A doctoral dissertation by German Gonzales (2007, Arizona State University) is dedicated to the life and conducting career of David Whitwell through the year 1977. David Whitwell is one of nine men described by Paula A. Crider in *The Conductor's Legacy* (Chicago: GIA, 2010) as 'the legendary conductors' of the 20th century.

> 'I can't imagine the 2nd half of the 20th century—without David Whitwell and what he has given to all of the rest of us.' Frederick Fennell (1993)

www.ingramcontent.com/pod-product-compliance
Lightning Source LLC
Chambersburg PA
CBHW081347230426
43667CB00017B/2750